This book is to be returned on or before
the last date stamped below.

| 11 FEB 1999 | -7 ... 2007 |
| | 0 7 JAN 2008 |

in Modern Society

The South East Essex
College of Arts & Technology

30130504173836

X
STL
ESF REF
302.23
JAC

Mass Media
in Modern Society

Edited by
Norman Jacobs

With a New Introduction by Garth S. Jowett

Transaction Publishers
New Brunswick (U.S.A.) and London (U.K.)

New material this edition copyright © 1992 by Transaction Publishers, New Brunswick, New Jersey 08903. Originally published in 1959 by D. Van Nostrand Co., Inc.

All rights reserved under International and Pan-American Copyright Conventions. No part of this book may be reproduced or transmitted in any form or by any means, electronic or mechanical, including photocopy, recording, or any information storage and retrieval system, without prior permission in writing from the publisher. All inquiries should be addressed to Transaction Publishers, Rutgers—The State University, New Brunswick, New Jersey 08903.

Library of Congress Catalog Number: 91-46668
ISBN: 1-56000-612-9
Printed in the United States of America

Library of Congress Cataloging-in-Publication Data

Culture for the millions?
    Mass media in modern society/edited by Norman Jacobs; with a new introduction by Garth S. Jowett.
    p.   cm.
    Previously published: Culture for the millions? Princeton, N.J.: Van Nostrand, 1961.
    ISBN 1-56000-612-9
    1. Mass media—United States. 2. Popular culture. 3. United States—Popular culture. I. Jacobs, Norman, 1914— . II. Title.
P92.U5C86   1992
302.23′0973—dc20   91-46668
                                                           CIP

46099

Contents

Introduction to the
Transaction Edition

Mass Media in Modern Society (*Culture for the Millions?*) is a collection
of essays and discussions that were originally presented at a symposium
held in June, 1959 by the Tamiment Institute and *Daedalus*, the journal of
the American Academy of Arts and Sciences, and where most of the
material originally appeared. The collection was edited by Norman Jacobs,
the education director of the Tamiment Institute, and contained an
introduction by the eminent social scientist, Paul Lazarsfeld. Writing the
foreword to a new edition of a thirty-year-old book is a rather daunting
experience for a scholar. The presumption is that, given the enormous
number of new books that are being published every year, this book is
being reprinted because it was historically significant in its time, and/or
has continued relevance to readers today. The task then is to decide why
this particular volume is worthy of rescue from the detritus of the past, and
to enlighten modern readers as to what they can expect to learn from this
collection that will be of use to them today. In making the historical
relevance case for *Mass Media in Modern Society* there are two significant
hurdles that must be overcome. The first is that the book's original
intended academic "fields," listed on the back cover by the publisher as
"sociology and communications" have both undergone major shifts in how
they approach the study of culture in the period since 1961. No longer the
isolated preserve of these two disciplines, the study of "media culture" is
now a part of a larger academic enterprise called "critical and cultural
studies" found in almost all of the humanities and social sciences.[1] The
second obstacle is that the precise subject of *Mass Media in Modern
Society*—"mass culture"—is a term and concept which has been largely
discredited and dismissed by the new school of "critical theorists." Why
then after thirty years should this book be worthy of republication?

There are several reasons that can be advanced to justify the rescue of
Mass Media in Modern Society from the relative obscurity that it has fallen
into since the emergence of critical and cultural studies. First and foremost
is the validation that the book's major themes and problematics, the role
and effect of the mass media in the shaping of modern culture, are still
central issues for any study of culture today. Second is a direct challenge to

the currently fashionable position that "mass culture" is an outdated, outworn idea, by arguing that, on the contrary, the terms, historical facts, and concerns evidenced in this collection precisely contribute toward establishing the intellectual viability of this concept. Third, that the arguments developed in the book provide us with an significant "snapshot in time" of the positions taken in an important and ongoing debate, and that such perceptions have shaped, and continue to shape modern positions on the issue of "media and culture." Finally, in a matter of pure intellectual style, these essays offer modern critical theorists a model of reason, clarity, and erudition that is sadly lacking in most current "critical studies" scholarship. To paraphrase a famous Monty Python sketch, "we only dreamed of writing like this!"

Mass Media in Modern Society was one of a series of important books that appeared in the short period between 1956 and 1962 that gave shape to the intellectual arguments surrounding the issue of "mass culture" as well as laying the groundwork for the emergence of popular culture studies in the university. The first was the anthology *Mass Culture: The Popular Arts in America* (1957) edited by Bernard Rosenberg and David Manning White; this was followed by Reuel Denney's wonderful collection of analyses of various forms of popular culture, *The Astonished Muse* (1957), William Kornhauser's *The Politics of Mass Society* (1959), Leon Bramson's *The Political Context of Sociology* (1961), which dealt with the history of the mass society theories, and Dwight Macdonald's acerbic, but stimulating diatribe *Against the American Grain* (1962). These works and collections provided a splendid confirmation of the potential for the academic study of the history of popular culture and opened up an entirely new world of intellectual concerns about the importance of the mass media in the reshaping of modern culture.

It was no accident that these and other studies on the topic of mass culture appeared from the mid-fifties onward. It was in the immediate postwar period that the specter of consumerism gone wild, together with the advent of television and the increasing significance of the other media, crystallized traditional American concerns about the extent to which individuals can be "free" while at the same time they are "controlled" by social and cultural institutions. It wasn't only communism which raised fears in fifties America; the concern for the future of all forms of cultural expression in the face of what Dwight Macdonald had called "the spreading ooze of Mass Culture"[2] was being sounded loudly across a variety of intellectual landscapes. The range of these concerns are articulated in the various positions presented in *Mass Media in Modern Society*.

The Emergence of "Mass Society" Theory

Why should anyone care about the mass society/mass culture debate in the 1990s? Daniel Bell, writing in 1960, suggested that with the exception of Marxism, the theory of mass society was "probably the most influential theory in the western world today."[3] In the interim the validity of these concepts has been challenged and downplayed in social science theory and especially in the emerging critical/cultural studies approaches. Nevertheless, from the historical perspective, the intellectual significance of "mass society" theories should neither be underestimated nor ignored, because it is impossible to understand the emergence of political and social attitudes and public responses toward the mass media and mass culture without examining the evolution of these ideas. While they may have been eclipsed by other theoretical approaches in academic circles, mass society theories still provide the context in which the majority of our public perspectives on mass culture are formed. Also, the notion of mass society is still implicit in much of current communications research that suggests a "large, undifferentiated audience" for mass media content (which could be defined as "mass culture").

Mass Media in Modern Society is a clear product of the period in the late 1950s when the study of popular and mass culture was still in academic limbo. A perusal of the biographies of the contributors and the nature of their essays reveals that few of them had actually systematically studied the content of media; their concerns lie more with impressionistic evaluations of the role of the media in shaping modern culture. This does not lessen their insights, but a similar conference today would elicit a very different set of papers. In fact, if some enterprising institute wished to engage this topic in the 1990s, it would have to be retitled "Mass Culture: The Myth and the Reality" because, as indicated above, the concepts of "mass society" and "mass culture" are currently the site of considerable academic disagreement. To many of the new generation of "critical theorists" these terms denote the acceptance of an outdated and elitist perspective on culture. As an example, in their recent book *Key Concepts in Communication* the authors note that

> "mass society/mass culture" . . . has been refuted by historical evidence, but its continuation as an ideology can be accounted for by attending to the term most often used as the polar opposite of "mass," namely "elite." This indicates the politics of mass society theorists—they are advocates of various kinds of cultural *elite* who should be privileged and promoted over the masses, claiming

> for themselves both exemption from and leadership of
> the misguided masses. These terms, mass and elite, are
> of course convenient "erasures" or euphemisms for
> *class*.[4]

There is no doubt that the description of what constitutes mass
society/mass culture depends upon the political and ideological perspective
of the theorist. As the British critical scholar Tony Bennett notes of the
mass society tradition, "it by no means constitutes a unified and tightly
integrated body of theory. It should rather be viewed as a loosely defined
'outlook' consisting of a number of intersecting themes." [5]

Mass Society: Toward a Definition

In order to understand the evolution of mass culture and its reception in
the United States, it is crucial to deal with the concept of "mass society,"
and to arrive at some meaningful definition. As with so many other social
and cultural phenomena in our society, we must turn back to the late
eighteenth and early nineteenth centuries to discover its origin. While the
validity of the historical terms "industrial revolution" and "mass society"
are still heavily debated, it is obvious that much of the world has
experienced dramatic shifts in economic, political and social structure
since the late eighteenth century. These shifts have been marked by rapid
and sustained rises in real output per capita; extensive increases in
mechanization, high energy output, and consumption; a decline in the
percentage of the labor force engaged in agriculture and other primary
sectors of the economy; and most significantly, the enormous growth of
urban centers. Correspondingly, there has been a rise in the percentage of
the population engaged in industrial and manufacturing sectors of the
economy.[6] These economic and demographic changes have been
accompanied by an expansion in transportation and communications
facilities, and especially in the West, a significant increase in literacy due
to improvements in the systems of formal education. There have also been
attendant shifts in social structures, cultural practices, and public values
and expectations. These shifts, varying in intensity and application from
country to country depending upon a variety of economic, political, and
social conditions, have affected all societies and cultures in the last one
hundred and fifty years.

Many sociologists and historians have suggested that since the mid-
nineteenth century, we in the West have been part of a developing "mass
society" (although there is still basic disagreement as to what mass society
is, or whether or not it is a positive or negative phenomenon.) It is clear

however, that the original concepts of mass society were developed by nineteenth century European sociologists, who, like all social theorists, were working in a very specific historical and social context that shaped their intellectual perspectives. Everywhere they looked was the disquieting evidence that industrialization and urbanization had caused a drastic shift in the traditional patterns of (rural) community life. Leon Bramson, who has closely examined the history of the concept of mass society, summarizes this influence:

> Indeed, the theory of mass society seems to have developed out of 19th century sociology in a direct line of continuity . . . [and has] . . . a preoccupation with "social disorganization" and "social disintegration." The idea of breakdown of the primary group in modern society was a fundamental theme of 19th century sociology, as it is for the theory of mass society. [7]

Thus we find in the work of the early European social theorists such as August Comte, Ferdinand Tönnies, Herbert Spencer, George Simmel, Emile Durkheim, Max Weber, and, the most complete of them all, Karl Marx, various theoretical approaches to describe and analyze the transition from a traditional (mainly rural-based) to a modern (mainly urban-based) society.[8] The effects of the fundamental shift from a rural to an urban-based society was obviously a central and highly visible issue throughout the nineteenth century and well into our own era. Almost all of these theorists interpreted the effects of urbanization and industrialization as having essentially negative social and cultural consequences, that ultimately caused the destruction of traditional communal life, depersonalization of the individual, and ultimately the emergence of materialistic urban values with an emphasis on money and distraction. While none of these late nineteenth century social theories encompassed all of these negative attitudes, each of these concerns was articulated at one time or another.

There was an even more insidious threat implied in this shift. Whereas before the French Revolution aesthetic standards and moral values were assumed to exist as part of a "natural order" in society (essentially ordained by God, or by elite secular powers), in the emerging democratic societies the highly volatile (and therefore untrustworthy), will and opinion of the mass seemed to prevail, and these were open to constant manipulation. For many Europeans the final danger of "the rise of the masses" within the mass society was that the individual loses a coherent sense of self. When the entire society is subject to such malaise, it sets the stage for the emergence of the charismatic leader who promises to supply the much needed new faith that will provide an identity for the individual, and restore the society to its former glories destroyed by the bland egalitarianism of the mass society. It seemed to some that the mass society theorists had predicted the emergence of the horrors of the European communist and fascist states that were based upon unquestioned support from the masses, manipulated by the control of the mass media and led by the charismatic figures of Lenin, Stalin, Franco, Mussolini, and Hitler.

It is not difficult to see how this philosophical-sociological approach, which emphasizes the breakdown of the close-knit traditional community, has led to a great deal of negative thought concerning the development of mass society. Further, because the advent of the mass media occurred in this same period, these new forms of communication and entertainment and their product—mass culture—were often considered to be an integral part of the development of mass society and are therefore viewed in the same negative light. When combined with the equally critical and cynical views about the nature of collective human behavior ("mass" behavior), this formidable synthesis formed the basis of a very powerful critique of mass society, mass media, and ultimately mass culture.

The concept of mass society took a different form within the context of American intellectual thought. Beginning with the work of Robert Park, Herbert Blumer, and others in the field of "collective behavior," together with that of John Dewey, Walter Lippmann, and others in the movement that Michael Sproule has so aptly called the "progressive propaganda critique,"[9] American intellectuals tended to take a more sanguine tone. Because they were not hampered by the trappings of feudalism, and the resulting obsession with destructive alterations in "class" structure, Americans were more accepting of the mass society as a natural result of the pluralistic and inclusive nature of American society. The dangers lay in the unscrupulous use of the new agencies of mass influence—the mass media and advertising—to subvert the democratic political process. It was this issue that attracted most of the attention from American intellectuals in the period before the Second World War.

Mass Culture

There has never been a universally accepted definition of "mass culture." For purposes of this essay, it will be defined as *the intensified and commercialized form of expressive culture, created by and disseminated throughout the society by the communications media.* Using a market-based model, mass culture can be seen as a series of standardized cultural products manufactured solely for a mass market. As a "product," in order to be successful, it cannot vary too far from what the majority of the audience will accept as part of the publicly articulated cultural norm, otherwise it runs the risk of being too specialized, or fails to attract an audience large enough to sustain commercial sponsorship. One of the major objections by current critical scholars to the traditional concept of a "mass culture" as articulated in the 1950s and 1960s is that it appears to denote a monolithic form of culture, and further implies that the audience are merely passive recipients of the "messages" to which they are exposed. This runs counter to the contemporary view that cultural messages are polysemic and are "read" in a wide variety of ways by heterogeneous audience actively making choices about their participation in media culture. While this objection may reflect the reality of current schools of interpretation, it ignores the purely historical fact, obvious to any who would look, that a "mass culture" did emerge in twentieth-century America. Granted that it was not monolithic, and that it did not convey the same meanings to an undifferentiated audience, nonetheless the increased role of the mass media in shaping our culture cannot be contested. To put it succinctly, the way in which our culture is surveyed, collated, reshaped, and disseminated is vastly different in 1991 than it was in 1891 or 1791. This is due almost entirely to the new agencies of information transmission in modern society, that is, the mass media.

For those scholars whose essays are contained in this and similar volumes of the period, the issue of mass culture and its impact on society was a very real one. If anything, the debate about mass culture—its origins, its role as social integrator or handmaiden of the ruling class, its aesthetics, and its effects on all expressive cultural activities—is even more complex than that concerning the reality of the concept of mass society. Here we are dealing with a problem that is seldom open to satisfactory empirical investigation, but is, instead, subject to the highly subjective taste preferences of individuals. We have all had the experience of having enjoyed a novel or a film, then reading a scathing critical attack on it, and wondering if our own tastes were suspect. (Usually we justify the difference in opinion by saying that it is the critic who has poor judgment.) This problem is particularly acute with television. Since its beginnings, the general critical or intellectual response to television has been so overwhelmingly negative that we have fostered almost two generations of "intelligent" television viewers who are ashamed to admit publicly that they really do enjoy the medium and spend a great deal of time viewing it. As Wilensky pointed out in the early 1960s, "Education has a lot more to do with how people *feel* about TV than what they *do* with it. College graduates criticize TV programming, but they choose to watch extensively."[10]

The problem of subjective judgment and concern about declining aesthetic standards has always plagued the popular arts, and with the advent of mass culture the level of attack was escalated. As the physical presence of popular and later mass culture became more obvious with increased urbanization, so did the critical response. Not that all of the critical attacks were unwarranted; on the contrary, some aspects of mass culture warrant criticism, especially on aesthetic grounds, but it was the idea of the very existence of a "mass culture" that most disturbed those who complained about it.

Of all the critiques of mass culture, the most enduring one has been the "elitist critique," which suggests that as the quantity and ubiquitousness of mass culture has increased, so the quality and quantity of high culture has decreased as the two have tended to move toward each other. (Some astute elite critics correctly point out that even in the best of times, there was very little worthy of being called high culture.) As Ernest van den Haag notes in this volume, the crucial issue was "Is it possible to extend a higher civilization to the lower classes without debasing its standard and diluting its quality to the vanishing point? Is not every civilization bound to decay as soon as it begins to penetrate the masses?" One of the most articulate and widely quoted of these elitist critics was Dwight Macdonald who was even more vociferous in his condemnation of what he called "masscult." In his very provocative collection of essays, *Against the American Grain*, Macdonald, who made a living as a professional literary and film critic, attacked masscult as "at best a vulgarized reflection of High Culture and at worst a nightmare." He was particularly concerned that "while High Culture could formerly address itself only to the *cognoscenti* [those who understand and appreciate], now it must take the *ignoscenti* [those who are ignorant and lack appreciation] into account. . . . For Masscult is not merely a parallel formation to High Culture, as Folk Art was; it is now a competitor."[11] Comments such as van den Haag's and Macdonald's, while patronizing toward the democratic aspirations of mass culture, nevertheless reflect a genuine concern for the survival of their version of high culture in a world increasingly dominated by industrially produced forms of expressive culture. It is easy to see how the critiques of mass society and mass culture are essentially two sides of the same discursive coin.

Despite the most ardent entreaties of cultural analysts who decry such elitist bias, the concern about the encroachment of mass culture, and the resulting debasement of high cultural standards has not diminished, and has, on the contrary, continued to attract the attention of many modern intellectuals. The intellectual odyssey of Daniel Bell on the subject of mass culture is an excellent example of such an attitude. Although he had been mildly positive about the benefits of the social organization of mass society in the early 1960s, by 1976 Bell, in his book, *The Cultural Contradictions of Capitalism*, was voicing a very pessimistic view of the effects of mass culture on "post-industrial" society. He suggested that there was general chaos in society, and the arts in particular, because of the pervasive influence of the mass media and the breakdown in the boundaries between high and mass culture. He attacked television and film, because they

> impose their pace upon the viewer and, in emphasizing images rather than words, invite not conceptualization but dramatization. In the emphasis news places upon disasters and human tragedies, it invites not purgation or understanding but sentimentality and pity, emotions that are quickly exhausted, and a pseudo-ritual of pseudo-participation in the events. And, as the mode is inevitably one of over-dramatization, the responses soon become either stilted or bored. [12]

For Bell, it is the "culture," by which he means both "modernism"—the avant garde in high culture—together with the mass media (mass culture) which are the sources of disruption in modern society. It is the culture which emphasizes "apocalyptic moods and anti-rational modes of behavior" as opposed to the "rational, technological-economic sphere." This is the inherent cultural contradition—"the most fateful division in the society"—which is "the historic cultural crisis of all Western bourgeois society," and which threatens the very nature of the democratic political system. [13] There are some inconsistencies and biases in this argument, for as Patrick Brantlinger points out, "Bell does not squarely confront the question of the possible irrationality of the supposedly rational technological order." [14]

More recently with *The Closing of the American Mind*, the best-selling book by the philosopher Alan Bloom, there has been a revival of the mass culture critique. The phenomenal and unexpected success of this polemical account of the decline of American education in a mass cultural age indicates that the old suspicions about the deleterious effects of mass culture remain deeply ingrained in American society. Bloom virulently attacks the very foundation of modern youth culture—rock music—and lays the blame for the low quality of modern education squarely at its feet. [15] That this book touched a raw cultural nerve in American society was reinforced by the success of E.D. Hirsch's *Cultural Literacy: What Every American Needs to Know*, a similar evaluation of the failure of American education to correctly "acculturate" the population. [16] Hirsch went so far as to compile actual lists of "cultural facts" that he felt "cultured" individuals should be familiar with. Both of these books remain the subject of intense debate, especially since their basic philosophies on the need for a defined "cultural" education were given endorsements by William Bennett, then the secretary of education in President Ronald Reagan's cabinet.

Despite what the academics promoting the seemingly more egalitarian theories of expressive culture may wish, elitist-based fears about the effects of mass culture refuse to succumb in the face of mere academic analysis, and are still very prevalent in current cultural criticism. While most modern cultural theorists may decry such conservative perspectives as historically invalid, representative of an outdated social power structures, and lacking theoretical rigor, the fact remains that they continue to exercise a significant influence in the real world of educational policy, legislation, and social control. The main concern is that the increased availability of, and participation in, mass culture has gradually made high culture, together with its historically and universally agreed upon standards of quality, less relevant to modern society. It is felt that without reference to these traditional aesthetic standards as guidelines, all forms of culture assume the same level of significance. In this view, the result of such egalitarianism has been a disaster for expressive cultural activities in general, and especially for the quality of popular and mass culture. We can see examples of this concern as manifested by attacks upon the perceived poor quality of popular music, together with its provocative sexuality and peculiar dress codes;[17] the triviality of the content of television, and the increasing amount of time spent watching it;[18] and the general decline in education and the failure to study the "great works" of civilization that embody all that high culture represents. [19]

Views supporting the validity of mass culture are equally as diverse as the critiques. Leo Lowenthal, a pioneer in the study of mass culture, pointed out in his essay in this volume that the debate about high versus low culture has been going on a long time, and has been clearly articulated since the eighteenth century.[20] There have always been defenders of the rights of the "mass" to have their particular cultural pursuits, but the advent of mass culture created a wider philosophical problem. No longer was a specific form of cultural activity, such as the movies, dancing, picnics, saloons, or the theater being defended;[21] the issue now coalesced around the more universal question of what effect the development and increasing importance of the popular arts was having on the high arts. The enlarged scope of the debate created a need for a broader understanding of how mass culture interacted with its audiences.

It is important to note that the elitist critics no longer deny the right of mass culture to exist, or even to flourish within its own sphere; their concern is with the increasing centrality of the mass media and mass culture at the expense of high culture, and the failure to establish any recognized aesthetic standards that might serve to improve their quality. This last concern is, obviously, a matter of personal taste and ideological perspective, and ignores the fact that comparative and internal critical standards are increasingly being applied to mass culture. It is extremely difficult to establish universally accepted aesthetic standards for such a wide range of expressive cultural activities. Does one judge the quality of creation, production, or the level of audience reception as the mark of success? These three elements are relatively easy to evaluate, and even to quantify in certain cases such as the size of the audience. (There is the suggestion, usually made by the producers, that the only true evaluative criterion for mass culture is success and survival in the marketplace.) However, it would be almost impossible to critically evaluate all of the specific and special meanings that the audiences take from such activities. Nonetheless, despite continued misgivings on the part of creators, performers, and even audiences, recognized critical standards have evolved in mass culture, especially for such media as film, popular music, and more recently, television.

The key question is: Have these critical standards been developed specifically for mass culture, taking into account its unique modes of production, audience reception, and historical and cultural function? Or are they merely a reworking of the traditional high culture critical standards? Clearly, if we are to understand mass culture, we need to evaluate it using critical approaches more appropriate to its own historical framework and cultural and social role.

The Rise and Decline of the Mass Society/Mass Culture Theories

By the end of the Second World War a variety of historical circumstances combined to bring about a new focus on the issues of mass society and mass culture in the United States. The most obvious of these was the unprecedented consumerist spree generated by the pent-up needs of returning servicemen and servicewomen for everything from nylon stockings to cheap tract housing in the new treeless suburbs. Less obvious was the gradual emergence in the next decade of a highly materialist, youth-oriented culture in stark contrast to the austerity of the Depression years. But without doubt, the major catalyst or shifting the focus from the political implications of mass *society* to the cultural and educational implications of mass *culture* was the introduction of television in the period after 1947. The extent to which the American public embraced television, and the obvious grip that the medium had on American culture and consumerism was seen by many intellectuals as a graphic symbol of the decline of traditional culture. (By 1959, eighty-six percent of American households had a television set).[22] While everyone had their own specific definition of what encompassed "traditional" culture, there was no denying that cultural practices were changing. While there had been complaints about every new medium of communication and entertainment since the nineteenth century, the sheer ubiquity of television and the increasing number of hours being devoted to it, was the harbinger of a new age in which all forms of culture were thought to be in danger. A careful reading of this volume shows exactly how much the issue of television is insinuated into the various essays, and becomes a dark specter hovering over the debate.

A major part of the intellectual problem with assessing the cultural content of the mass media was that the study of mass media and mass culture had taken divergent paths in the post-World War II period. It was in the late 1920s that we find the first tentative research studies using empirical research strategies especially devised to gauge the impact of communications on different aspects of modern life. During the 1930s and through the Second World War there was an increasing interest in using the mass media for active persuasive or information purposes. This interest came from two sources, the desire of advertisers for greater effectiveness, especially in the medium of commercial radio, and from governments as the propaganda efforts from competing political forces intensified on an international scale. These articulated needs were met by a new generation of social scientists led by Paul Lazarsfeld and his associates at Columbia University, and provided some of the first empirical work on the cultural influence of the media, especially radio.[23] However, after 1945 the field of communications research was dominated by positivistic empirical research, and the study of mass culture was relegated to a more philosophical and political role.

Because mass culture is essentially the product of the media it is natural to assume that an interest in the two areas would follow automatically in any research design. However, this has not necessarily been the case, and for a variety of reasons, the cultural component of communications research was increasingly ignored as the level of methodological sophistication increased. First, as communications research designs moved to a more positivistic position and adopted a variety of complex quantitative techniques, the content of the media became less important than the measurement of audiences and attitudinal changes in the aggregate (the "effects" of media). Second, an additional problem was that "culture," as has been noted at some length, is a difficult concept to define, let alone reduce to manageable terms where it can be "quantified" to provide "scientific" theories of change. Third, the persistence of mass society theory as a viable political and historical framework had a tendency to remove the mass culture debate away from empirical research, and place it more in the arena of sociological and aesthetic theorizing. Fourth, the differences in the primary concerns of the two areas dictated a difference in the style of approach. The characteristics of cultural studies tend to be subjective, theoretical, historical, and narrative; while those for communication research tend to be objective, empirical, current, and presented in a dry, scientific form. Finally, academic politics had an important part in this history. For, despite the increasing interest in mass communications research in universities, there was a lingering intellectual stigma attached to actually studying popular or mass culture in many of these same institutions that would last almost until the late 1970s.

The unfortunate dichotomy between communications research and cultural studies has been widely commented upon in recent years. In a perceptive analysis of these differences, Paul Hirsch named the two perspectives the "social problem" (reflecting the lingering mass society influence) and the "communications research" orientations, and noted that "The relation between social science and popular culture is best characterized as one of long-standing and mutual incomprehension and distaste."[24] Elihu Katz has noted that there has long been a debate between those asking "What are the mass media doing to us?" and those who are more interested in examining "what are the uses to which people put the mass media."[25] The first approach stems from the historical concern to understand the implications of the media to change political attitudes and to satisfy media industry's needs, while the latter is more conducive to the study of mass culture. Contributing to this was the increasing importance of the "client-centered research" commissioned by the media industries, which concentrated efforts on seeking to measure the size and characteristics of audiences and media effectiveness in shaping consumer behavior. Few media industries were willing to subsidize research to confirm for their critics how influential the media really were in shaping American culture. In some ways this stance was understandable, for they were fearful of government regulation if this acculturation role became too obvious or seemed out of control. The long, controversial battle over censorship, which had befallen the movie industry ever since its introduction precisely because of its great popularity, was a lesson not lost on the other media industries.

Social scientists, using mainly survey research methods on relatively large population samples, concentrated on trying to measure the impact of media on society by examining single programs, or specific political campaigns. When these methods yielded very cautious results about the power of the media to effect change, it was naturally assumed that the content of the media (mass culture) would also have minimal effect. Unfortunately, these survey methodologies were not sensitive enough to measure or explain the potential long-term and cumulative effects brought about by exposure to mass media content. Simply put, most survey research methodologies cannot reveal the way in which the audiences for mass culture actually uses and enjoys this form of expressive culture. Measurements of audiences in the aggregate fail to explain how mass culture helps to reinforce existing attitudes, beliefs and values, or how mass culture reorganizes elements from the core of culture to create new, and yet seemingly familiar themes and perspectives.

The study of the cultural role of the mass media was not entirely ignored, quite the contrary, for even as empirical research of mass communications was receiving increased attention in the period after 1939, there were competing voices which suggested that "effects research," concentrating as it did on the degree of "exposure" to given content and the measurement of resulting attitude or opinion changes, did not provide a comprehensive picture of mass communication influence. In particular, the philosophical perspectives of the members of that group of social scientists and philosophers known as the Frankfurt School, especially the critiques of Theodor Adorno and Walter Benjamin, provided an intellectual platform for later examinations of the role of the mass media and its content forms within the entire social and cultural fabric. [26]

However, throughout the 1950s and 1960s while some American sociologists and literary intellectuals were engaged in the intense debate on the merits of "mass society" and "mass culture," the newly emerging, specialized researchers from recently created doctoral programs in communications were busy developing highly refined, empirically-based models of mass media influence. It was the empirical, limited-effects model which provided the dominant paradigm for media studies until the mid-1970s.[27] However, while much of the "mass society" debate proved to be incompatible with, and antithetical to, most empirical research, in recent years the revival of interest in the study of expressive culture has rekindled an awareness of the fundamental political and social concerns which underlay the mass society theories, albeit from the opposite side.

In recent years mainstream communications research has begun to concern itself more and more with issues of long-term change, the nature of cognitions rather than attitude or opinion change, and shifts in structures of belief, ideology, and cultural patterns. Perhaps the greatest shift has been in the growing interest shown in all aspects of the practices and ideologies of the institutions that are responsible for the creation and dissemination of media messages.[28] In particular, the interrelationship between the economic base of these industries and the "production of culture" has been a pivotal point in the understanding of the "media messages" which shape and perpetuate the dominant ideologies in a society.[29]

The New Critique: Critical and Cultural Studies

The emergence of the cultural and critical studies approaches to mass communication in the 1970s signalled a major shift in the direction of media studies away from the concentration on "effects" toward a broader range of perspectives.[30] Starting in Europe, where the tradition of Marxist and neo-Marxist scholarship and analysis is more accepted, and building upon the earlier work of the Frankfurt School of theorists, a new, more culturally centered focus began to emerge in communication studies. Once these approaches achieved some recognition, it was not long before empirical research found itself under justified attack from American as well as European scholars for its failure to deal adequately with the totality of media impact on a society. It was suggested that research which used surveys and experimental designs was "individualistic and microanalytical," and therefore did not reveal much about the social and cultural context of the communication act. As James Curran and his colleagues have pointed out, "The initial response [on the part of critical and cultural theorists] . . . was to dismiss out of hand empirical communications research as being uniformly uninteresting. The media, they argued, were ideological agencies that played a central role in maintaining class domination; research studies that denied media influence were so disabled in their theoretical approach as to be scarcely worth confronting (or indeed, even reading)."[31] There was, as expected, a natural response from empirically oriented media researchers that past work in metatheorizing about the media (in the form of the mass society/mass culture theories) had been equally inadequate in its attempts to explicate the role of media in society.

What is critical studies, and how has it contributed to our understanding of the mass media in the creation of mass culture? A good place to start would be to examine the Summer 1983 issue of the *Journal of Communication*, entitled "Ferment in the Field." In this special issue, which symbolized the changes then taking place in the field of communications research, fifty-one authors from ten countries assessed the current and future state of the field, and in so doing represented the amazing diversity of approaches sheltering under the general umbrella of "critical studies." The editor of the journal, Dr. George Gerbner had the unenviable task of summarizing the results of this symposium. Gerbner's observations provide a good place to begin our search for answers, for only by appreciating the fact that communication scholars now view the mass media as much more than merely news and entertainment vehicles, can we hope to understand the potential impact of these new, culturally-based approaches. Gerbner noted that

> Social and symbolic structures cultivate tacit agreement on the terms of their existence. People growing up and living with these structures come to assume their existence as unwittingly as the proverbial fish in the ocean does salt water. Any scholarly inquiry that explicitly recognizes these structures is inherently critical. It poses a challenge to unthinking acceptance. It extends the possibility of conscious control and deliberate change. It brings some degree of autonomy, self-direction, and the development into the realm of human social possibilities. Posing that challenge is a unique task of an academic discipline and the only legitimate justification for its admittedly limited but still significant freedoms.

The different perspectives offered in this issue of the *Journal of Communication* clearly indicates that in the last decade there had been a gradual, but significant innovation in the curricula of many schools of journalism and communication, as well as departments of English, history and sociology—the emergence of a sometimes defiantly antiempirical, humanistically based perspective known as "critical studies."[32] The basic subject matter—the "critical" evaluation of the mass media—is not really new; after all, an element of criticism and evaluation has always been an integral part of the approach to studying the media. What is different, however, about this particular approach to media criticism is the impressive body of intellectual theory and political ideology which underlies and impels it.[33] Unlike previous *ad hoc* forms of idiosyncratic media criticism, critical studies has become a recognized and accepted, if not always clearly understood or appreciated, approach to the study of mass media in our society. The critical studies approach has already had an observable impact on the published research in the field, and is the subject of sometimes intense debate at academic conferences. Its proponents, and some of its detractors, feel that it is only a matter of time before critical studies achieves the same status as the statistically based empirical research approach which is currently predominant in the study of mass communication in the United States. In fact, critical studies' strongest supporters have as their stated aim the displacement of so-called "objective" empirical research from its lofty perch by a more socially and politically aware hybrid combination of empiricism and critical research.

What exactly is "critical studies?" Once again, it is not easy to come up with a precise definition of the term, as it covers a number of different theoretical perspectives and techniques. However, there are some centrally identifiable concerns common to all of these approaches. In 1982, Everett Rogers, one of the leading communication scholars in the United States, wrote in *Communication Yearbook 5* that the "main concerns of the critical school today are to criticize empirical communication studies of development and modernization, to champion a new international information order, [which would encourage the "free and open" flow of information, while discouraging the imperialistic domination of third world media systems by the industrialized nations], and to question the consequences of new communication technology."[34] Just three short years later, in 1985, Rogers' appreciation and understanding of critical studies had evolved to the point that in a revision of this essay he altered the definition to now read: "the essence of the critical school is its philosophical emphasis, its focus on the broader social-structural context of communication, an original basis in Marxist thought, and a central concern with the issue of who controls mass communication systems."[35] The shift in Rogers' definition also mirrors the increasing acceptance that certain aspects of critical studies have found among the more traditional communications researchers.

Whatever the precise definition, supported by an impressive and often controversial body of published work, critical studies approaches to the study of mass communication have obviously gained the attention of the mainstream media scholars. Since the middle of the 1970s there has been a melding of the two methodologies—critical studies and empiricism—which has begin to enrich all of communications research. (In reality they were not as far apart as some scholars would have had us believe.) Researchers working within the critical tradition have begun to rely upon data generated by empirical methods, such as surveys and audience measurements, while those working in empirical communications research have been sensitized by the Marxist critiques that "more attention needs to be paid to the influence of the media on the ideological categories and frames of reference through which people understand the world."[36] To emphasize this point, one of the leading American critical theorists, Lawrence Grossberg has suggested that

> We need to bring some of the sophisticated research techniques available to us today into critical research. At the very least, the nature of the mass media and the sheer size of its audience (not to mention the differences between them) seems to demand new forms of critical research.[37] . . . the attempt to study communication in the contemporary world—in which messages are effective in part because of their proliferation and repetition, and in which the mass audience is no longer conceivable as either a simple aggregate of sociological fractions or a common psychological structure—may, in fact, demand the appropriation of such research practices.[38]

As Grossberg notes, the two fields—empiricism and critical studies—have much to offer the other. It is unfortunate that the histories of these two fields developed in such a way as to foster both ignorance and hostility toward each other. Part of the explanation lies in the dominance exerted by large media organizations in the development of communications research in the United States; while in Europe, a similar dominance was partially balanced by the accepted tradition of the public examination of social and cultural conditions and phenomena by intellectuals and scholars. Nowhere were these differences between the industrial pragmatism of the United States, and the academic theorizing of Europe more evident than in the work of the members of the Frankfurt School and the other theoretical perspectives on mass culture developed out of Marxist philosophy.

The end result of this "unnatural" separation between the study of mass media and mass culture was that it hindered the development of the full potential of both approaches. An examination of the literature reveals that popular and mass culture studies have often suffered badly, in the academic and qualitative sense, from a lack of empirical evidence, and relatively few attempts have been made to encompass and deal with the enormous amount of reliable data generated by researchers in other fields. (Of course, not all studies of mass culture need to use empirical methods, but many that should, do not!)[39] On the other hand, communications research in the purely methodological and "intellectual respectability" sense has probable suffered less, but here too much of the work in this field could benefit from a greater sensitivity to the historical and social contexts of the forms of expressive culture created by and disseminated through the media.[40] It is heartening to note that since the 1970s, and the emergence of a new set of largely European-inspired cultural theories, that some "rapprochement" between the two fields has been effected. The result has been an increased interest in the study of media and culture, and a widened appreciation for the complex interrelationships between the audience and expressive cultural activity in modern society.

Mass Media in Modern Society: A Review

It is only against the historical background outlined above that the essays in *Mass Media in Modern Society* can be understood. Paul Lazarsfeld noted at the conclusion of his introductory essay that "Matters often look bad, but somehow they always stop short of being disastrous.... It is the tragic story of the cultural crusader in a mass society that he cannot win, but we would be lost without him." These essays reflect a real sense of concern for the future of culture in the United States, but there are also points of optimism. For the modern reader some of the arguments and dire predictions may now seem moot, (Frank Stanton's comments about CBS's news and documentary activities are particularly poignant) but there are themes and tropes that are clearly still part of the current debate about the interrelationship between media and culture.

The keynote essay "Mass Society and Its Culture" by the sociologist Edward Shils is considered a classic, and has been widely reprinted in various anthologies. It has also been the center of an ardent debate over the years. In this, and other similar essays,[41] Shils defended mass society by claiming that there were positive attributes in the threads of this new integrative type of large-scale social organization. In his view the development of modern society has been greatly facilitated by the growth of the mass media with their ability to reduce perceived distance between individuals, groups, and even institutions. There was also some evidence that the growth of the media had led to a wider recognition of common needs and values in society as a whole. Thus, as the mass media became a more powerful social and cultural force, geographic separation appeared to decrease; the end results, the mass society defenders argued, were a greater degree of internal unity and a tendency toward centralization. As Shils noted, "The new society is a mass society precisely in the sense that the mass of the population has become incorporated *into* society. . . . Most of the population (the 'mass') now stands in a closer relationships to the center than has been the case in either premodern societies or in the earlier phases of modern society." Thus, when American society was in the throes of the politically, and culturally, divisive Age of McCarthyism, Shils was attempting to turn the negative image of mass society into a positive, and particularly American "liberal-pluralist" perspective. This enabled him to attack the elitist views of the mass society critics, while extolling the virtues of both political and cultural democracy.

Shils's views had the advantage of offering explanations that appeared to fit in with the empirical observations about mass media usage, whereas many of the "pessimistic" theories—based as they were on personal philosophical, political and historical perspectives—did not. Of course, there are those who continue to argue that the very conditions that Shils described served only to provide an illusion (the classic Marxist notion of "false consciousness") to these pluralistic groups that they are participating meaningfully in the central decision-making institutions of American society.

As part of his optimism toward the social reorganization of mass society, Edward Shils also provided a defense of mass culture by making the point that a considerable amount of what he called "mediocre" culture retained its value over long periods, "and even though mediocre taste varies, as does superior taste, there are stable elements to it, too, so that some of the mediocre culture of the past continues to find an appreciative audience." He made a cogent historical point that the number of consumers of high culture had never been very large and have usually been limited to a small group of people with a specific intellectual preparation, such as university teachers, scientists, writers, lawyers, and a scattering of those from other occupations. (He could also have said that this cultural elite were usually high on the socioeconomic scale.) However in modern society, mainly through the mass media, a larger number of people, especially the middle classes, have "come into contact with and consumed a larger quantity of extra-religious, superior culture than has ever been the case throughout the course of modern history." Also, according to Shils, in spite of their exposure to the mass media the working class and rural populations have maintained a great deal of their traditional culture. While Shils did attack some of the negative aspects of mass culture (he was especially concerned about the preoccupation of "youth" with what he called "brutal culture"), he remained optimistic about the prospects for "superior culture" (high culture), precisely because it overlapped with mass culture at certain points and hence reached a wider audience.

Shils's views did not go unchallenged at this symposium. Hannah Arendt and Ernest Van Den Haag both disputed aspects of his central thesis. Arendt was much more concerned with the nature of mass culture in that emerged as a result of the formulation of a mass society: "Mass society . . . wants not culture but entertainment, and the wares offered by the entertainment industry are indeed consumed by society just as they are any other consumer goods." Arendt's concern was for the future of high culture in a consumerist society. She observed: "If we understand by culture what it originally meant (the Roman *cultura*—derived from *colere*, to take care of and preserve and cultivate) then we can say without any exaggeration that a society obsessed with consumption cannot at the same time be cultured or produce a culture." The issue of the decline of high culture is also taken up by other essayists, most notably the poet Randall Jarrell in his famous essay, "Sad Heart at the Supermarket," in which he laments that "Our culture is essentially periodical: we believe that all that is deserves to perish and to have something else put in its place."

It is left, however, to Van Den Haag to examine the reality of Shils's contention that mass society had a positive function in the modern world. Van Den Haag asks the key question: "Of course we have more communication and mobility than ever before. But isn't it possible that less is communicated?" These are among the many issues that confront the reader of this fascinating volume. In light of social and cultural developments in the last thirty years the optimistic faith that Shils placed on the integrative role of mass society must be examined against the decay of our inner cities and the continued racism in American society.

Mass Media in Modern Society remains a classic, not only for what it represents as an historical document, but also because of the centrality of its discussions about the nature of cultural participation and aesthetics in modern societies. While the terms "mass society" and "mass culture" may not be as widely used as they were in the past, they continue to have a specific relevance for historians in that the denote the very definite change in the quality and quantity of cultural production and consumption which began in the mid-nineteenth century. This volume is symbolic of the continuous intellectual quest to understand the nature and extent of these changes.

Garth S. Jowett

NOTES

1. This is evidenced by the growing number of academic journals devoted exclusively to cultural studies. See *Critical Studies in Mass Communication, Cultural Studies, Media, Culture and Society,* and *The Journal of Communication Inquiry* as examples.
2. Dwight Macdonald, "A Theory of Mass Culture," in *Mass Culture; The Popular Arts in America,* ed. Bernard Rosenberg and David Manning White (Glencoe, Ill.: The Free Press, 1957), 73.
3. Daniel Bell, "America as a Mass Society: A Critique," *The End of Ideology* (Glencoe, Ill.: The Free Press, 1960), 21.
4. Tim O'Sullivan, John Hartley, Danny Saunders, and John Fiske, *Key Concepts in Communication* (New York: Methuen, 1983), 131.

5. Tony Bennett, "Theories of Media and Society," in *Culture, Society and the Media*, eds. Michael Gurevitch, Tony Bennett, James Curran, and Janet Woolacott (London: Methuen, 1982), 32.

6. Of course, there has been a gradual decrease in the number of people employed in these sectors in the late twentieth century. For an excellent historical account of the "development process" see Frederick W. Frey, "Communication and Development," in *The Handbook of Communications*, eds. Ithiel de Sola Pol and others (Chicago: Rand McNally, 1973), 337-432.

7. Leon Bramson, *The Political Context of Sociology* (Princeton, N.J.: Princeton University Press, 1961), 31.

8. There is a fairly extensive literature on the development of social theory which examines the work of these and other nineteenth century social philosophers. In particular see Nicholas S. Timasheff, *Sociological Theory: Its Nature and Growth*, 3rd ed. (New York: Random House, 1967); and Randall Collins and Michael Makowsky, *The Discovery of Society* (New York: Random House, 1972).

9. Michael Sproule, "Propaganda and American Ideological Critique," in *Communication Yearbook 14*, ed. James Anderson, (Newbury Park, Cal.: Sage, 1991), 211-38.

10. Harold L. Wilensky, "Mass Society and Mass Culture," in *Public Opinion and Communication*, eds., Bernard Berelson and Morris Janowitz (New York: The Free Press, 1966), 295.

11. Dwight Macdonald, *Against the American Grain: Essays on the Effects of Mass Culture* (New York: Random House, 1965), 34. These are particularly well written, but very provocative and largely pessimistic essays on the dangers of mass culture to many aspects of modern civilization.

12. Daniel Bell, *The Cultural Contradictions of Capitalism* (New York: Basic Books, 1976), 108.

13. Ibid., 84

14. Patrick Brantlinger, *Bread and Circuses* (Ithaca: Cornell University Press, 1983), 286. This book contains an excellent analysis of the "post-industrial" theorists of mass society and its consequences. See 287-97.

15. Alan Bloom, *The Closing of the American Mind* (New York: Simon and Schuster, 1987).

16. E.D. Hirsch, Cultural Literacy: *What Every American Needs to Know* (Boston: Houghton Mifflin, 1987).

17. For a useful overview of popular music and its cultural implications, see Iain Chambers, *Urban Rhythms: Pop Music and Popular Culture* (New York: St. Martin's Press, 1985).

18. See Neil Postman, *Amusing Ourselves to Death: Public Discourse in the Age of Show Business* (New York: Viking, 1985).

19. This viewpoint was expressed in Alan Bloom, *The Closing of the American Mind.*

20. See also chapter 2, "Popular Culture and Its Enemies," in J.M. Goldby and A.W. Purdue, *The Civilisation of the Crowd* (New York: Schocken Books, 1985), 41-62.

21. The introduction of these various forms of entertainment was always accompanied by concern, while others rose to their defense. See Robert C. Toll, *The Entertainment Machine* (New York: Oxford University Press, 1981).

22. Christopher Sterling and John Kittross, *Stay Tuned* (Belmont, Cal.: Wadsworth, 1978), 535.
23. See Paul Lazarsfeld and Frank Stanton, *Radio Research, 1941* and *Radio Research, 1942-43* (New York: Duell, Sloan and Pearce, 1941, 1944).
24. Paul M. Hirsch, "Social Science Approaches to Popular Culture: A Review and Critique," *Journal of Popular Culture* 9, 2 (Fall 1977), 401.
25. Elihu Katz and David Foulkes, "The uses of mass media as 'escape': clarification of a concept," *Public Opinion Quarterly* 25 (1969), 377-388.
26. The work of the members of the Frankfurt School has been discussed extensively in many publications. For an outstanding evaluation of their contribution to modern thought, see the detailed history of this group by Martin Jay, *The Dialectical Imagination: A History of the Frankfurt School and Institute of Social Search, 1923-1950* (Boston: Little, Brown and Company, 1973). For a useful summary of their influence in the development of mass communication theory see Bennett, "Theories of the Media, Theories of Society," 41-47.
27. Everett Rogers has noted that "the empirical school of communication research is characterized by quantitative empiricism, functionalism [which postulates a view of society with relatively stable relationships and a tendency toward stability], and positivism [which sees the media as a generally positive force in society]," in Everett M. Rogers, "The Empirical and Critical Schools of Communication Research," in Rogers and Balle, eds., *The Media Revolution in America and Western Europe* (Norwood, N.J.: Ablex Publishing, 1985) 222-23.
28. There are many examples of this new interest in the critical approach to studying media institutions. One excellent introduction is Joseph Turow, *Media Industries: The Production of News and Entertainment* (New York: Longman, 1984).
29. The study of the "political economy" of media institutions can provide historians with a great deal of useful data for assessing their historical role. This is not an area which has received a great deal of attention from historians, but as industry files are becoming available, we can expect to see more such studies. See for example, Janet Wasko, *Movies and Money: Financing the American Film Industry* (Norwood, N.J.: Ablex Publishing, 1982); and Graham Murdock, "Large Corporations and the Control of the Communications Industries," Michael Gurevitch, et al., *Culture, Media and Society*, 118-150.
30. The definitions of "cultural studies" and "critical studies" can be quite amorphous. For a useful introduction to this subject see Albert Kreiling, "Toward a Cultural Studies Approach for the Sociology of Popular Culture," *Communication Research* 5, 3 (July, 1978), 240-63; James Carey, "Communication and Culture," *Communication Research* 2, 2 (April 1975), 173-91; and Everett M. Rogers, "The Empirical and Critical Schools of Communication Research," in Rogers and Balle, eds., 219-35.
31. James Curran, Michael Gurevitch and Janet Woollacott, "The Study of the Media: Theoretical Approaches," Michael Gurevitch, et al. *Culture Society and the Media*, 13.
32. In this essay, I have preferred to use the term "critical studies" as a generic term to describe the approaches that emerged out of European inspired interpretations of Marxist theory. The term "cultural studies" is a specific

form of critical studies, coming largely out of the American experience, and more clearly based in the disciplines of anthropology and ethnography.

33. A useful taxonomy of various critical approaches is found in Lawrence Grossberg, "Strategies of Marxist Cultural Interpretation," *Critical Studies in Mass Communication*, 1, 4 (December 1984), 392-421.

34. Everett M. Rogers, "The Empirical and critical schools of communication research," in Michael Burgoon, ed., *Communication Yearbook 5* (New Brunswick, N.J.: Transaction Books, 1982), 133.

35. Everett M. Rogers, "The empirical and critical schools of communication research," in Everett M. Rogers and Francis Balle, eds., p. 226.

36. Ibid., 16.

37. Lawrence Grossberg, "Critical Theory and the Politics of Empirical Research," in Michael Gurevitch and Mark R. Levy, eds., *Mass Communication Yearbook 6* (1987), 87.

38. Ibid., 97.

39. One of the best examples of the use of empirical data as the base for generating cultural analysis is Pierre Bourdieu, *Distinction: A Social Critique for the Judgement of Taste* (Cambridge, Mass.: Harvard University Press, 1984).

40. This argument is developed at length in Garth S. Jowett, "Toward a History of Popular Culture," *Journal of Popular Culture* 9, 2 (Fall 1975), 493-94.

41. A more fully developed examination of mass society is found in Edward Shils, "The Theory of Mass Society," in *America as a Mass Society*, ed. Philip Olsen (New York: The Free Press, 1963), 30-47.

Introduction to the Original Edition

PAUL F. LAZARSFELD

Mass Culture Today

OVER THE last thirty years much has been written about mass society, mass culture, and the mass media. Two variations make the present volume different from previous symposia on the same topic.

One is the composition of the group of contributors. There are some of the expected names: Gilbert Seldes who, in 1927, with his book *The Seven Lively Arts*, put the mass media on the agenda of intellectual discussion and has contributed to it ever since; Bernard Berelson, one of the empirical research specialists who, over the last two or three decades, has made mass communication one of the best documented aspects of the American scene. The mass media themselves are mainly represented through spokesmen who have had serious research backgrounds: Frank Stanton, who has done some of the pioneering work in radio research and who is now president of the Columbia Broadcasting System; Leo Rosten who, with his *Washington Correspondent*, made one of the early contributions to the study of the "communicator," and who is now an influential policy adviser for *Look* Magazine. Two of the contributors are affiliated with magazines that have continuously paid great attention to the study of mass culture: Irving Kristol, the former Managing Editor of the *Reporter*, and Nathan Glazer, a regular contributor to *Commentary*. And there are the social scientists who are professionally concerned with analysis of the contemporary scene: Edward Shils, Professor of Social Thought at the University of Chicago; Ernest Van den Haag, co-author of an outstanding book, *The Fabric of Society*; and the well-known author Hannah Ahrendt, who won the Goethe Prize for her book on *The Human Condition*.

Three other types of participants are not usually represented in this kind of symposium. We find professional historians of prominence in their own fields, like Oscar Handlin, Arthur Schlesinger, Jr., and Stuart Hughes, all of Harvard University. Then, there are three well-known philosophers: Ernest Nagel and Charles Frankel

25

from Columbia, and Sidney Hook from New York University. Most unusual, however, is the participation of artists. As far as I know, this is the first time people who write about culture and those who create it have confronted each other. Among the participants are: Randall Jarrell, the poet; James Baldwin, the novelist; and Arthur Berger, the composer.

The second interesting feature of this volume is a very careful record of the discussion which followed the original presentation; it gives an additional element of depth to what is offered in the formal papers. Many discussants made important contributions but wrote no papers. Their comments will be found in the summaries of the discussions at the end of this volume. Some of those whose prepared statements are included in this volume often said more personal, and therefore more important, things in the discussion. These will also be found at the end of the book.

I consider it my task and my privilege to give the readers some help in the perusal of all this material.

Mass Society and Mass Culture

The keynote paper by Edward Shils is indeed an illuminating presentation of the whole problem. It is important, however, to distinguish two strands in it. Shils gives a coherent presentation of almost all the issues, but at many points he also adds his own observations of the situation. The reader might do well to separate these two aspects and to consider first the formal structure of Shils' contribution.

He begins with a brief description of what he considers the essence of mass society. One should not worry too much about the definition. We all know from direct experience that tremendous growth of the population, the complexity of urban life, the mechanization of the productive system, and a changed political structure have engendered in many countries a way of life quite different from the one existing, say, a hundred years ago. In the United States we have to add the rapidly rising standard of living and the development of a large entertainment industry. What the essential features of this new type of society are and how they affect human existence is, as we shall see, one of the major topics of this symposium. The main facts are known to everyone and only the term "mass society" might be new to some.[1] Shils describes the culture of this mass society; he distinguishes three levels of culture which in colloquial terms are often called highbrow, middlebrow, and lowbrow culture. The classification, although vague, is useful and perhaps inevitable. When we talk of highbrow culture we think of enduring works of art and the contemporary efforts of avant-gardists who deserve respect because of the seriousness of their intentions. We think of the average movie, the family magazine, or the respectable television program when we use the term middlebrow. By lowbrow we mean such things as comics, detective stories, and vaudeville. It is no coincidence that the examples are cultural products offered to people rather than activities in which they themselves engage.

Little was said at the symposium about lowbrow culture. But a distinction between the first two levels is crucial. For in a nutshell one can say that everyone is concerned with two main problems: What happens *to* highbrow culture in mass society? And what does the great increase in middlebrow culture *do* to people? The focal point at which both these problems can be unraveled appeared to Shils to be the mass media. All through the symposium this emphasis on the mass media is hardly ever questioned, and yet I shall try to show that this is not a completely obvious point of view.

Shils also deals with the consumers and the producers of the various forms of cultural products. He briefly summarizes what is known of the social stratification of "audiences." It is useful to learn that a simple classification of the population by education or by some index of social economic status permits reasonably safe predictions of what people will select on their television sets or do with their free time. [2] But Shils adds an observation which has rarely been made. The cultural activities of *young* people at least in this country are much less related to their social status. Here he implies an interesting problem indeed: Will these young people twenty years hence recreate the stratified pattern of their parents or should we expect greater homogeneity of cultural interests in the future?

In the latter part of the keynote paper, some of the most urgent issues are laid out. There is the question of historical comparisons. Certainly many more people participate in "culture" today than took part, say, one hundred years ago, and that has necessarily made for lowering the level of the average supply. But if we were to look at strata comparable to the upper class and aristocracy of the nineteenth century, would the same be true? The tendency toward and the difficulty of seeing historical trends is very marked in such discussions.

Handlin's paper in this volume provides a characteristic example.

He sees a great difference between the folk art of the past and today's mass culture. But a careful reading of his contribution shows that what he means by folk art could have played only an occasional role in people's lives. What did they do on long winter evenings? Were they desperately bored? Or is boredom itself an experience which has developed in industrial society? From Handlin's personal remarks one gathers that historians know very little about how people used to spend their time, so comparisons become speculations. But Shils correctly raises a second question: Is there an inherent threat to highbrow culture in mass society? Where does this threat come from? Are commercial interests corrupting the public? Or is it that a mediocre audience, which can afford to pay for entertainment, is distracting valuable talent from more worthy pursuits? Is there a withering away of elites who are a necessary breeding ground for cultural innovations? The keynote paper also introduces a notion of "mediocre intelligentsia." These are the men and women who, while highly trained themselves, produce the middlebrow culture. We shall later see that they are a special problem for the creative artist.

Shils is optimistic on most of the points and it was this strongly expressed optimism which obscured for many participants the merits of his general formulations.[3] Both Van den Haag and Arendt more or less explicitly stressed that Shils had omitted one important category. Their argument was that one should not only look at the nature and content of the cultural supply; one should be much more concerned with the way it is received. Van den Haag argues that people in mass society have lost the ability to take cultural issues seriously. The whole idea is symbolized in a statement by T. W. Adorno: "Radio has made of Beethoven's Fifth Symphony a hit tune which is easy to whistle." The theme of Miss Arendt's contribution is related; she says popular culture has made of the classics something to be consumed rather than understood. In a way, Handlin's paper belongs in the same group. When he compares the folk culture of an earlier period with the mass culture of the industrial age, he finds a change in function. Folk art was not necessarily better but it was much closer to people's daily lives and their social traditions; "it dealt with the complete world intensely familiar to its audience and permitted a direct rapport between those who created and those who consumed this culture."

Nathan Glazer suggested that from a combination of the content level of the cultural product and the way it is received, one should derive four types of situations. In an oversimplified form, these are:

(a) Serious work seriously received;

(b) serious work denatured by the attitude of the "consumer" —looking at the reproduction of a great painting inserted in a picture weekly, listening to a Mozart aria preceded and followed by some popular hit in the frame of a television set;

(c) mediocre works received in a serious mood as exemplified by a woman who listens to a day-time drama in order to understand her family problems better or the Book-of-the-Month Club subscriber who honestly wants to improve himself;

(d) finally, there is bad stuff consumed to fill empty time, this being the enemy of the people.

Each of these situations might have been discussed in its own terms, but it would take a long time to explore them systematically. In retrospect, I can only urge the readers of this volume to penetrate in their own way and as best they can this notion of functional variation in *reception* which is the common theme of Handlin, Arendt, and Van den Haag.

Attention should be drawn to characteristic differences between various contributions. The social scientist Van den Haag e.g., in the last part of his contribution, gives a list of properly numbered indictments of the deterioration of human relations in mass society: we have lost the taste for privacy and contemplation, have replaced sincere personal contacts with an empty gregariousness, and so on. Randall Jarrell, the poet, in the first part of his paper, uses—purposely, he says—a stream of metaphors and impressive aphorisms which he feels communicate more. One other comparison should not be missed. Shils characterizes mass society in terms which show his basic optimism: Social participation has increased, the rights of each individual are more respected, rationality is more widespread. Van den Haag, in the second part of his paper, takes up all these points and so to say reverses their sign: Social participation is uninformed and vulnerable to slogans, individualism has broken all human bonds, rationality comes about at the expense of deep and sincere experiences. The interchange might give some readers the feeling which Hughes at one point expressed only half facetiously: that whomever he listens to he has to agree with. Perhaps the fact that positive and negative elements are so interwoven in the contemporary scene is one of its most characteristic features.

Mass Culture and Mass Media

The first papers in the symposium, while supposed to deal with mass culture in general, devote much space to the mass media. As the sequences progress, the mass media increasingly become the center of attention, with television receiving the major share. By the end of the volume, one can tell that they have become the main topic of the program. In some ways this should not cause surprise. Since the participants are mostly people who make their living from writing, problems of communication are nearest to their hearts. Still this bias deserves some further comment. I have for a long time noticed the intensity with which topics related to broadcasting and to a lesser degree movies and the printed media are discussed in the United States. I may be permitted to repeat an interpretation I made more than ten years ago.

"Twenty or thirty years ago liberal organizations were concerned almost exclusively with questions of social betterment—child labor, woman suffrage, economic insecurity, the exploitation of workers, and so on. These same liberal organizations are today almost as exclusively concerned with the danger of radio, the danger of newspapers, and the bad effects of motion pictures. . . . Broadcasters think of themselves as honest, hard-working, and decent people; why is it then, that doctors and preachers and teachers dislike them? The liberals of today feel terribly gypped. For decades they and their intellectual ancestors fought to attain certain basic goals—more leisure time, more education, higher wages. They were motivated by the idealistic hope that when these goals were reached, the "masses" would develop into fine human beings. But what happened? After the liberals had won their victories, the people spent their newly acquired time and money on movies, radio, magazines. Instead of listening to Beethoven, they listen to Johnny Mercer, instead of going to Columbia University, they go to the Columbia Broadcasting System. The situation of the liberals is much like that of the high school boy who, after weeks of saving, accumulates enough money to buy a bracelet for a girl, and who then learns that the girl has gone out with another boy to show off her nice new trinket."[4]

It seems that this interpretation is still valid today. And the position of the spokesmen for the mass media has also remained unchanged. Rosten and Stanton stress that they make considerable contributions to adult education. Of course they are first of all responsible to their stockholders but they plow much of their profits back into public service features. The manager of and advisers to the mass media feel that their economic success is proof that they do "what the people want"—and that in addition they provide cultural leadership. Interestingly enough, a similar attitude is reported as characteristic of the attitude of businessmen even if their own profits are not involved. One contributor to this volume, Mr. Sweeney, at the time Director of the Museum of Modern Art, blames the board members of many museums for resorting to mass appeal when it is not economically necessary. Museums have the double function of serving the trained mind and being educational agents for a broader public. It is regrettable that no expert in adult education was included in the symposium. His opinion would have helped to develop further Mr. Sweeney's interesting observations.

The emphasis on the mass media is characteristic of the American scene and obscures certain other aspects of mass culture. This can be somewhat remedied by a short digression into the way similar discussions are conducted in another country, France.

In one respect the French and the American situations are like one another. The social scientist and the man of letters in both countries are likely to be politically left of center. But in France, because they have as a frame of reference strong labor parties, they debate cultural values more in their relations to political militancy. The central theme in discussion of mass culture is usually the use of leisure time. Mass media only play a marginal role. The great symbol of the first labor government under Leon Blum in 1936 was the enactment of laws guaranteeing paid vacations and regulating details of week-end arrangements. Equally characteristic are a number of government supported activities like the popular theatre and the youth sport movement. The issue hidden behind the intensive theoretical discussions about leisure time is whether it will lead to an independent labor class culture or whether it will end in assimilation of all workers into a middle-class pattern.

One gets a good picture of this climate of thinking through an issue of the magazine *Esprit* which appeared in June, 1959, simultaneously with the symposium, which led to the present volume. The issue is devoted to "Le Loisir." The theoretical papers are primarily concerned with the relation btetween leisure time and participation in social movements. Empirical studies analyze how the legally guaranteed vacation period is utilized by various groups of employees. Data on mass media exposure are used to bring out the sociological meaning of various types of work. Thus, for instance, one study compares two groups of white collar people who have about the same income but differ according to the degree their work is mechanized. The group with more interesting work shows a normal distribution of activities like movie attendance or listening to the radio. Those who have monotonous work show bimodal behavior, they either engage in an excessive amount of mass media activities or they retreat into an isolation, which takes them either to the saloon or leads to an impoverished family life. It is this retreatism which is considered the main cultural danger by many authors. One has the impression that mass media exposure is looked on as a hopeful sign of incipient concern with the larger world. [5]

Quite a number of other aspects are often crowded out from discussions of mass culture among American intellectuals. Only Hazard in this symposium points out that the objects of daily use have an aesthetic aspect which is definitely part of the surrounding culture. He seems to feel, for instance, that by and large the design of home equipment achieves quite high standards. The social scientist might make a distinction between objects which have high social visibility and lend themselves to social competition and which are often in bad taste—some types of cars would be a good example. Other objects like refrigerators and dictating equipment are more easily left to the control of the professional designer, and do indeed often display considerable taste. In poorer countries, alcoholism is usually an important topic in mass culture discussions.

The Voice of the Artist

While the scope of this symposium is restricted in one direction, it is enlarged in another. Included in the present volume are the statements of three creative artists and the record of the discussion includes the comments of some others. I have tried to extract from all this a statement of their position.

They all agree that the goal and task of the artist is to interpret human experience. There is some disagreement as to whether he does so mainly by describing other people's lives or by being especially articulate about himself. But they have no doubt that life for everyone would be much harder if art didn't help to make sense out of it.

Some idea of a division of labor is implied. Not every human being can, by himself, add this kind of depth to what happens to him. Only the artist is in a position to perform this task because he lends all his efforts to it; but throughout history he has done this at a great sacrifice. Because the artist's social function is intangible and its importance not easily appreciated, he is usually economically insecure and the contact with his audience, if it exists, is precarious and frustrating. Today additional difficulties are added because of the nature of mass society, the role of the mass media, and in the United States also because of some consequences of its economic system. On the first point the main complaint is that the mass man is unreceptive to contemplation; that a complete separation has come about between artistic production on the one hand and occupational and community life on the other; that it has become less and less clear for whom the creative artist is working; and that he is often restricted to addressing himself to just a small group of experts.

The mass media complicate the matter in a variety of ways. By providing endless diversion, they corrode people's willingness to pay attention to serious thought. The mass media emphasize the fleeting events of the moment and weaken people's connection with the past, as it is expressed in myths and the kind of symbolism which epics or the Bible provide. This has grievous consequences for the artist, for his creativeness consists essentially in providing new variations on pervasive themes.

The record is most explicit on two dreaded features of the American scene. The one could be called institutional temptation. It is true that artists are not likely to starve as they did a century ago; there are fellowships, foundation grants, and teaching positions at the universities. But they all require the artist to do a great many things that are not essential to him. He is rarely paid for performing his most creative function. The objection was made that nothing keeps him from starving as his ancestors did and working on what the spirit moves him to. But I think there was real understanding that in an overpowering institutional setting such individual solutions are hardly possible.[6]

The second target of the artist's complaints—and also pointed out at length by Miss Arendt—is the role of the popularizers. The existence of a large audience wanting some easy information and eager to pay for it creates a new group of technicians who take the original and make it palatable, be it fashioning a movie out of a drama or a magazine article out of a serious piece of analysis. This again increases the sense of despair for the serious artist. In terms of fame and material success, he finds himself pushed into the background as compared to the mass communicator; compared with the past, he suffers less absolute and increasing relative deprivation. This point lends additional complexity to the debate with the defenders of the mass media. Rosten in his paper points out how hard he and his colleagues try to popularize important subject matters. However, the artist can more easily condone the ineptness of a bad writer than the slickness of a popularizer. The grievance, incidentally, does not seem to be restricted to the artist. The physicist Holton mentioned in the discussion that he and his colleagues resent the image of the scientist portrayed by the mass media.

It was surprisingly difficult to get artists to talk in terms of their own experience. Notice, for instance, how Mr. Jarrell's paper clearly falls into two parts. In the first he describes mass society mainly in the same detached way as any social scientist would—but his style is different from Van den Haag's. Only in the second part of his paper does he write about his own experiences. And the most personal and revealing remarks of Mr. Baldwin are found in the record of the discussion and not in his paper. Perhaps in such a symposium the artists resent playing the role of guinea pigs. In this sense then the presence of the creative writers was a noble experiment but not a complete success. The partial failure shows, however, how important it would be to pursue the effort further. What is needed are men and women who are willing to talk to us social scientists about themselves as artists in the world of mass culture, rather than about the nature of art.[7]

Interestingly enough, it is the musician Arthur Berger who is most specific and articulate. Perhaps it is reading and explanation of musical scores which gave him analytical training. He makes many interesting points. Among these is the idea that one should not be overjoyed by the extensive performance of classical music over radio, because the unanticipated effect might be a freezing of musical taste. The trend in artistic style has always been toward increasing complexity, and it usually takes a new generation of laymen to accept what was considered revolutionary and unharmonious in their parents' day. Such acceptance might now take much longer because broadcasting puts all its weight behind works which people are accustomed to hearing. Berger singles out quite a number of other impediments which are built into the technology and social structure of the mass media. New works, e.g., are difficult to play and require a great deal of rehearsal. But because of union rules and other traditions developed in broadcasting, lengthy rehearsals become almost prohibitive today. Incidentally, magazines too develop a style of their own, and television has producers who are believed to know what the medium requires. All this means that in many areas professional techniques interpose themselves between the artist and the public. Whatever the need for or the justification of this trend, the artists do not seem to take it kindly.

Berger suggests concretely that broadcasters should make unconditional grants to modern writers and composers. Their contribution should not be linked to the suitability of a work for television or radio. It should rather be looked on as an additional tax, because a broadcasting license turns over a public property—the airwave—for the benefit of a private businessman. While he did not put it quite this way, the remarks of A. W. Brown went in the same direction. A former president of the Metropolitan Educational Television Association (which provides educational television stations with program material), he pointed out that, because of lack of funds, only about 50 education channels have been put in operation out of 250 available channels. More such stations would give artists a larger number of outlets. If one adheres to the formula that commercial broadcasters should make somewhat less money than their franchises permit in the free market, it is easy to conclude that they should give active financial support to educational television.[8]

I might be permitted to add one remark which is personal in the sense that it concerns only my own professional specialty. The artists in the symposium request effort and respect for difficult modern art. At the same time they are impatient when they are confronted with the corresponding problem in the social sciences. Mr. Jarrell said at one point that he loved anthropologists but hated sociologists. The context made it quite clear that what he dislikes are statistical tables difficult to read and what he is pleased by are essays on cultural subjects more akin to poetry. Two men who took pessimistic positions in the discussion have a similar record. The *Reporter*, of which Mr. Kristol was the Managing Editor, and *Commentary*, of which Mr. Glazer is a frequent contributor on social sciences, have been consistently hostile to all modern trends in the social sciences. As Mr. Hazard put it in an aside, empirical social research might be the counterpart of atonal music. It seems to create the same hostility among modern artists which their work creates among the general public.

And yet there is one type of research which might help on some of the problems which the artists brought up. I mentioned above that the way people receive or "consume" cultural products is of considerable concern to some of the participants. Seldes, for instance, comments on the passivity of modern audiences; Hook, on the other hand, insists that he does not understand what is meant by this frequently used term. Now it so happens that mass communication research has developed sophisticated interviewing techniques which bring out what people feel while they watch a movie or television program, at what points they are involved, where they misunderstand the content, and so on. Such analysis of the listening experience has been used mainly for the purpose of improving the effectiveness of propaganda, commercial or otherwise.[9] There is no reason, however, why it should not be used for more objective ends.

As a matter of fact, such an effort was made once by I. A. Richards, who was one of the pioneers of the "New Criticism" which started in England after the First World War.[10] His Cambridge group was mainly interested in substituting for the romantic approach to the personality of the author a structural analysis of the work of art itself. Richards wanted, in addition, to look at the other side of the coin and to study the structure of the readers' experience. He developed a procedure which seems to be little known and to which more attention should be given.[11]

Richards asked a number of his students to read carefully and repeatedly an array of poems ranging from serious pieces to conventional trash. He then requested them to describe in detail all the reactions, associations and opinions they had. These reports he analyzed and classified carefully. The main product is a detailed description of what today we would call the audience experience. The purpose of Richards' experiment as well as the organization of his book are best described in his own formulation of his three aims:

> "First, to introduce a *new kind of documentation* to those who are interested in the contemporary state of culture whether as critics, as philosophers, as teachers, as psychologists or mainly as curious persons. Secondly, to provide a new technique for those who wish to discover for themselves what they think and feel about poetry (and cognate matters) and why they should like or dislike it. Thirdly, to prepare the way for *educational methods* more efficient than those we use now in *developing discrimination* and the power to understand what we hear and read." [Emphasis supplied]

I have never quite understoood why Richards' idea has rarely been pursued further. Perhaps it falls in a no-man's land between psychologists and students of literature. Perhaps Richards' rather primitive techniques seem disappointing. But as the studies quoted above show, we now know that one can give a very good picture of how a specific type of person understands a work of art, how he is affected by it, and how it fits into the stream of his personal experiences. I would strongly urge that a convergence of these research techniques with serious artistic concerns be more widely tried. Obviously, the goal is not to custom tailor creative production to the wishes of the man in the street. But a great many interesting and mostly unpredictable outcomes can result from a systematic confrontation of the artist with his actual and potential audiences. To say the least, the type of controversies which the present symposium exemplifies could be referred to a firmer body of facts.

Dilemmas of Reform

Stuart Hughes in his paper takes the position that one cannot have political without cultural democracy; we are paying for our freedom of opinion by letting the people have the freedom of choice in cultural matters. Phillips in the discussion objects: he does not see any necessary connection. A somewhat different formulation might make the issue more concrete.

The expression "paying for" is indeed somewhat vague and perhaps fatalistic. What actually happens is that, in the mass media field, we are confronted with a set of basic values which we hold equally dear but which cannot be all fully realized. Schlesinger, for instance, argues for a stronger role of the government in broadcasting policies. Even if television is accepted as a business, the idea of free enterprise does not preclude some government regulation. He correctly points out that at many points in our economic system we have laws on wages and hours and similar business decisions. In the communications field, however, we run into a conflict with the First Amendment which specifically precludes government interference in the realm of ideas. Even if this difficulty could be resolved by stating that television, like the movies, conveys mainly entertainment and, therefore, doesn't fall under the First Amendment, a realistic problem remains. American broadcasting is really quite free so far as political controversy goes. It is questionable whether the opposition party would have a fair chance in a government controlled system. One would, therefore, have to look for a form of regulation which affected cultural matters only.

Once this is conceded, another question comes up. In a democracy, is there any justification for imposing elite standards on the whole country? In this connection a distinction which is often overlooked must be made. The realistic issue is not whether the majority should accept what the intellectual minority prefers. The problem is whether *within* the realm of what was referred to as middlebrow culture standards could be developed and should be maintained. The Federal Communications Commission, for instance, receives many complaints about the abundance of violence in television dramas. The question then arises whether one does not find less violence there than, for instance, in *Hamlet*. Everyone has an uneasy feeling that this is a specious argument, but it would be difficult to articulate clearly under what conditions an overbundance of violence is regrettable. While there is no answer on this specific problem, there are similar issues on which communication research can provide answers. Everyone is familiar with the programs called "soap operas." They are about families which get into trouble, solve a predicament somehow, only to start a new episode of difficulties. It is certainly not high art, but it is sometimes entertaining and listeners should not be deprived of this kind of relaxation. However, even if one accepts the basic formula, one can point to some specific deficiencies. Arnheim has analyzed a score of such plots and has shown that the troubles in which the families find themselves are usually created by men while the happy solution is provided by women. It is not difficult to understand the purpose of this tradition: it makes the soap opera more attractive to women, and this is the audience in which the advertisers are primarily interested. But the same type of entertainment could be provided without such elements of bias and this would be an intrinsic improvement.

What I am trying to say is that even if we accept the legitimacy of middlebrow culture, it is still possible to develop standards which make for improvement on its own terms. The role of the elite then would not be that of dictators but of advisers. Concretely this role can take a variety of forms. Hyman's contribution to this symposium describes what he as a college teacher does to influence the standards of his students. On another occasion Robert Hutchins stressed the importance of periodic reviews. One of the proposals of his Commission on the Freedom of the Press was that the content of mass media be sampled under appropriate categories so they could be subjected to the limelight of public opinion. This is supposed to make for improvement without specific regulation. The success of such a scheme depends very much of course on the introduction of creative descriptive ideas like the ones exemplified by Arnheim's study.

A third dilemma which deserves attention is due to a special piece of broadcasting legislation. The Federal Communications Act provides that, in order to avoid collusion on the setting of advertising rates, the anti-trust laws should apply to broadcasting. On this it proved ineffectual. But in present application it also precludes concerted action on program content. Stanton in his paper points with justified pride to the many fine programs one finds in an average week on CBS. Competing networks could make the same claim. But what would be overlooked is the fact that for competitive reasons all of these programs are usually heard at the same time. The value of the existing program supply could be greatly enhanced by a very simple procedure. Now the networks pit against each other programs with mass appeal at one time and programs with elite appeal at another time. Nothing but legal traditionalism prevents an arrangement by which on some days one network has a large audience and another network has a smaller number of connoisseurs: on other evenings the situation would be reversed by agreement. It is not so much the commercial nature of broadcasting but a narrow interpretation of commercial competition which accounts for some of these difficulties.

Since this symposium was held, interest in the problematics of the mass media has extended, at least temporarily, to broader public groups. It is rather characteristic that this interest was not aroused by the cultural critics but by moral indignation over cheating on a television show. This raises the question whether discussions like the one published in this book have any practical utility at all. And here we can once more turn to the teachings of history. The contribution of Leo Lowenthal shows that every technological innovation in the field of communication was experienced by some people as a cultural danger: the less expensive book, the lending library, the magazine and so on. It is really startling how timely the discussions which Lowenthal reports from the 17th and 18th century sound today. Stimulated by his material, I went back to the first recorded discussion of mass communication: Plato's *Phaedros*, the dialogue concerned with the skills and the social implications of the public orator. Socrates, of course, takes the position which the pessimistic critics in this volume take and he, too, goes back to history. He feels that the misery started with the discovery of writing.[12]

"For this discovery will create forgetfulness in the learners' souls, because they will not use their memories; they will trust to the external written characters and not remember of themselves. . . . They will appear to be omniscient, and will generally know nothing; they will be tiresome company, having the show of wisdom without the reality."

In spite of this dire foreboding, writing, orating, printing and now broadcasting have spread, and society still survives. Matters often look bad, but somehow they always stop short of being disastrous. True, as in other fields, especially in social legislation, it was often an accidental event which triggered an improvement. But this would not have happened if a continuous stream of criticism had not kept us prepared to take advantage of such opportunities. It is the tragic story of the cultural crusader in a mass society that he cannot win, but that we would be lost without him.

REFERENCES

1 Since this symposium was held, a very instructive summary of the pertinent literature has been published. Kornhauser, in the first part of "The Politics of Mass Society" shows that the idea has two historical roots: fear that traditional standards will be destroyed by the political movements following the French Revolution; and fear that democratic rights will be lost, engendered by the experience of fascistic dictatorships. Instead of trying one unitary definition of "mass society" Kornhauser shows the types of meanings the concept has acquired in varying contexts.

2 What people read or watch is well known from numerous studies. For a first orientation, one may consult several chapters in a "Reader on Public Opinion and Communications Research," Bernard Berelson and Morris Janowitz (eds.) (Glencoe, Ill.: The Free Press, 1953).

3 Actually, toward the end of his paper he expresses interesting ideas of what in his opinion are the shortcomings of the American scene. But these points were not picked up during the symposium and therefore will not be reviewed here.

4 Paul Lazarsfeld, "Role of Criticism in Management of Mass Communications," *Communications in Modern Society* (Urbana: University of Illinois Press), 1948, pp. 191-192.

5 They actually play a different role than they do in the United States. The government-owned radio-television system has definite cultural and social assignments which are maintained by advisory councils of artists and other professional groups attached to the broadcasting agency. It is indicative that the French literature has not created special words for mass media but taken over the English words. Especially interesting are papers which deal with education for leisure utilization. To give just one characteristic example, the French beaches are as crowded as ours, but the problem is raised as to what people should do when they find themselves in such a situation. Instead of frantically trying to preserve a square yard of pseudoprivacy, they should think of joint activities and organize equitable use of available facilities.

6 I was recently struck by the observation that in countries like Switzerland and Austria mountain climbing is rapidly declining; the number of profes-

sional guides, for instance, has greatly decreased. This is due to the fact that more and more cable cars and hard surface automobile roads are being built. Here again the point could be made that no one has to use these technical devices; one could still reach mountain peaks by his own strength. But it is obvious that such pursuits lose their sense if at the end of such a climb one meets all the people who have come up with the help of some technical gadget.

7 During the discussion Berelson especially stressed the need for better communications between the various agents active in the communications field. In another symposium sponsored by Notre Dame University he contributed an imaginary exchange between three such characters: the philosopher who pursues ideals, the operator who has to make a success of the mass media and the academician who tries to be guided by empirical research. His paper makes good contributory reading to the point of view represented in the present collection.

8 Little is known about the actual audiences of educational stations, the needs they could serve and the types of programs they could develop. There is, however, great hope that this gap will be filled. The recently legislated Defense Education Act provides grants for research and several major grants have been made to research groups working in areas in which educational stations are in operation.

9 It is not possible to give a complete picture of this procedure without devoting much more space to it. The best examples can be found in the studies that the Army did during the last war on the reaction of soldiers to films designed to give an understanding of the contemporary historical situation. The results are summarized in the third volume of *The American Soldier* (Princeton, N.J.; Princeton University Press, 1949, Ch. 4). A more detailed discussion of the technique I am referring to is given by Merton *et al.*, in *The Focused Interview* (Glencoe, Ill.: The Free Press, 1958), and in Tore Hollonquist and E. A. Suchman, "Listening to the Listener," in P. F. Lazarsfeld and F. N. Stanton (eds.), *Radio Research 1942-43* (New York: Duell, Sloan and Pearce, 1944).

10 A vivid description of how this movement originated can be found in F. N. W. Tillyard, *The Muse Unchained* (London: Bowes and Bowes, 1958).

11 I. A. Richards, *Practical Criticism* (London: Kegan, Paul, Trench, Trubner & Co., Ltd., 1929).

12 *The Philosophy of Plato* (Jewett translation), (New York: Modern Library), p. 323.

EDWARD SHILS

Mass Society and Its Culture

Mass Society: Consensus, Civility, Individuality

A NEW ORDER of society has taken form since the end of World War I in the United States, above all, but also in Great Britain, France, Northern Italy, the Low and Northern European countries, and Japan. Some of its features have begun to appear in Eastern and Central Europe, though in a less even manner; more incipiently and prospectively so, in Asian and African countries. It is the style to refer to this new order as the "mass society."

This new order of society, despite all its internal conflicts, discloses in the individual a greater sense of attachment to the society as a whole, and of affinity with his fellows. As a result, perhaps for the first time in history, large aggregations of human beings living over an extensive territory have been able to enter into relatively free and uncoerced association.

The new society is a mass society precisely in the sense that the mass of the population has become incorporated *into* society. The center of society—the central institutions, and the central value systems which guide and legitimate these institutions—has extended its boundaries. Most of the population (the "mass") now stands in a closer relationship to the center than has been the case in either premodern societies or in the earlier phases of modern society. In previous societies, a substantial portion of the population, often the majority, were born and forever remained "outsiders."

The mass society is a new phenomenon, but it has been long in gestation. The idea of the *polis* is its seed, nurtured and developed in the Roman idea of a common citizenship extending over a wide territory. The growth of nationality in the modern era has heightened the sense of affinity among the members of different classes and regions of the same country. When the proponents of the modern idea of the nation put forward the view that life on a contiguous, continuous, and common territory—beyond all divisions of kinship, caste, and religious belief—united the human beings living within that territory into a single collectivity, and when they made a common language the evidence of that membership, they committed themselves, not often wittingly, to the mass society.

An important feature of that society is the diminished sacredness of authority, the reduction in the awe it evokes and in the charisma attributed to it. This diminution in the status of authority runs parallel to a loosening of the power of tradition. Naturally, tradition continues to exert influence, but it becomes more open to divergent interpretations, and these frequently lead to divergent courses of action.

The dispersion of charisma from center outward has manifested itself in a greater stress on individual dignity and individual rights. This extension does not always reach into the sphere of the political, but it is apparent in the attitudes toward women, youth, and ethnic groups which have been in a disadvantageous position.

Following from this, one of the features of mass society I should like to emphasize is its wide dispersion of "civility." The concept of civility is not a modern creation, but it is in the mass society that it has found its most complete (though still very incomplete) realization. The very idea of a *citizenry* coterminous with the adult population is one of its signs. So is the moral equalitarianism which is a trait unique to the West, with its insistence that by virtue of their sharing membership in the community and a common tongue men possess a certain irreducible dignity.

None of these characteristic tendencies of mass society has attained anything like full realization. The moral consensus of mass society is certainly far from complete; the mutual assimilation of center (i.e., the elite) and periphery (i.e., the mass) is still much less than total. Class conflict, ethnic prejudice, and disordered personal relations remain significant factors in our modern mass societies, but without preventing the tendencies I have described from finding an historically unprecedented degree of realization.

Mass society is an industrial society. Without industry, i.e., without the replacement of simple tools by complicated machines, mass society would be inconceivable. Modern industrial techniques, through the creation of an elaborate network of transportation and communication, bring the various parts of mass society into frequent contact. Modern technology has liberated man from the burden of physically exhausting labor, and has given him resources through which new experiences of sensation, conviviality, and introspection have become possible. True, modern industrial organization has also been attended by a measure of hierarchical and bureaucratic organization which often runs contrary to the vital but loose consensus of mass society. Nonetheless, the fact remains that modern mass society has reached out toward a moral consensus and a civil order congruous with the adult population. The sacredness that every man possesses by virtue of his membership in society finds a more far-reaching affirmation than ever before.

Mass society has aroused and enhanced individuality. Individuality is characterized by an openness to experience, an efflorescence of sensation and sensibility, a sensitivity to other minds and personalities. It gives rise to, and lives in, personal attachments; it grows from the expansion of the empathic capacities of the human being. Mass society has liberated the cognitive, appreciative, and moral capacities of individuals. Larger elements of the population have consciously learned to value the pleasures of eye, ear, taste, touch, and conviviality. People make choices more freely in many spheres of life, and these choices are not necessarily made for them by tradition, authority, or scarcity. The value of the experience of personal relationships is more widely appreciated.

These observations are not meant to imply that individuality as developed in mass society exists universally. A part of the population in mass society lives in a nearly vegetative torpor, reacting dully or aggressively to its environment. Nonetheless, the search for individuality and its manifestations in personal relations are distinctly present in mass society and constitute one of its essential features.

The Culture of Mass Society

The fundamental categories of cultural life are the same in all societies. In all the different strata of any given society, the effort to explore and explain the universe, to understand the meaning of events, to enter into contact with the sacred or to commit sacrilege, to affirm the principles of morality and justice and to deny them, to encounter the unknown, to exalt or denigrate authority, to stir the senses by the control of and response to words, sounds, shapes, and colors—these are the basic elements of cultural existence. There are, however, profound variations in the elaboration of these elements, for human beings show marked differences in capacity for expression and reception.

No society can ever achieve a complete cultural consensus: there are natural limitations to the spread of the standards and products of superior culture throughout society. The tradition of refinement is itself replete with antinomies, and the nature of creativity adds to them. Creativity is a modification of tradition. Furthermore, the traditional transmission of superior culture inevitably stirs some to reject and deny significant parts of it, just because it is traditional. More fundamental than the degrees of creativity and alienation is the disparity in human cognitive, appreciative, and moral capacities. This disparity produces marked differences in the apprehension of tradition, in the complexity of the response to it, and in the substance of the judgments aroused by it.

Thus a widely differentiated "dissensus" has become stabilized in the course of history. The pattern of this "dissensus" is not inevitably unchanging. The classes consuming culture may diminish in number, their taste may deteriorate, their standards become less discriminating or more debased. On the other hand, as the mass of the population comes awake when its curiosity and sensibility and its moral responsiveness are aroused, it begins to become capable of a more subtle perception, more appreciative of the more general elements in a concrete representation, and more complex in its aesthetic reception and expression.

The Levels of Culture. For present purposes, we shall employ a very rough distinction among three levels of culture, which are levels of quality measured by aesthetic, intellectual, and moral standards. These are "superior" or "refined" culture, "mediocre" culture, and "brutal" culture.*

* I have reservations about the use of the term "mass culture," because it refers simultaneously to the substantive and qualitative properties of the culture, to the social status of its consumers, and to the media by which it is transmitted. Because of this at least three-fold reference, it tends to beg some important questions regarding the relations among the three variables. For example, the current conception of "mass culture" does not allow for the fact that in most countries, and not just at present, very large sections of the elite consume primarily mediocre and brutal culture. It also begs the important questions as to whether the mass media can transmit works of superior culture, or whether the genres developed by the new mass media can become the occasions of creativity and therewith a part of superior culture. Also, it does not consider the obvious fact that much of what is produced in the genres of superior culture is extremely mediocre in quality. At present, I have no satisfactory set of terms to distinguish the three levels of cultural objects. I have toyed with "high," "refined," "elaborate," "genuine," or "serious," "vulgar," "mediocre," or "middle," and "low," "brutal," "base" or "coarse." None of these words succeeds either in felicity or aptness.

Superior or refined culture is distinguished by the seriousness of its subject matter, i.e., the centrality of the problems with which it deals, the acute penetration and coherence of its perceptions, the subtlety and wealth of its expressed feeling. The stock of superior culture includes the great works of poetry, novels, philosophy, scientific theory and research, statues, paintings, musical compositions and their performance, the texts and performance of plays, history, economic, social, and political analyses, architecture and works of craftsmanship. It goes without saying that the category of superior culture does not refer to the social status, i.e., the quality of their attainment, of the author or of the consumers of the works in question, but only to their truth and beauty.

The category of mediocre culture includes works which, whatever the aspiration of their creators, do not measure up to the standards employed in judging works of superior culture. Mediocre culture is less original than superior culture; it is more reproductive; it operates largely in the same genres as superior culture, but also in certain relatively novel genres not yet fully incorporated into superior culture, such as the musical comedy. This may be a function of the nature of the genre or of the fact that the genre has not yet attracted great talent to its practice.

At the third level is brutal culture, where symbolic elaboration is of a more elementary order. Some of the genres on this level are identical with those of mediocre and refined culture (pictorial and plastic representation, music, poems, novels, and stories) but they also include games, spectacles (such as boxing and horse racing) and more directly expressive actions with a minimal symbolic content. The depth of penetration is almost always negligible, subtlety is almost entirely lacking, and a general grossness of sensitivity and perception is a common feature.

The greatest difference among the three levels of culture, apart from intrinsic quality, is the tremendous disparity in the richness of the stock available in any society at any given time. What any given society possesses is not only what it creates in its own generation but also what it has received from antecedent generations and from earlier and contemporaneous generations of other societies. Superior culture is immeasurably richer in content because it contains not only superior contemporary production but also much of the refined production of earlier epochs. Mediocre culture tends to be poorer, not only because of the poorer quality of what it produces in its own generation, but because these cultural products have a relatively shorter life span. Nevertheless, mediocre culture contains much that has been created in the past. The boundaries between mediocre and superior culture are not so sharp, and the custodians of superior culture are not so discriminating as always to reject the mediocre. Furthermore, a considerable amount of mediocre culture retains value over long periods; and even though mediocre taste varies, as does superior taste, there are stable elements in it, too, so that some of the mediocre culture of the past continues to find an appreciative audience.

At the lowest cultural level, where the symbolic content is most impoverished and where there is very little original creation in each generation, we come again to a greater, if much less self-conscious, dependence on the past. Games, jokes, spectacles, and the like continue traditional patterns with little consciousness of their traditionality. If the traditional element in brutal culture has been large, this is due to the relatively low creative capacities of those who produce and consume it. Here, until recently, there has been little professional production, machinery for preservation and transmission is lacking, and oral transmission plays a greater part in maintaining traditions of expression and performance than with superior and mediocre cultures.

The Magnitudes: Consumption. The quantity of culture consumed in mass society is certainly greater than in any other epoch, even if we make proper allowance for the larger populations of the mass societies at present. It is especially at the levels of mediocre and brutal culture that an immense expansion has occurred, but the consumption of superior culture has also increased.

The grounds for this great increase, and for the larger increase in the two lower categories, are not far to seek. The most obvious are greater availability, increased leisure time, the decreased physical demands of work, the greater affluence of the classes which once worked very hard for long hours for small income, increased literacy, enhanced individuality, and more unabashed hedonism. In all these, the middle and the lower classes have gained more than have the elites (including the intellectuals, whatever their occupational distribution).

The consumption of superior culture has increased, too, but not as much as the other two categories, because the intellectual classes were more nearly saturated before the age of mass society. Moreover, the institutions of superior culture—the collections of connoisseurs, academies, universities, libraries, publishing houses, periodicals—

were more elaborately and more continuously established in the pre-mass society than were the institutions which made mediocre and brutal culture available to their consumers.

Thus in mass society the proportion of the total stock of cultural objects held by superior culture has shrunk, and correspondingly the share of mediocre and brutal culture has grown.*

Note on the Value of Mediocre and Brutal Culture. Mediocre culture has many merits. It often has elements of genuine conviviality, not subtle or profound perhaps, but genuine in the sense of being spontaneous and honest. It is often very good fun. Moreover, it is often earnestly, even if simply, moral. Mediocre culture, too, has its traditions; many of the dramas and stories which regale the vulgar have a long history hidden from those who tell and enjoy them. Like anything traditional, they express something essential in human life, and expunging them would expunge the accumulated wisdom of ordinary men and women, their painfully developed art of coping with the miseries of existence, their routine pieties and their decent pleasures.

There is much ridicule of *Kitsch*, and it *is* ridiculous. Yet it represents aesthetic sensibility and aesthetic aspiration, untutored, rude, and deformed. The very growth of *Kitsch*, and of the demand which has generated the industry for the production of *Kitsch*, is an indication of a crude aesthetic awakening in classes which previously accepted what was handed down to them or who had practically no aesthetic expression and reception.

The Reproduction and Transmission of Culture

In medieval society, the church and, to a less effective and more limited degree, the schools (which were immediate or indirect adjuncts of the church) brought the culture of the center into the peripheral areas of a very loosely integrated society.† Protestantism

* This change in the relative shares of the three levels of culture has been distorted by contrast with the preceding epochs. The cultural life of the consumers of mediocre and brutal culture was relatively silent, unseen by the intellectuals. The immense advances in audibility and visibility of the two lower levels of culture is one of the most noticeable traits of mass society. This is in turn intensified by another trait of mass society, i.e., the enhanced mutual awareness of different sectors of the society.

† A society which was far less "organic" in its structure and outlook than the critics of modern society allege and less "organic" also than the modern society which is so unsympathetically assailed by these critics.

and printing led to a pronounced change which showed the direction of the future. The cheapened access to the printed word and the spread of a minimal literacy (which became nearly universal within European societies only at the beginning of the present century) resulted in an expansion of each of the three strata of culture. In this expansion, the chief beneficiaries were mediocre and brutal culture.

The increased wealth, leisure, and literacy of the lower classes, and the flowering of hedonism which these permitted, would undoubtedly have produced the great expansion in mediocre and brutal—as well as superior—cultural consumption, even without the further technological developments of communication in the twentieth century. This technological development did, however, supply a mighty additional impetus. The popular press of the last decades of the nineteenth century showed the way. The development of new methods of graphic reproduction in lithography and in both still and moving pictures, new methods of sound recording and the transmission of sound and picture, increased the flow of communication from the center to the periphery. Where previously the custodians of superior culture and its mediocre variants had nearly a monopoly—through their quasi-monopoly of the institutions of transmission—the new methods of mass communication have transformed the situation.

The quest for a larger audience, which would make it feasible to obtain a subsidy (in the form of advertising) to cover the difference between what the consumers pay and what it costs to produce cultural objects, has been of the greatest importance to the interrelations of the various strata of culture. The dependence of the subsidy on greatly extended consumption would in itself have required a reaching-out toward a heterogeneous audience. The increased overhead of communication enterprises in television, for example, as compared with book printing, has intensified the need for large and heterogeneous audiences.

Before the emergence of the most recent forms of mass communication, with their very large capital requirements, each stratum of culture had its own channels and institutions. As long as books were the chief means of impersonal cultural transmission, the cultural segregation of the classes could be easily maintained. The drive toward a maximum audience has helped change this, and the change has had momentous repercussions. The magazine is the embodiment of this new development. The form of the magazine is an eighteenth-century phenomenon; but the enlargement of its role in the reproduction and transmission of culture is the product of the latter-day need to gain the maximum audience, one in its turn impelled by the economic necessity of the subsidy. To speak to the largest possible audience, it has been necessary to make the content of what is transmitted in a single issue as heterogeneous as the audience sought.

The general principle of providing something for everyone in the family became well established in the first decades of the popular press. The principle was developed to the point where every class which could possibly increase the total audience was offered something. This principle has not succeeded in dominating the entire field. There are still specialized organs and institutions which seek to please only one particular stratum of consumers, and in Europe the tradition of a unitary public still persists—but even there not without making very substantial concessions to the new principle. Even the universities (which do not necessarily seek large numbers) in Europe, although not as much as in America, have also diversified their programs in order to meet the diversified demand. In popular periodicals like *Time, Life, Look, Picture Post, Match, Der Spiegel, Esquire,* and in distinguished daily newspapers like *The New York Times,* and recently, even in a cumbersome way, *The Times* of London, there is an intermixture of superior, mediocre, and brutal culture which is historically unique. The same can be observed in television and, of course, in the film: a single network presents a wide variety of levels, and films of genuinely high artistic and intellectual merit may be produced in the same studio which produces numerous mediocre and brutal films.

The Consumption of Culture

In modern society, the number of consumers of superior culture has never been very large; in premodern societies, it was even smaller. The chief consumers of works of superior culture are the intellectuals, i.e., those whose occupations require intellectual preparation, and in practice, the application of high intellectual skills. In the contemporary world this category includes university teachers, scientists, university students, writers, artists, secondary-school teachers, members of the learned professions (law, medicine, and the church), journalists, and higher civil servants, as well as a scattering of businessmen, engineers, and army officers.

Outside the intellectual occupations, where the largest number are found, the consumers of superior culture are spread thin and at random. This situation has probably never been different, even in periods when the princes of the church were patrons of painting and sculpture, or when in most grand-bourgeois households one could find sets of Goethe, Nietzsche, Fielding, the memoirs of Sully, or the letters of Mme. de Sévigné.

The political, technological, military, ecclesiastical, and economic elites have not usually been intellectuals, even though their members have had intellectual training and followed intellectual careers before entering their particular profession. Politican and intellectual come closest in regimes just established by revolution or by a successful nationalist movement (their quality as intellectuals, however, is usually not particularly distinguished). In established political regimes, although there may be a significant number of politicians who were once intellectuals of a respectable level, over a long period the demands of the profession of politics leave little time, strength, or sensitivity for the continued consumption of intellectual goods.

Among the leading Western countries, it is in the United States that the political elite gives a preponderant impression of indifference toward works of superior culture. The situation is probably not very different in Great Britain, France, Germany or Italy—though there, the political elite, living amidst aristocratic and patrician traditions, possesses an external gloss of intimacy with high culture. In the United States, however, despite Woodrow Wilson, Franklin Roosevelt, the Plutarch-reading Harry Truman, and the *De re metallica*-editing Herbert Hoover, the political elite gives a definitely unintellectual impression.

The same is true of the American plutocracy: as a body of collectors of the works of painting and sculpture and as patrons of learning, it will take an outstanding place in the history of the great Maecenases. Yet the dominant impression is one of indifference and inhospitality to intellectual work. The great industrial system of the United States has required a large corps of engineers and applied scientists, men of great imagination and even high creativity; yet their cultural consumption (not only of superior culture but also of mediocre culture) is rather small. The vigor and pre-eminence of these sectors of the American elite, and the conventions of the media of information through which their public image is formed, fortify intellectuals with the sense that they alone in their society are concerned with superior culture.

Among the middle classes the consumption of the traditional genres of superior culture is not large. Popular periodicals, best-selling novels, political books of transient interest, inferior poetry, inspirational works of theology and moral edification and biographies—these made up and still make up the bulk of their consumption. More recently, the films and radio, and most recently, television, have provided the substance of their cultural consumption. Their fare is largely philistine—mediocre culture and brutal culture. Nonetheless, because of exposure to the "mass media," e.g., periodicals like *Life* and a narrow band of the output on television, film, and radio, a larger section of these classes has come into contact with and consumed a larger quantity of extra-religious, superior culture than has been the case throughout the course of modern history.

Finally, the industrial working class and the rural population remain to be considered. Together, these classes consume almost nothing of the inheritance and current production of superior culture. Very little mediocre culture of the conventional genres reaches them except in such periodicals as *Life, Look,* and *The Reader's Digest.* Much of their culture as transmitted by mass media is brutal—crime films and television spectacles, paperbacks of violence, pornographic oral and printed literature, and the culture of the world of sports.

It would be a mistake, however, to think that the culture possessed by these classes is exhausted by what comes to them through the mass media. A large amount of traditional religious culture (and of sectarian variants of traditional religious culture) flourishes in all the nonintellectual classes. Much of regional and class culture, maintained by family, by colleagues, neighbors, and friends and by local institutions, survives and is unlikely to be supplanted by the larger culture which emanates from the center. This places limits on what is incorporated from the current flow of the mass media.*

A special stratum of the population that cuts across all classes and gives a particular tone to mass society is the younger generation, the maligned and bewildering "youth." The coming forth of youth in contemporary society rests on primordial foundations which exist in all societies. In most societies, however, the institutional structure and the niggardliness of nature have kept youth in check. In modern times, romanticism and increased wealth and (more deeply) the expanding radius of empathy and fellow-feeling have given

---

* Also, it should be added, this persistence of traditional and orally transmitted culture renders fruitless the effort to diagnose the dispositions and outlook of a people by analyzing what is presented to them through films, television, and wireless broadcasts, the press, etc.

youth opportunities never before available. The enhanced productivity of the economy of Western countries has, on the one hand,
allowed young people to remain outside the hard grind of work for
a longer time; it has given them opportunities to earn and spend
substantial individual incomes. The resulting cultural manifestations are largely responsible for what is called "mass culture."

Before the advent of mass society, a small proportion of the youth
were rigorously inculcated with superior culture; the rest were
exposed to the brutal culture of their seniors. It is one of the marks
of mass society, however, that youth has become a major consumer
of the special variants of mediocre and brutal culture that are
produced for transmission through the mass media. An extraordinary quantity of popular music, mediocre and brutal films, periodical literature, and forms of dance is produced for and consumed by
youth. This is something unprecedented, and this is the heart of
the revolution of mass culture.

Most of the "youthful mass" comes from strata of society which
have had little connection except through religious education with
high or superior culture. Not yet enmeshed in the responsibilities
of family and civic life, and with much leisure time and purchasing
power, youth constitutes both an eager and a profitable public which
attracts the attention of the mass media. The eagerness of youth for
the mediocre and brutal culture provided by the mass media, and
that youth's own creative poverty are a universal phenomenon.
Where the political elite does not grant this eagerness the right of
direct expression, but seeks instead to divert it into ideological channels or to dam it up, it still remains powerful and indomitable.
Where the political order allows this passionate and uncultivated
vitality to find a free expression, the result is what we see throughout
the Western world.

The Production of Culture

The High Intelligentsia. A differentiated creative intelligentsia
is the oldest stratum of Western society with a set of continuous
traditions. Such a stratum still exists today, far broader than ever
before, far more extended and with international ties exceeding
that of any other section of our own or any other society.* There is

* The internationality of the medieval church and of the European aristocracy
in the eighteenth century was thin and parochial in comparison with the scope
and intensity of that exhibited by present-day intellectual classes.

today more internal specialization than in the past: it is impossible for any one man to be fully conversant with the inherited and currently produced stock of cultural objects. The productive intelligentsia is perhaps less intensely like-minded now than in the past, when it was smaller and the body of what it had to master was smaller. Nonetheless, despite changes in society, in the modes of financial support and in the organization of intellectual life, this creative stratum is constantly reproducing and increasing.

The Mediocre Intelligentsia. The modern age, however, has seen growing up alongside this creative intelligentsia a much larger stratum of producers of mediocre culture. In the seventeenth and eighteenth centuries, when letters and the arts began to offer the possibilities of a professional career, thanks to the advance of printing and to an enlarging public, there emerged, besides those whose creative capacities achieved the heights of greatness, a wider group of writers, artists, and scholars. From these were recruited the residents of Grub Street, who, while still trying to reach the highest levels, had to live by producing for a less discriminating public. The nineteenth century saw the stabilization of the profession of those who produced almost exclusively for the public that consumed mediocre culture. The popular press, the film, radio, and television have deepened and extended their ranks. The enlargement of university populations and the corresponding increase in the number of university teachers, the increased opportunities for careers in research, in the applied natural and social sciences, have similarly added to the producers of mediocre culture.*

The professional practitioner with a mediocre culture has developed traditions, models, and standards of his own. More frequently than in the past he engages directly in the professional production of mediocre culture without first essaying the production of works of superior culture. He can attain an excellence within his own field that often brings him satisfaction and esteem. Indeed, in certain genres of mediocre culture that are new or at least relatively

---

* The increase in numbers of persons in intellectual occupations and those that require intellectual training might well be pressing hard against the supply. The supply of high talent is limited; improved methods of selection and training can somewhat increase it, but they cannot make it limitless or coterminous with the population of any society. Hence as the numbers expand, modern societies are forced to admit many persons whose endowments are such as to permit only a mediocre performance in the creation and reproduction of cultural works.

new, he can reach heights of unprecedented excellence, to the point where, if the genre is admissible, his work can take on the lineaments of superior cultural achievement.

Yet despite this approximation to autonomy, the autonomy remains incomplete. The producer of mediocre culture is exposed to the standards of superior culture, and he cannot entirely escape their pressure. If he prospers and his colleagues on the level of superior culture do not, then he is guilt-ridden for having "betrayed" higher standards for the sake of the fleshpots.

This troubling juxtaposition of two consciences is rendered more acute by the physical juxtaposition of the two levels of cultural objects and the social contact of their producers in the media through which mediocre culture chiefly finds its audience, namely, the media of mass communication. The professionals of mediocre culture cannot, even if they would, forget the standards of superior culture, because they mix with persons who often attain them, because the media from time to time present works composed according to those standards, and because critics continually refer to them. These factors provide an increasing stimulus to an awareness of and a concern for high standards, even when they are not observed.

The Brutal Intelligentsia. The producers of brutal culture confront a quite different situation. They have neither a similarly compelling historical past nor the connections with superior culture which their "colleagues" in the field of mediocre culture possess. They do not, so far as I know, justify their performance by reference to the great masters of their art. There are some exceptions among crime-story writers, boxers, jockeys, and certainly among a few of the best sports writers. But these are new professions. Their practitioners feel no continuity with their forerunners, even though the objects they produce have been produced for a long time. Brutal culture therefore has only recently developed a differentiated professional personnel.

Brutal culture has not shown great potentialities for development. Nonetheless, certain genres of brutal culture have produced works of great excellence, so that these reach through mediocre culture into the outer confines of superior culture. Some works of pornography have found a place in superior culture, some horror stories have done the same, as have the chronicles of sports. Since brutal culture is by no means restricted to the uncultivated classes for its audience, works of brutal culture, which reach a form of high refinement, also make their way upward, and with them, their producers move in the same direction. In the main, however, there is a wall which separates the producers of brutal culture from the producers of superior culture. Even where they find the same audience, the tradition of superior culture is such as to erect a barrier to a massive interpenetration.*

A few words should be said here about another kind of cultural production: the anonymous production of folk art and literature and linguistic innovation. In their highest manifestations, the production of these arts was probably never very widely spread. They grow on the edge of craftsmanship, of religious worship and of brutal entertainment. Considerable creative talents must have impelled them into existence. Their creators must have been men of genius, working with subterranean traditions that scarcely exist any more, and that had only a small direct connection with the great tradition of superior culture. In so far as they were inspired by craftsmanship, machine production has greatly restricted their emergence; the traditions which sustained them have atrophied.

It is sometimes asserted that the anonymous cultural production of craftsmen and peasants in the Europe of the later Middle Ages and of early modern times has been destroyed by the growth of mass culture. This is possible, but it is not the only possibility. If we assume that the proportion of geniuses and outstandingly gifted intelligences and sensibilities in any population remains fairly constant (not an unreasonable assumption) and that modern Western societies with their increasing cultivation of science, literature, art, enterprise, administration, and technology have been drawing more and more on their reservoirs of talent, then it appears quite plausible to assert that the talents of the type once manifested in the anonymous productions of folk culture have been recruited and diverted into other spheres and are active at different levels of culture and social life.

The Position of Superior Culture in Mass Society

Has the culture created in the past forty years—the approximate age of mass society—deteriorated as much as its detractors claim?

---

* The bohemian sector of the high intelligentsia, past and present, is an exception to this generalization. The mingling of poets and cut-purses has a long and special history which runs down to the occasional highbrow glorification of the hipster.

The task of assessment is most difficult.

Let us for the moment grant that contemporary refined culture may be poorer than the superior culture produced in any comparable span of years in the past. There may be any number of reasons or causes, totally unrelated to the development and impact of mass society on culture. For example, the distribution and efflorescence of genius are matters that still await full understanding. It is conceivable, if unlikely, that our neural equipment is poorer than that of our ancestors. And even if it is as good, it is also possible that our cultural traditions have passed their point of culmination, that they contain no possibilities of further development, that they offer no point of departure even for creative minds. Another important consideration is whether the alleged deterioration is being evaluated in the light of standards that are applied equally to other periods. We must be sure to comprehend in our assessment the whole range of intellectual and artistic activities. We must remember that the genius which is expressed in refined culture may be of diverse forms, and that it can flow into some domains in one age, and into other domains in other ages.

Yet these might be idle reflections. The evidence of decline is not by any means very impressive. In every field of science and scholarship into which so much of our contemporary genius flows (in physics, chemistry, and in mathematics, in biology and neurology, in logic, linguistics, and anthropology, in comparative religion, in Sinology and Indology), outstanding work is being done, not only in the older centers not yet afflicted by the culture of mass society, but in the United States as well, that most massive of all mass societies. Theology seems to be in a more vital and powerful state than it has been for several centuries. Economics proceeds on a high level, higher on the average than in past periods; sociology, barbarous, rude, and so often trivial, offers at its best something which no past age can match in the way of discovery and penetration. In political philosophy, in which our decay is said to be so patent, we have no Aristotle, Hobbes, or Bentham, but there are probably only a half dozen such masters in all human history. On the other hand, in France and America there are men and women who are at least as deep and rigorous in their analysis of central issues as John Stuart Mill or Walter Bagehot or de Tocqueville were. In the novel, we have no Tolstoy, no Stendhal or Dostoievsky or Flaubert; still, the level of achievement is high. In poetry and in painting, there may indeed have been a falling-off from the great heights; in drama there is no Aeschylus, no Shakespeare, no Racine. But these are among the highest peaks of all human history, and the absence of any such from our two-fifths of a century can scarcely constitute evidence of a general decline in the quality of the products of superior culture in our own time.

That there is, however, a consciousness of decline is undeniable. Intellectuals are beset by a malaise, by a sense of isolation, of disregard, of a lack of sympathy. They feel they have lost contact with their audiences, especially that most important of all audiences, those who rule society. This is nothing new. Romanticism is still far from dead, and it is a cardinal tenet of romanticism that the creative person is cut off from his own society and especially from its rulers. The contemporary romantic intellectual has in addition an acute sense of being cut off from the people.

The noisy, visible, tangible presence of mediocre and brutal culture has heightened his anguish. Whereas intellectuals in earlier ages of modern society could remain ignorant of the cultural preferences of those who consumed cultural objects other than their own, this is not really possible for contemporary intellectuals. By virtue of their own relations to production, the vigor with which mediocre and brutal cultures are promoted, and the evident enjoyment of their consumers, intellectuals are forced to be familiar with what takes place on these levels of culture.

But what are the specific threats to superior culture in mass society? To what extent do they differ from earlier dangers? To what extent do these dangers derive from mass society itself? For superior culture is and has always been in danger. Since it never is and never has been the culture of an entire society, it must necessarily be in a state of tension *vis-à-vis* the rest of society. If the producers and consumers of superior culture see further and deeper than their contemporaries, if they have a more subtle and more lively sensitivity, if they do not accept the received traditions and the acknowledged deities of their fellow countrymen, whatever they say or believe or discover is bound to create tension.

Are intellectuals more endangered in the age of mass society by the jealousy and distrust of the powerful than in other social eras? Surely, censorship, arrest, and exile are nothing new. Can the occasional anti-intellectual flurries of American politicians and businessmen be equated with the restraints imposed on intellectuals in Soviet Russia, Fascist Spain, or National Socialist Germany? None of these countries, it should be noted, are or were mass societies in the sense that the contemporary United States is, or as the United Kingdom, Western Germany, and France are becoming. Does the role played by advertising on the television screen represent a greater intrusion into the creative sphere than did the prosecutions of Flaubert and Baudelaire in nineteenth-century France, or the moral censorship which Mrs. Grundy used to exercise so coarsely in the United States and which she still does in Britain, or the political and religious censorship practiced in eighteenth-century France? Athenian society was no mass society, and there were no advertisers there, yet Socrates was executed. I do not wish to belittle the present or recent attacks on intellectual or artistic liberty in the United States, but I do wish to stress that they are not unique to mass society.

It is sometimes asserted that the culture of mass society produces its insidious effects in roundabout ways that constitute a greater danger than the crude external pressures employed by the rulers of earlier societies. It seduces, it is said, rather than constrains. It offers opportunities for large incomes to those who agree to the terms of employment offered by institutions of mediocre and brutal culture. But does this opportunity, and even its acceptance, necessarily damage superior culture? The mere existence of the opportunity will not seduce a man of strongly impelled creative capacities, once he has found his direction. And if he does accept the opportunity, are his creative talents inevitably stunted? Is there no chance at all that they will find expression in the mass medium to which he is drawn? The very fact that here and there in the mass media, on television and in the film, work of superior quality is to be seen, seems to be evidence that genuine talent is not inevitably squandered once it leaves the traditional refined media.

It is, of course, possible for men to waste their talents, to corrupt themselves for the pleasures of office, for the favor of authority, for popularity, or for income or for the simple pleasure of self-destruction. Qualitatively, the financial temptations of work in the media of mass communication are of the same order as the other temptations intellectuals encounter. Quantitatively, it is difficult to estimate the magnitude of the temptation. There are certainly more opportunities now for intellectuals to earn much money in the production of mediocre and brutal cultural objects than there were before the development of the mass media. It is clear, however, that the large majority of literary men, poets, scholars, painters, scientists, or teachers have not been tempted nor have they yielded to the temptation—even if we concede, which we do not, that their experience in the mass media prevents them from finding creative expression either in the mass media or outside them.

Popularization is sometimes cited as one of the ways in which superior culture is being eroded. Does the contact between mediocre and refined culture which occurs in popularization do damage to refined culture? Raymond Aron's thought does not deteriorate because he occasionally writes in *The New York Times Magazine* and much more frequently in *Le Figaro*; Bertrand Russell suffers no injury from an article in *Look Magazine*. There is no reason why gifted intellectuals should lose their powers because they write for audiences unable to comprehend their ordinary level of analysis and exposition. An intellectual who devotes all his efforts to popularization would soon cease to have anything of his own to popularize and would have to become a popularizer of the works of other persons. But there is no convincing evidence that persons who are capable of refined cultural production and who are strongly impelled to it are being gradually drawn away from their calling by the temptations of popularization. What has been the loss to American, British, and French science in the past forty years from the development of the new branch of journalism which is involved in scientific popularization?

The production of mediocre or brutal culture need not (so the argument goes) destroy superior culture by striking at its producers, either constrainingly or seductively. It can deprive them of their market, and especially of the discriminating appreciation they need to keep their skills at the highest pitch. The corruption of public taste, of those consumers whose natural discriminative powers are not so great that they can dispense with the cultivation which a refined cultural environment provides, is certainly a possibility. In contrast to this possibility, however, is the fact that in the United States today discrimination in a small minority (certainly no smaller than at the end of the nineteenth century or in England today) is as acutely perceptive as it ever was. The quality of literary criticism in *The Partisan Review, The Hudson Review, The Sewanee Review,* and *The New Yorker* is as informed, as penetrating, and as reflective as it was fifty years ago in the best American or British periodicals.

The demand for the products of mediocre and brutal culture certainly affects the market for the products of superior culture. If there were no inferior cultural products available and if the purchasing power were there, there certainly would be a larger body of purchasers of the products of superior culture. This was the situation in Britain during the war, and it is probably the situation in the Soviet Union today. As to whether this represents an improvement in public taste is another matter. In Britain, after the war, once inferior cultural objects became available in larger supply, the prosperity of serious booksellers markedly declined. The same would probably occur in the Soviet Union if a larger range of consumer goods, cultural and other, were to enter the market.

Therefore, when public demand is free to obtain the objects it desires, the market for superior cultural objects, given the present distribution of tastes, is restricted, and enterprisers with capital to invest will not rush in to use their resources in areas of the market where the return is relatively poor. Yet are there many manuscripts of books of outstanding merit lying unpublished today?

The relative unprofitability of the market for superior cultural objects is compensated for in part by the existence of enterprises motivated by other than profit considerations. There is no reason to assume that such uneconomically oriented investors will be fewer in the future than in the recent past. In part, the unprofitability of the market is circumvented by subsidy or patronage.

We often hear the old system of patronage praised by those who bemoan its passing. It is well to remember, however, what misery and humiliation it imposed on its beneficiaries, how capricious and irregular it was, and how few were affected by it during the period from the seventeenth to the nineteenth centuries when intellectuals were growing in numbers. Many more were supported by administrative sinecures in church and state.

The private patronage of individual intellectuals by individual patrons still exists, but it plays a scant role. The place of this older form of subsidy has been taken over by the universities, the state, and the private foundations, and they appear to be more lavish, more generous, and more just than their predecessors were in earlier centuries.

There is, however, a major deficiency in the institutional system of high culture in the United States, one that can be largely attributed to the successful competition among the best of the newer organs of mass communication. America lacks a satisfactory intellectual weekly press, and, ironically, this is in part the achievement of *Time Magazine*. *The Nation* and *The New Republic*, which thirty years ago provided something quite comparable in journalistic and intellectual quality to *The Spectator*, have declined in quality and influence.

The absence of a passable intellectual weekly* does damage to American intellectual life. The country is so large and the intellectuals so scattered that a continuous focus on intellectual concerns (including the evaluation of political and economic affairs in a manner acceptable to a sophisticated, intellectual public) would serve invaluably to maintain standards of judgment and to provide a common universe of discourse.† There is a danger in the United States today of a centrifugal force within the intellectual classes, arising from their numbers, their spatial dispersion and their professional specialization. These factors tend to weaken the sense of community among our intellectual classes. Without this sense of community, the attachment to high standards might slacken or even collapse altogether.

Puritanism, Provincialism, and Specialization

If the arguments of those who attribute to mass society the alleged misery of contemporary culture are not sound, there is no gainsaying the fact that the consumption of superior culture does not rest in a perfectly secure position in the United States. The culture of the educated classes, who in America as elsewhere should be its bearers, leaves much to be desired. One is distressed by the boorish and complacent ignorance of university graduates, by the philistine distrust of or superciliousness toward superior culture which is exhibited by university professors in the humanities and social sciences or in the medical and law schools of this country, and by journalists and broadcasters. The political, economic, military, and technological elites are no better. The near illiteracy of some of the better American newspapers, the oftentimes raucous barbarism of our weeklies and our one widely circulated fortnightly, the unletteredness of many of our civil servants, the poverty of our bookshops, the vulgarity of our publishers (or at least those who write their jacket blurbs and their advertising copy) can give little comfort.

There is undeniably much that is wrong with the quality of culture consumed by the more or less educated classes in America. Very

* *Commonweal* exists on a higher intellectual plane than that of our two secular weeklies, but its religious preoccupations restrict the generality of its appeal.

† The excellent highbrow reviews are no substitute for an intellectual weekly. They are too infrequent, they are too apolitical, and even where they are not, as in the case of the *Partisan Review* or *Commentary*, they cannot maintain a continuous flow of comment and coverage.

little of what is wrong, however, can be attributed to the mass media, particularly to the films, television, radio, and popular magazines.

It is not that the cascade of mediocre and brutal culture which pours out over the mass media is admirable. Quite the contrary. The culture of the mass media is not, however, the reason that the distribution and consumption of superior culture disclose (alongside so many profoundly impressive achievements) many things that are repellent.

What is wrong, is wrong with our intellectuals and their institutions and with some of our cultural traditions, which have little to do with the culture created for and presented by the mass media.

The dour Puritanism that looked on aesthetic expression as self-indulgence does not grow out of mass society. Nor does the complacent and often arrogant provincialism that distrusts refined culture because it believes it to be urban, Anglophile, and connected with a patrician upper class. America was not a mass society in the nineteenth century, it was a differentiated society in which pronounced equalitarian sentiments often took on a populistic form. Certain tendencies which have culminated in a mass society were at work in it. However, much of its culture, although mediocre and brutal, was not produced by the institutions or by the professional personnel now producing the culture of mass society.

Refined culture in nineteenth-century America, reflecting the taste of the cultivated classes of New England and the Middle Atlantic States, did not enjoy a hospitable reception in the Middle West, as a result of the usual hostility of province against metropolis and of those who arrived later in America against those who arrived earlier and who became established sooner. American provincial culture in the nineteenth century was a variant of the British provincial dissenting culture that Matthew Arnold criticized unsparingly in *Culture and Anarchy.* Whereas this culture collapsed in England after World War I, in America it has continued powerful almost up to the present.

These are some of the special reasons for the present uncongeniality of superior culture to so many Americans. It springs from a general distrust that superior culture must always encounter in any society. In this country it expresses itself with greater strength, virulence, and freedom because the political and economic elites of American society feel little obligation to assume a veneer of refined culture, as in Great Britain and France.

Against this background of tradition and sentiment, the development of education in the United States in the past decades has created a technical intelligentsia that does not form a coherent intellectual community. While secondary education became less intellectual in its content and undergraduate education dissipated itself in courses of study of very low intensity and little discipline, a very superior and vigorous type of postgraduate education developed. In trying to make up for lost ground and in seeking to make a deep and thorough penctration into a rapidly growing body of knowledge, postgraduate training in each discipline has had to become highly specialized.

This impetus toward specialization has been heightened by the natural development of science and by the growth of the percentage of the population that pursues postgraduate studies. The development of science has greatly increased the volume of literature a student must cover in each discipline; the increasing number of students, and the necessity for each to do a piece of research no one has ever done before have tended to narrow the concentration within the discipline imposed by the internal evolution of the subject.*

The product of these educational and scientific developments has been the specialist who is uncultivated outside his own specialty. Except for those strong and expansive personalities whose curiosity and sensitivity lead them to the experience of what their education has failed to give them, even the creative American scientist, scholar, or technologist often possesses only a narrow range of mediocre culture.

The ascent of the universities to preponderance in the life of superior culture in the United States, and increasingly (though still not to the same extent) in Europe, has meant that trends within the university tend to become the trends of intellectual life as a whole to a much greater degree than in earlier periods of modern society. As the universities have become more internally differentiated and specialized, superior cultural life has also tended to become more specialized.

What we are suffering from is the dissolution of "the educated public," coherent although unorganized, with a taste for superior cultural objects with no vocational import. The "universitization" of superior culture—most advanced in America but already visible

---

* The romantic idea of originality, which claimed that genius must go its own unique way, has been transposed into one that demands that the subject matter should be unique to the investigator. This has led to much specialized triviality in humanistic research.

in Great Britain, too, though not at all a completely realized tendency—is part of this process of the dissolution of the body of consumers of superior culture.

At the same time, it would be disregarding the truth to overlook the extraordinary vitality of the contemporary American university. Vitality by its nature is diffuse and inflammatory. It is possible, therefore, that despite the densely specialized clutter of the postgraduate system and the prevailing pattern of research which is partly a cause and partly a result of that system, this vitality will do more than withstand the pressure; it is possible that it will ignite interest along a broader front than specialized training commands. It is also possible that the waste of undergraduate education will turn into lively cultivation through the vitality of the new generation of college teachers who are at present among the chief consumers and reproducers of superior culture.

Specialization has lessened the coherence of the intellectual community, comprising creators, reproducers and consumers; it has dispersed its focus of attention, and thus left ungratified cultural needs which the mediocre and brutal culture of the mass media and of private life have been called in to satisfy. The consumption of brutal and mediocre culture is the consequence, not the cause, of developments which are quite independent of the specific properties of mass society. As a matter of fact, the vitality, the individuality, which may rehabilitate our intellectual public will probably be the fruits of the liberation of powers and possibilities inherent in mass societies.

The Prospects of Superior Culture in Mass Society

The problems of superior culture in mass society are the same as in any society. These problems are the maintenance of its quality and influence on the rest of the society.

To maintain itself, superior culture must maintain its own traditions and its own internal coherence. The progress of superior culture (and its continued self-renewal and expansion) require that the traditions be sustained, however much they are revised or partially rejected at any time.

Respect for the traditions in one's own field, together with freedom in dealing with those traditions, are the necessary conditions for creative work. The balance between them is difficult to define, and it is no less difficult to discern the conditions under which that balance can be achieved and maintained. Of great importance is the morale (in its broadest sense) of the intellectuals who take on administrative and teaching responsibilities for the maintenance and advancement of high culture. Within this section of the intellectual class, there must be an incessant scrutiny of every institutional innovation, with regard to its possible impact on intellectual morale. An essential element in this internal state is a balance between respect and freedom in relation to the immanent traditions of each field of intellectual work.

Serious intellectuals have never been free from pressure on the part of sectors of society other than their own. The intellectual sector has always been relatively isolated, regardless of the role of intellectuals in economic and political life. The external world is always jealous of the devotion of the intellectuals to their own gods, and of the implicit criticism which that devotion directs against the ruling values of the other spheres. Intellectuals have always been faced with the task of continuing their own tradition, developing it, differentiating it, improving it as best they could. They have always had to contend with church, state, and party, with merchants and soldiers who have sought to enlist them in their service and to restrict and damage them in word and deed if they did not yield to temptations and threats. The present situation has much in common with the past. The responsibilities of intellectuals also remain the same: to serve the standards they discern and develop and to find a way of rendering unto Caesar what is Caesar's without renouncing what belongs to their own proper realm.

There is no doubt in my mind that the main "political" tradition by which most of our literary, artistic, and social-science intellectuals have lived in America is unsatisfactory. The fault does not lie exclusively with the intellectuals. The philistine Puritanism and provincialism of our elites share much of the blame, as does the populism of professional and lay politicians. Nonetheless, the intellectuals cannot evade the charge that they have done little to ameliorate the situation. Their own political attitudes have been alienated, they have run off into many directions of frivolity. The most recent of such episodes in the 1930's and 1940's were also the most humiliating, and temporarily the most damaging, to the position of intellectuals in American society.

One of the responsibilities implied by their obligation to maintain good relations with the nonintellectual elite is the "civilization" of political life, i.e., the infusion of the standards and concerns of a serious, intellectually disciplined contemplation of the deeper issues of political life into everyday politics. Our intellectuals have in the main lectured politicians, upbraided them, looked down their noses at them, opposed them, and even suspected those of their fellow intellectuals who have become politicians of moral corruption and intellectual betrayal.

The intellectuals who have taken on themselves the fostering of superior culture are part of the elite in any country; but in the United States they have not felt bound by any invisible affiliation with the political, economic, ecclesiastical, military, and technological elites.*

The "civilization" of political life is only one aspect of the "process of civilization," which is the expansion of the culture of the center into the peripheries of society and, in this particular context, the diffusion of superior culture into the areas of society normally consuming mediocre and brutal culture.

Within the limits mentioned earlier in this essay, the prospects for superior culture seem to be reasonably good. The overlapping at certain points on the part of the producers of superior culture and those of mediocre culture has resulted in an expansion of the elements of superior culture which reaches persons whose usual inclinations do not lead them to seek it out. Popularization brings a better content, but not all of this expansion is popularization; much of it is the presentation (and consumption) of genuinely superior cultural work. An improvement in our educational system at the elementary and secondary levels, which is assuredly practicable and likely, will also further this process of civilization. A better education of taste, which a richer, less scarcity-harassed society can afford, the opening and enrichment of sensitivity, which leisure and a diversified environment can make possible, and a more fruitful use of available intelligence can also push forward the "process of civilization."

Of course, men will remain men, their capacities to understand, create, and experience will vary, and very many are probably destined to find pleasure and salvation at other and lower cultural levels. For the others, the prospect of a more dignified and richer cultural life does not seem out of the question. It would certainly be an impossible one, however, if all intellectuals devoted themselves to education and popularization. In a short time the superior culture which would be transmitted through the "process of civilization" would fade and dessicate.

* This is not a condition unique to the United States. Only Great Britain has managed to avoid it for most of the period since the French Revolution, yet there, too, the past few years have not provided notable examples of Britain's good fortune in avoiding this separation.

Thus, if the periphery is not to be polished while the center becomes dusty, the first obligation of the intellectuals is to look after intellectual things, to concentrate their powers on the creation and reproduction and consumption of particular works of philosophy, art, science, literature, or scholarship, to receive the traditions in which these works stand with a discriminating readiness to accept, elaborate, or reject. If that is done, there will be nothing to fear from the movement of culture in mass society.

LEO LOWENTHAL

An Historical Preface to the Popular Culture Debate

POPULAR ART is not a specifically modern phenomenon; but, until the modern era, it was not a source of intellectual or moral controversy. Under feudalism, for example, leisure-time activities were firmly regulated by Church and State, with a set of rules for each class. There was no point of cultural contact between the elite and the masses, nor was there a middle class to complicate the picture or to bridge the gap. Contact or conflict between the two estates in this as in any other area of life was inconceivable.

Controversy arose only after they had come into contact. The exact date of this is difficult to determine; the process that led to the change was gradual, but there is little doubt that it was associated with broad social and technological changes which led to the birth of a middle class. The artist, traditionally dependent for his subsistence on the direct consumers of his art, no longer had to please only one rich or powerful patron; he had to worry about the demands of an increasingly broad, more "popular" audience. The process took place in all great European nations with varying speed. By the middle of the eighteenth century, there had arisen in each of them a group of writers or playwrights who specialized in catering to the needs of these broader audiences. It was about then that the controversy over the threat of popular art to civilization was given voice.

Montaigne first formulated the controversy in terms that have stayed with us. In his analysis of entertainment as a means of meeting a universal human need, he unwittingly fired the opening shot in the conflict over the moral, aesthetic, psychological, and social functions of entertainment—to be contradicted intentionally by Pascal a generation later.

The difference between the two, insofar as their ideas have a bearing on modern discussions, may be summed up as follows: In Mon-

70

taigne's skeptical view of man, the demands of human nature cannot be changed, and we must make the best of them; there is no point in denying them gratification (illusory or real). Pascal, his inspiration and motivation deeply religious, stands for spiritual progress: entertainment and escape are not ineradicable needs; man's nobler impulses must be mobilized against them. A heightened consciousness of our inner selves, which we can achieve only in solitude, away from the distractions of entertainment, opens the way to salvation. Pascal's language naturally lends itself to translation into the language of modern reformers and champions of moral and cultural change; Montaigne's superficially resembles that of the modern box office manager: "The public wants or needs it." Actually, Montaigne's view goes deeper. He has a keen sense of the audience as participant, and his conception of the function of entertainment leaves no room for the possibility of manipulation or passivity, which later are to become serious problems.[1]

The period represented by Montaigne and Pascal marks the emergence of modern national states following the breakdown of the medieval supra-national political, economic, and cultural hierarchies. The intellectual task of the new period was to reconcile the individual's religious and moral heritage with the harsh requirements of an emerging national and capitalist economy. It is therefore not surprising that it was the philosophers who played leading roles in these discussions. Looked at today, the discussions seem a bewildering speculation over whether the individual should ever be allowed to indulge in any leisure-time activities except those that may contribute to the salvation of his soul. For the first time in modern history discussions pose the problem of the value of serious as against relatively frivolous leisure-time pursuits.

The stage for the future was set in the eighteenth century, particularly in England. Most of the problems inherent in modern commercial popular culture were being faced in England in the eighteenth century. Many of the media forms, as well as audience-building devices for their promotion, first became widespread there more than two hundred years ago. It was also at this time that the writer, as a member of a skilled social group, first became dependent for his financial support on the public instead of on aristocratic patronage. The reading public ceased to be limited to scholars and members of the privileged classes and began instead to represent the population at large. For the first time, too, the writer emerged as a distinct professional; authors began writing on commission for the rapidly growing book-seller trade. While the hitherto privileged leisure classes, the landed gentry, were gradually forced to abdicate their commanding positions, the urbanized members of the emerging middle classes began to find themselves with leisure time, presently to be occupied by those forms of diversion and entertainment which an accommodating market was ready to supply.

As a result, "mass" media, in the sense of marketable literary goods, began to be produced to meet the interests and demands of the new reading public. And these media comprised prototypes of practically all the popular literary products familiar to us today: the newspaper, which not only covers the news proper but peddles social gossip, topical commentaries, and special features catering to diverse segments of the audience; the "family" magazine, ranging over as wide a variety of topics as those covered in *Reader's Digest* today, but offering, in addition, advice to the lovelorn and question-and-answer columns on a hundred and one topics; news digest magazines parading "the news of the week in review"; magazines of gossip retailed from the world of the theatre and the world of opera; book reviewing journals; book digests; and the prototypes of our *Love Story* and *True Story* slicks.

The novel became a more popular stock item than it had ever been and in the course of the century it approached pocket-book dimensions for the optimal convenience of the reader. It was customary for a novel to be published in three handy, portable volumes, so that milady could finish a volume in one sitting at the hairdresser's. Enterprising eighteenth-century book publishers (who were booksellers as well) also hit upon the remunerative device of publishing fiction in cheap weekly installments, printed and illustrated on news sheets. Portable volumes of "selections" from classical and contemporary writers, on the order of our pocket anthologies, became popular after the middle of the eighteenth century. During the last decades, inexpensive reprints, second-hand books, and remainder sales became commonplace not only in London—then as now the center of the book trade—but in all major urban centers throughout Britain.

Booksellers and other energetic entrepreneurs made the most of a wide variety of "audience building" institutions. The first circulating library was established in 1740; by the turn of the century over a thousand such libraries existed in London and the provinces. Frequently the bookseller bought controlling interests in these libraries —making sure that each novel he distributed to them carried conspicuous front- and back-page itemized lists and blurbs for other novels published under his aegis. The bookseller likewise encouraged the various book clubs and literary societies which sprang up among the middle classes all over the country; he distributed annual catalogues; and by the end of the century, he had established the rudiments of a mail order business.

Approximately half of the advertisements which appeared in eighteenth-century magazines took the form of book blurbs, or "puffery," as this device was called in the trade. Catchy titles were considered of paramount importance, second only to the device of building up the author in the public mind as a person famous, or mysterious, or immoral, or, preferably, all three. "Men of distinction" were called upon to write endorsements. Book reviewers were bribed or otherwise influenced, and many booksellers owned controlling interests in book-reviewing journals. The more unscrupulous members of the book-selling professions resorted to yet more fraudulent tricks: books that had failed in the market were called in and reissued under new titles; or they were reissued, carrying upon their title-pages the bald-faced announcement that the first issue having sold so immensely well, the present version was a second, revised, and up-to-date edition especially prepared "by popular request." All sorts of devious means were adopted to suggest to the public that a certain book was the work of an eminently famous personage, when in fact it had been thrown together by a Grub Street hack writing in a garret to keep alive.

In short, the decisive change which took place in the world of literary communication in the seventeen hundreds was the change, substantially, from private endowment and a limited audience to public endowment and a potentially unlimited audience. This change was to have the most far-reaching effects both in the aesthetic and ethical domains, on the body as well as the form of literature, to say nothing of its effect on the author's own daily habits and concerns. An earlier study[2] has attempted to describe at some length the types of literature and literary institutions which were affected by this change and which, in turn, fostered it; the shifting ideational patterns (the sentimental craze, the gothic mode, and the like) which illuminate it; and the specific issues and controversies (the controversy, principally, between the artist on the one hand and the consumer of poplar culture on the other) which attended it. The historical stages are noted by the sensitive optimism of Addison as he endeavored to educate the public by means of delightful moral small talk; the outright antagonism of Fielding and Goldsmith to the mass media;

the willingness of Johnson to recognize the claims of the common reader; and finally, toward the close of the century, the disposition to search for a basis of reconciliation between art and popular culture. If these concerns sound unduly modern to the reader, he may be assured that, rather than representing a transfer of contemporary terms to meet an outdated situation, they grow from the social sub-soil of middle class society; and they clearly demonstrate that the whole controversy, far from depending on the introduction of electronics, is part and parcel of the historical development.

By 1800, the changes which were merely incipient in the century of Montaigne had taken place: nearly all remnants of the feudal system had been destroyed, at least in political and economic fields; industrialization and the resulting division of labor in a predominantly middle class society were well under way. Artists and intellectuals had freed themselves from dependence upon both Church and State and were struggling to establish well defined roles in this society. They experienced the growing emancipation of the middle classes as a threat and feared that, as this group became more prosperous, it would use philosophy and art as a kind of mass ornament, threatening the scholars' and artists' integrity which had been so newly wrested from Church and State. The artists and scholars were not concerned with the salvation of their souls as their predecessors had been, but with the preservation of a mission—the search for truth and beauty. The artists therefore bent their efforts to educating the public for the difficult task of art appreciation and, at the same time, to fighting the literary manipulators and imitators who corrupted the public before it could be educated. In this period, then, the artist— and especially the writers—felt it their mission to establish on every level of society the reading of great works as the only permissible pastime in literary matters. From the point of view of the relations between the producers and the consumers of art, these concerns reflect an intermediary stage of development: the interests of the producers and consumers no longer coincide but they are not felt to be completely divergent either.

By 1850, the middle classes had achieved unchallenged rule in much of Europe and America, and the modern form of mass society had emerged. Mass media of communication—especially the newspapers—had established their dominance, and the literary market was flooded by products designed to attract the broadest possible public. Those writers or artists who held an esoteric conception of their vocation began to be and to feel isolated. Some of them—

beginning with Stendhal—met the challenge of the times by further accentuating the rift, proclaiming the mission of art as art for art's sake—by its very nature to be understood and enjoyed only by the few, "happy" or otherwise.

England during the nineteenth century represents the richest source for a study of middle class debate on standards for high and low culture. To understand why this is so, one must consider the impact of the French Revolution and its aftermath on the Establishment. The ruling groups, fearing revolt from below, sought to channel and control the emerging educational maturity of the lower strata of the population by nourishing them exclusively on religious tracts and paternalistic pedagogical trash. In a period of transition from an aristocratic to a middle-class policy the Establishment was successful in keeping the wolf of revolution from its door and, at least for the first decades of the century, was almost equally successful in protecting elite culture from the "vulgar" participation of "vulgar" people. At the same time—representing an almost opposite trend— the rapid rate of industrialization in England brought with it new methods of paper production and more efficient machinery which accelerated the rate of publication. This increased the amount of printed material available to the masses who more and more spurned the tracts spoon-fed to them.[3] What was true for the poor was even more true for the middle classes whose popular fare of newspapers, magazines, novels, and banal comedies was plentifully supplied.

This economy of abundance in available means of entertainment aroused a vivid debate concerning the threat to high culture from middlebrow and lowbrow entertainment. In comparison with this debate, the eighteenth century controversies seem pallid. Even the briefest effort to describe and understand the problem as it emerged in the nineteenth century would have three important themes.

One of these would be to tell the story of the development of diverse agencies for marketing popular literature and the arguments that arose among their defenders as well as their detractors. Attention would have to be paid to the commercial libraries which had already begun to make inroads during the eighteenth century. A hymn-writing bookseller by the name of Charles Edward Mudie developed this type of business into a mammoth affair during the century. At its end, his firm had about three and one-half million books in circulation. Among other tricks of the trade he knew how to market remainders successfully, very much in the style of modern enterprises. He even developed "for those subscribers who were unable to come" to his libraries in person "his famous door-to-door van service, forerunner of today's bookmobile, which daily kept eight vehicles in operation."[4]

An important innovation in the course of industrialization was the introduction of so-called "railway literature." Publishers stocked the bookstalls at English railroad stations with printed merchandise for purchase or loan during the ride. They even engaged in a germinal form of audience research; the biggest entrepreneur in railway literature sent out his agents in order to observe the buying habits of the traveling public; or as his admiring biographer expressed it, young booksellers "were educated to gauge the literary taste of the various districts."[5] It would be intriguing to study the presumptuous claims for civic betterment made by the purveyors of these literary wares, as well as the vituperative attacks on these allegedly degrading practices by such people as the influential Samuel Phillips of the London *Times* and others, who joined him in denouncing what, after the prevailing cover color, were called the "Yellow Backs."[6]

A second route to an understanding of the debate over cultural standards would be to study the views expressed by some of the major English writers. Here a few brief, but significant, illustrations must suffice.

William Wordsworth's famous Preface to the second edition of his *Lyrical Ballads* gave classic formulation, as early as 1800, to the view that popular art was an expression of deeper social conditions. Wordsworth voiced his alarm about the extent to which the "beauty and dignity" represented in true art was threatened by "frantic novels, sickly and stupid German tragedies, and the deluge of idle and extravagant stories in verse."

In analyzing the spread of this popular literature, Wordsworth made use of a psychological construct which by now has become familiar to us: the need of modern man for "gross and violent stimulants," tends "to blunt the discriminating powers of the mind," whereas the function of true art is to stimulate these powers. Popular literature reduces people to an attitude of passivity or, in the words of Wordsworth, to "a state of almost savage torpor." He finds these predispositions activated by social change, by "the great national events which are daily taking place, and which the increasing accumulation of intelligence hourly gratifies." And he offers his own works as a modest endeavor to counteract the new degrading tendencies.

Matthew Arnold in contrast to Wordsworth and in a manner remi-
niscent of Pascal, was more concerned with spiritual than aesthetic
values. He was deeply troubled lest the rapid spread of industrialization overwhelm "culture," which for him is the "idea of perfection as
an inward condition of the mind and spirit." This role of true culture,
he believed, is more essential to mankind than ever before as civilization, more than ever before, tends constantly to become increasingly
"mechanized and external." Arnold at times dealt with specific
phenomena of popular culture. Not unlike Pascal (or, for that matter,
contemporary critics of our college mores), he indicted games, sports,
and mass media as various manifestations of the same trend away
from the true essence of life:

> . . . the result of all the games and sports which occupy the passing
> generation of boys and young men may be the establishment of a better
> physical type for the future to work with . . . our generation of boys and
> young men is in the meantime sacrificed.[7]

In the same context, he attacked the producers of literature for mass
consumption:

> Plenty of people will try to give the masses as they call them, an intellec-
> tual food prepared and adapted in the way they think proper for the
> actual condition of the masses. The ordinary popular literature is an
> example of this way of working on the masses.

Such manipulation, he believed, was incompatible with culture which
"works differently." He, too, singled out the newspaper (particularly
the American newspaper) for special attack.

Arnold did not view as alternatives esoteric artistic production and
substitute products seeking the market for popularity. He and other
critics of the time formulated a concept of art which makes it neither
exclusive nor condescending but which certainly grants no living
space to the products of popular culture. They believed that the basic
function of art, and particularly literature, is to bring about the universal liberation of mankind; to provide for his emancipation from any
sort of social manipulation by teaching truth and freedom.

The crucial question of the role of "public taste," that is to say, the
impact of the market place on public opinion in a liberalistic if not
democratic society, is a recurrent topic in pre-Victorian and Victorian
discussions. One could arrange most of the literati of this era on a
continuum, ranging from strong agreement to strong disagreement
with the following statements of William Hazlitt (1778-1830):

The highest efforts of genius, in every walk of art, can never be understood by the generality of mankind. [8]
The public taste hangs like a millstone round the neck of all original genius that does not conform to established and exclusive models. [9]

It is on these premises that Hazlitt became apprehensive about the denigration of art. Popular culture, he said, was bringing about the decay of high culture under the dictates of the buying customers' taste. Hazlitt:

> The public taste is, therefore, necessarily vitiated, in proportion as it is public; it is lowered with every infusion it receives of common opinion. The greater the number of judges, the less capable must they be of judging, for the addition to the number of good ones will always be small, while the multitude of bad ones is endless, and thus the decay of the arts may be said to be the necessary consequence of its progress. [10]

He came very close to using our contemporary categories in describing mass culture and mass leisure by pointing to the social configuration of official pontificators in matters artistic, the role of money, and the eagerness of the general public to keep up appearances whenever they make for social success. To quote from an article in the *Examiner* (1816), in which he took the selection policy of the British Museum to task:

> . . . the Royal Academy are a society of hucksters in the Fine Arts who are more tenacious of their profits as chapmen and dealers, than of the honour of Art. . . . A fashionable artist and a fashionable hair-dresser have the same common principles of theory and practice; the one fits his customers to appear with *eclat* in a ball-room, the other in the Great Room of the Royal Academy. [11]

Hazlitt's contempt for the public culminated in the following statement:

> It reads, it admires, it extols only because it is the fashion, not from any love of the subject or the man. [12]

And Hazlitt summed up: "The diffusion of taste is not the same thing as the improvement of taste." [13]

With Sir Walter Scott we encounter a radically different attitude toward the relation between the artist and the public. First of all, he considered the trade of writing a legitimate business which deserved its monetary rewards: "I care not who knows it—I write for general amusement." [14]

In an intimate journal entry he very frankly confessed that "the public favor is my only lottery" and he proudly added, "I have long enjoyed the foremost praise." [15] We might perhaps say that he formulated the credo of the middlebrow in assuming a pre-stablized harmony between books which sell and the healthy tastes of the reading public:

> . . . it has often happened, that those who have been best received in their own time, have also continued to be acceptable to posterity. I do not think so ill of the present generation, as to suppose that its present favour necessarily infers a future condemnation.[16]

In strict contrast to the esoteric concept of art defended by Hazlitt or the early Hunt—not to speak of Coleridge, Wordsworth and Shelley—Scott advocated a "cultivation" of literature "useful" for the business of society:

> A taste for poetry . . . is apt if too much indulged, to engender a fastidious contempt for the ordinary business of the world, and gradually to unfit us for the exercise of the useful and domestic virtues, which depend greatly on our not exalting our feelings above the temper of well-ordered and well-educated society. . . . Cultivate, then, sir, your taste for poetry and the belles-lettres, as an elegant and most interesting amusement, but combine it with studies of a more serious and solid cast.[17]

What Scott did was to turn art into a residual category of activity, thereby robbing it of aesthetic principle. For Scott there were no critical rules by which to judge the adequacy or beauty of artistic works. He was alarmed when he decided that the standards of his class were being lowered by the popularity of certain types of art—but again he substituted a conventional moral standard for an aesthetic one. For if the standards of society prevail, then the audience to whom it is directed is the legitimate critic.

A study of the leading magazines of the period would provide the third route to understanding the issues of the nineteenth century debate over popular art. *The Edinburgh Review*, founded in 1802, is perhaps the most fruitful periodical source for locating the main themes of the discussion. To its pages, almost all the major figures of English literary life contributed unsigned articles.

A subject which came under frequent scrutiny by the *Review* was the role and influence of the press, as representative of the mass media. Newspapers, as one contributor wrote in a review article, are:

> . . . an essential element and symbol of the peculiar spirit and tendency

which characterize our civilization. There is no place to which they do not penetrate; no object which they may not serve; no description of person to whom they are not welcome.[18]

Perhaps the most interesting facet of this article is its thesis that "the only adequate standard at any given period [namely for the measurement of the moral and intellectual level of a society] is the style of its popular writings and of its domestic buildings." This means:

> Under a free and cheap press, newspapers are perhaps the best representative, at any given time, of the real moral and intellectual state of the greater part of a population.[19]

But the crucial dilemma of, a public opinion dependent on newspapers and, writers under pressure to satisfy the reading public is evaded by this writer, who views the growth of the press with optimism:

> Books, how cheap soever, and however popularly written, are not likely to be read by the uninformed. To buy, or to get, and to begin reading a volume, indicates a certain progress in improvement to have been already made. But all men will read THE NEWS; and even peasants, farm servants, country-day labourers, will look at, nay pore over the paper that chronicles the occurrences of the neighbouring markettown. Here then is a channel through which, alongst with political intelligence and the occurrences of the day, the friends of human improvement, the judicious promoters of general education, may diffuse the best information, and may easily allure all classes, even the humblest, into the paths of general knowledge.[20]

That this was a controversial issue is borne out by another article which appeared in 1846. It speaks about the "unfortunate effects" produced by "dependence on periodical literature."

> The constantly recurring demands of Periodical Literature are fatal to all deliberation of view,—to all care, or study, or selection of materials; in the case of those who engaged in it as a Profession.[21]

The article comments scathingly on the need to offer "novelty," "artificially fretted into foam," which prevents the public from learning to appreciate the

> calmness and repose of manner, and to that breadth and evenness of composition which are the distinguishing characteristics of those works which we regard as the classics of our language.[22]

Again, America looms on the horizon as the most telling example of the debasement of culture when the author goes on to say:

> We cannot but regard the condition of our own Daily Press, as a morning and evening witness against the moral character of the people; for if this kind of scurrility were as distasteful to the public, as the grosser kinds of licentiousness are, it would at once disappear. That its condition is still worse in America, we can . . . easily believe. . . . In the meantime, we hope that Mr. Dickens is mistaken as to the degree in which the Press in the United States impresses and influences the general feeling. . . . Does any well-educated man in America read these papers *with respect?* [23]

An interesting article, published in 1848, not only reiterates the thesis that the newspaper is the most appropriate yardstick for the state of culture, but declares that the newspaper is superseding the book:

> 'Give me a place to stand on,' said Archimedes, 'and I will move the world.' The modern Archimedes who should be content to use a moral lever, would take his stand upon the press. . . . Let one calmly reflect upon the enormous power, for good or evil, exercised by clever writers who are daily read by thousands. It is a well-known fact, which any leading book-seller will verify with a sigh, that, whenever public events of importance occur, or great changes are under discussion, it is useless to publish books. [24]

One remarkable article anticipated modern categories of social criticism such as those used by Riesman and others, categories which suggest that an individual's values must be neutralized if he is to remain an accepted member of a social team:

> A certain social uniformity ensues . . . insensibly destroying men's humours, idiosyncracies, and spontaneous emotions. It does so, by rendering their concealment an habitual necessity, and by allowing them neither food nor sphere. Men are thus, as it were, cast in a mould. Besides—the innumerable influences, intellectual and moral, which, at a period of diffused knowledge like the present, co-exist and cooperate in building up our mental structure, are often completely at variance with each other in origin and tendency: so that they neutralize each other's effects, and leave a man well stored with thoughts and speech, but frequently without aim or purpose. [25]

The article ended with a statement that art can only retain "but a feeble hold on the true and real" in a period which is characterized:

> by subserviency to Opinion—that irresponsible life which makes little things great, and shuts great things out from our view. [26]

A magazine with a social purpose, the *Edinburgh Review* again and again permitted its contributors to come back to the deplorable level of popular entertainment. A number of remedial measures were proposed at various times and by various contributors; they included increased and free education, legal measures against trash, a classification of the theaters, and a deliberate effort on the part of intellectuals to raise the standards of the general public so that their "casting vote" would be for works of "good taste." [27]

Throughout the nineteenth century, the writers who viewed the new developments with alarm were seldom contradicted. If the public continued to buy bestsellers, the champions of higher culture seemed to dominate the theoretical discussions. However, some limited oppostion to them did appear, and there were a few who took up the cudgels in defense of an art for and of the people. Their attitude was well expressed in the *Edinburgh Review* of 1896. The question was posed: Is it true that increased moral and material welfare of the masses "can only be obtained by making it more difficult for the man of intellect to make his mark on the age," that "the levelling up of the masses inevitably leads to the levelling down of genuis?" [28] If it be true, "the interests of the many must, we fear, prevail over the requirements of the few . . ." [29] But, it is not true:

> . . . material prosperity has been accompanied by moral progress; the life of our people is, on the whole, more healthy than it was fifty years ago . . . and their opportunities for sensible recreation greater. . . . there is no proof that, in levelling up the masses, we have levelled down genius. We have, on the contrary, argued that . . . there is no evidence of decay in our intellectual growth; and that an age which has done more to dominate nature, and to explain nature, than all the preceeding centuries, cannot rightly be charged with inferiority of intellect.[30]

It is on this note of optimism that the *Edinburgh Review* summarized the achievements of the century, and carried forward with new momentum the growing triumph of science and technology. Here are Arnold's Philistines victorious, relating popular culture to the grand march of Victorian progress in words which might be taken unaltered from the contemporary debate.

REFERENCES

1 See Leo Lowenthal, "Historical Perspectives of Popular Culture," *The American Journal of Sociology*, 1950, 55:324-325.

2 Leo Lowenthal and Marjorie Fiske, "The Debate Over Art and Popular Culture in Eighteenth Century England," *Common Frontiers of the Social Sciences*, ed. by Mirra Komarovsky, (Glencoe, Ill.: Free Press, 1957).

3 For details on the spread of reading among the lower classes, see the excellent book of Richard Altick, *The English Common Reader*, University of Chicago Press, 1957.

4 Robert A. Colby. "The Librarian Rules the Roost: The Career of Charles Edward Mudie, (1818-1890)" in *Wilson Library Bulletin*, April, 1952, p. 625.

5 Sir Herbert Maxwell, *Life and Times of the Rt. Hon. W. H. Smith*. London: Blackwell, 1893, vol. 1, p. 57.

6 For this whole complex see Sir Herbert Maxwell, *loc. cit.*; Samuel Phillips, *Essays from 'The Times,'* John Murray, 1871, Vol. I, pp. 311-325; "Railway Literature," the *Dublin University Magazines*, Vol. 34, September 1849, pp. 280-291; Michael Sadlair, "Yellow Backs" in John Carter (ed.) *New Paths in Book Collecting*, Constable, 1934, pp. 125-161; Robert A. Colby, "That He Who Rides May Read: W. H. Smith and Sons Railway Library," in *Wilson Library Bulletin*, December, 1952, pp. 300-306.

7 These and the following quotations are from Matthew Arnold, *Culture and Anarchy* (1869).

8 *The Round Table* (1817). *The Complete Works*. London: Dent, 1930, vol. 4, p. 164.

9 *Lectures on the English Poets* (1818). *Loc. cit.*, vol. 5, p. 96.

10 *Loc. cit.*, pp. 45-46.

11 *Loc. cit.*, vol. 18, pp. 105-108.

12 *Table Talk* (1821-1822). *Loc. cit.*, vol. 8, p. 99.

13 *Examiner* (1816). *Loc. cit.*, vol. 18, pp. 102-103.

14 Introductory epistle to *Fortune's of Nigel* (1822), London, 1892, vol. 1, p. xxxviii.

15 *Journal of Sir Walter Scott*, (1826), ed. by J. G. Tait. Edinburgh, 1950, p. 73.

16 Introductory Epistle to *Fortune's of Nigel, loc. cit.*, p. lii.

17 *Letters of Sir Walter Scott*, vol. II, p. 278, London, 1932.

18 *Edinburgh Review*, 65, 1837 (No. CXXXII): 197.——All contributions to the *Edinburgh Review* are anonymous. Wherever possible, the name of the contributor is supplied. The writer of the article quoted above is William Empson. For research on authorship, I am indebted to Ina Lawson of the Department of English, University of California, Berkeley. There is, however, a project now in progress at Wellesley College under the editorship of Walter E. Houghton. Known as *The Wellesley Index to Victorian Periodicals*, it will eventually give us, among other things, the authors' names.

19 *Loc. cit.*

20 *Loc. cit.*, 61, 1835 (CKXIII):184.

21 *Loc. cit.*, 83, 1846 (No. CLXVIII):383.
22 *Loc. cit.*
23 *Loc. cit.*, 76, 1843 (No. CLIV):520 [James Spaulding, author].
24 *Loc. cit.*, 88, 1848 (No. CLXXVIII):342 [A. Hayward, author].
25 *Loc. cit.*, 89, 1849 (No. CLXXX):360 [Aubrey de Vere, author].
26 *Loc. cit.*
27 *Loc. cit.*, 65, 1837 (No. CXXXII):204 [William Empson, author].
28 *Loc. cit.*, 183, 1896 (No. CCCLXXV):20.
29 *Loc. cit.*
30 *Loc. cit.*

HANNAH ARENDT

Society and Culture

MASS CULTURE and mass society (the very terms were still a sign of reprobation a few years ago, implying that mass society was a depraved form of society and mass culture a contradiction in terms) are considered by almost everybody today as something with which we must come to terms, and in which we must discover some "positive" aspects—if only because mass culture is the culture of a mass society. And mass society, whether we like it or not, is going to stay with us into the foreseeable future. No doubt mass society and mass culture are interrelated phenomena. Mass society comes about when "the mass of the population has become incorporated into society."* Since society originally comprehended those parts of the population which disposed of leisure time and the wealth which goes with it, mass society does indeed indicate a new order in which the masses have been liberated "from the burden of physically exhausting labor."† Historically as well as conceptually, therefore, mass society has been preceded by society, and society is no more a generic term than is mass society; it too can be dated and described historically. It is older, to be sure, than mass society, but not older than the modern age. In fact, all the traits that crowd psychology has meanwhile discovered in mass man: his loneliness (and loneliness is neither isolation nor solitude) regardless of his adaptability; his excitability and lack of standards; his capacity for consumption, accompanied by inability to judge or even to distinguish; above all, his egocentricity and that fateful alienation from the world which, since Rousseau, he mistakes for self-alienation—all these traits first appeared in "good society," where there was no question of masses, numerically speaking. The first mass men, we are tempted to say, quantitatively

*Edward Shils, see page 1.
†*Ibid.*, page 2.

85

so little constituted a mass that they could even imagine they constituted an elite, the elite of good society.

Let me therefore first say a few words on the older phenomena of society and its relation to culture: say them not primarily for historical reasons, but because they relate facts that seem to me little known in this country. It may be this lack of knowledge that leads Mr. Shils to say "individuality has flowered in mass society," whereas actually the modern individual was defined and, indeed, discovered by those who—like Rousseau in the eighteenth or John Stuart Mill in the nineteenth century—found themselves in open rebellion against society. Individualism and the "sensibility and privacy" which go with it—the discovery of intimacy as the atmosphere the individual needs for his full development—came about at a time when society was not yet a mass phenomenon but still thought of itself in terms of "good society" or (especially in Central Europe) of "educated and cultured society." And it is against this background that we must understand the modern (and no longer so modern) individual who, as we all know from nineteenth- and twentieth-century novels, can only be understood as part of the society against which he tried to assert himself and which always got the better of him.

The chances of this individual's survival lay in the simultaneous presence within the population of other nonsociety strata into which the rebellious individual could escape; one reason why rebellious individuals so frequently ended by becoming revolutionaries as well was that they discovered in those who were not admitted to society certain traits of humanity which had become extinct in society. We need only read the record of the French Revolution, and recall to what an extent the very concept of *le peuple* received its connotations from a rebellion against the corruption and hypocrisy of the salons, to realize what the true role of society was throughout the nineteenth century. A good part of the despair of individuals under the conditions of mass society is due to the fact that these avenues of escape are, of course, closed as soon as society has incorporated all the strata of the population.

Generally speaking, I think it has been the great good fortune of this country to have this intermediary stage of good and cultured society play a relatively minor role in its development; but the disadvantage of this good fortune today is that those few who will still make a stand against mass culture as an unavoidable consequence of mass society are tempted to look upon these earlier phenomena of society and culture as a kind of golden age and lost paradise, precisely because they know so little of it. America has been only too well acquainted with the barbarian philistinism of the *nouveau riche*, but it has only a nodding acquaintance with the equally annoying cultural and educated philistinism of a society where culture actually has what Mr. Shils calls "snob-value," and where it is a matter of status to be educated.

This cultural philistinism is today in Europe rather a matter of the past, for the simple reason that the whole development of modern art started from and remained committed to a profound mistrust not only of cultural philistinism but also of the word culture itself. It is still an open question whether it is more difficult to discover the great authors of the past without the help of any tradition than it is to rescue them from the rubbish of educated philistinism. And this task of preserving the past without the help of tradition, and often even against traditional standards and interpretations, is the same for the whole of Western civilization. Intellectually, though not socially, America and Europe are in the same situation: the thread of tradition is broken, and we must discover the past for ourselves— that is, read its authors as though nobody had ever read them before. In this task, mass society is much less in our way than good and educated society, and I suspect that this kind of reading was not uncommon in nineteenth-century America precisely because this country was still that "unstoried wilderness" from which so many American writers and artists tried to escape. That American fiction and poetry have so suddenly and richly come into their own, ever since Whitman and Melville, may have something to do with this.

It would be unfortunate indeed if out of the dilemmas and distractions of mass culture and mass society there should arise an altogether unwarranted and idle yearning for a state of affairs which is not better but only a bit old-fashioned. And the eager and uncritical acceptance of such obviously snobbish and philistine terms as highbrow, middlebrow, and lowbrow is a rather ominous sign. For the only nonsocial and authentic criterion for works of culture is, of course, their relative permanence and even their ultimate immortality. The point of the matter is that as soon as the immortal works of the past became the object of "refinement" and acquired the status which went with it, they lost their most important and elemental quality, which is to grasp and move the reader or spectator, throughout the centuries. The very word "culture" became suspect precisely because it indicated that "pursuit of perfection" which to Matthew Arnold was identical with the "pursuit of sweetness and light." It was not Plato, but a reading of Plato, prompted by the ulterior motive of self-perfection, that became suspect; and the "pursuit of sweetness and light," with all its overtones of good society, was held in contempt because of its rather obvious effort to keep reality out of one's life by looking at everything through a veil of sweetness and light. The astounding recovery of the creative arts in the twentieth century, and a less apparent but perhaps no less real recovery of the greatness of the past, began when good society lost its monopolizing grip on culture, together with its dominant position in society as a whole.

Here we are not concerned with society, however, but with culture —or rather with what happens to culture under the different conditions of society and of mass society. In society, culture, even more than other realities, had become what only then began to be called a "value," that is, a social commodity which could be circulated and cashed in on as social coinage for the purpose of acquiring social status. Cultural objects were transformed into values when the cultural philistine seized upon them as a currency by which he bought a higher position in society—higher, that is, than in his own opinion he deserved either by nature or by birth. Cultural values, therefore, were what values have always been, exchange values; in passing from hand to hand, they were worn down like an old coin. They lost the faculty which is originally peculiar to all cultural things, the faculty of arresting our attention and moving us. This process of transformation was called the devaluation of values, and its end came with the "bargain-sale of values" (*Ausverkauf der Werte*) during the 'twenties and 'thirties, when cultural and moral values were "sold out" together.

Perhaps the chief difference between society and mass society is that society wanted culture, evaluated and devaluated cultural things into social commodities, used and abused them for its own selfish purposes, but did not "consume" them. Even in their most worn-out shapes, these things remained things, they were not "consumed" and swallowed up but retained their worldly objectivity. Mass society, on the contrary, wants not culture but entertainment, and the wares offered by the entertainment industry are indeed consumed by society just as are any other consumer goods. The products needed for entertainment serve the life process of society, even though they may not be as necessary for this life as bread and meat. They serve, as the phrase is, to while away time, and the vacant time which is whiled away is not leisure time, strictly speaking, that is, time in which we are truly liberated from all cares and activities necessitated by the life process, and therefore free for the world and its "culture"; it is rather leftover time, which still is biological in nature, leftover after labor and sleep have received their due. Vacant time which entertainment is supposed to fill is a hiatus in the biologically conditioned cycle of labor, in "the metabolism of man with nature," as Marx used to say.

Under modern conditions, this hiatus is constantly growing; there is more and more time freed that must be filled with entertainment, but this enormous increase in vacant time does not change the nature of the time. Entertainment, like labor and sleep, is irrevocably part of the biological life process. And biological life is always, whether one is laboring or at rest, engaged in consumption or in the passive reception of amusement, a metabolism feeding on things by devouring them. The commodities the entertainment industry offers are not "things"—cultural objects whose excellence is measured by their ability to withstand the life process and to become permanent appurtenances of the world—and they should not be judged according to these standards; nor are they values which exist to be used and exchanged; they are rather consumer goods destined to be used up, as are any other consumer goods.

Panis et circenses truly belong together; both are necessary for life, for its preservation and recuperation, and both vanish in the course of the life process—that is, both must constantly be produced anew and offered anew, lest this process cease entirely. The standards by which both should be judged are indeed freshness and novelty— standards by which we today (and, I think, quite mistakenly) judge cultural and artistic objects as well, things which are supposed to remain in the world even after we have left it.

As long as the entertainment industry produces its own consumer goods, all is well, and we can no more reproach it for the nondurability of its articles than we can reproach a bakery because it produces goods which, if they are not to spoil, must be consumed as soon they are made. It has always been the mark of educated philistinism to despise entertainment and amusement because no "value" could be derived from them. In so far as we are all subject to life's great cycle, we all stand in need of entertainment and amusement in some form or other, and it is sheer hypocrisy or social snobbery to deny that we can be amused and entertained by exactly the same things which amuse and entertain the masses of our fellow men. As far as the survival of culture is concerned, it certainly is less threatened by those who fill vacant time with amusement and entertainment than by those who fill it with some haphazard educational gadget in order to improve their social standing.

If mass culture and the entertainment industry were the same, I should not worry much, even though it is true that, in Mr. Shils's words, "the immense advance in audibility and visibility" of this whole sector of life, which formerly had been "relatively silent and unseen by the intellectuals," creates a serious problem for the artist and intellectual. It is as though the futility inherent in entertainment had been permitted to permeate the whole social atmosphere, and the often described malaise of the artists and intellectuals is of course partly due to their inability to make themselves heard and seen in the tumultuous uproar of mass society, or to penetrate its noisy futility. But this protest of the artist against society is as old as. society, though not older; the great revival of nearly all the arts in our century (which perhaps one day will seem one of the great artistic—and of course scientific—periods of Western civilization) began with the malaise of the artist in society, with his decision to turn his back upon it and its "values," to leave the dead to bury the dead. As far as artistic productivity is concerned, it should not be more difficult to withstand the massive temptations of mass culture, or to keep from being thrown out of gear by the noise and humbug of mass society, than it was to avoid the more sophisticated temptations and the more insidious noises of the cultural snobs in refined society.

Unhappily, the case is not that simple. The entertainment industry is confronted with gargantuan appetites, and since its wares disappear in consumption, it must constantly offer new commodities. In this predicament, those who produce for the mass media ransack the entire range of past and present culture in the hope of finding suitable material. This material, however, cannot be offered as it is; it must be prepared and altered in order to become entertaining; it cannot be consumed as it is.

Mass culture comes into being when mass society seizes upon cultural objects, and its danger is that the life process of society (which like all biological processes insatiably draws everything available into the cycle of its metabolism) will literally consume the cultural objects, eat them up and destroy them. I am not referring to the phenomenon of mass distribution. When cultural objects, books, or pictures in reproduction, are thrown on the market cheaply and attain huge sales, this does not affect the nature of the goods in question. But their nature is affected when these objects themselves are changed (rewritten, condensed, digested, reduced to *Kitsch* in the course of reproduction or preparation for the movies) in order to be put into usable form for a mass sale which they otherwise could not attain.

Neither the entertainment industry itself nor mass sales as such are signs of, not what we call mass culture, but what we ought more accurately to call the decay of culture in mass society. This decay sets in when liberties are taken with these cultural objects in order that they may be distributed among masses of people. Those who actively promote this decay are not the Tin Pan Alley composers but a special kind of intellectuals, often well read and well informed, whose sole function is to organize, disseminate, and change cultural objects in order to make them palatable to those who want to be entertained or—and this is worse—to be "educated," that is, to acquire as cheaply as possible some kind of cultural knowledge to improve their social status.

Richard Blackmur (in a recent article on the "Role of the Intellectual," in the *Kenyon Review*) has brilliantly shown that the present malaise of the intellectual springs from the fact that he finds himself surrounded, not by the masses, from whom, on the contrary, he is carefully shielded, but by these digesters, re-writers, and changers of culture whom we find in every publishing house in the United States, and in the editorial offices of nearly every magazine. And these "professionals" are ably assisted by those who no longer write books but fabricate them, who manufacture a "new" textbook out of four or five already on the market, and who then have, as Blackmur shows, only one worry—how to avoid plagiarism. (Meanwhile the editor does his best to substitute clichés for sheer illiteracy.) Here the criterion of novelty, quite legitimate in the entertainment industry, becomes a simple fake and, indeed, a threat: it is only too likely that the "new" textbook will crowd out the older ones, which usually are better, not because they are older, but because they were still written in response to authentic needs.

This state of affairs, which indeed is equaled nowhere else in the world, can properly be called mass culture; its promoters are neither the masses nor their entertainers, but are those who try to entertain the masses with what once was an authentic object of culture, or to persuade them that *Hamlet* can be as entertaining as *My Fair Lady*, and educational as well. The danger of mass education is precisely that it may become very entertaining indeed; there are many great authors of the past who have survived centuries of oblivion and neglect, but it is still an open question whether they will be able to survive an entertaining version of what they have to say.

The malaise of the intellectual in the atmosphere of mass culture is much more legitimate than his malaise in mass society; it is caused socially by the presence of these other intellectuals, the manufacturers of mass culture, from whom he finds it difficult to distinguish himself and who, moreover, always outnumber him, and therefore acquire that kind of power which is generated whenever people band together and act more or less in concert. The power of the many (legitimate only in the realm of politics and the field of action) has always been a threat to the strength of the few; it is a threat under the most favorable circumstances, and it has always been felt to be more dangerous when it arises from within a group's own ranks. Culturally, the malaise is caused, I think, not so much by the massive temptations and the high rewards which await those who are willing to alter their products to make them acceptable for a mass market, as by the constant irritating care each of us has to exert in order to protect his product against the demands and the ingenuity of those who think they know how to "improve" it.

Culture relates to objects and is a phenomenon of the world; entertainment relates to people and is a phenomenon of life. If life is no longer content with the pleasure which is always coexistent with the toil and labor inherent in the metabolism of man with nature, if vital energy is no longer fully used up in this cycle, then life may reach out for the things of the world, may violate and consume them. It will prepare these things of the world until they are fit for consumption; it will treat them as if they were articles of nature, articles which must also be prepared before they can enter into man's metabolism.

Consumption of the things of nature does no harm to them; they are constantly renewed because man, in so far as he lives and labors, toils and recuperates, is also a creature of nature, a part of the great cycle in which all nature wheels. But the things of the world which are made by man (in so far as he is a worldly and not merely a natural being), these things are not renewed of their own accord. When life seizes upon them and consumes them at its pleasure, for entertainment, they simply disappear. And this disappearance, which first begins in mass culture—that is, the "culture" of a society poised between the alternatives of laboring and of consuming—is something different from the wear and tear culture suffered when its things were made into exchange values, and circulated in society until their original stamp and meaning were scarcely recognizable.

If we wish to classify these two anticultural processes in historical and sociological terms, we may say that the devaluation of culture in good society through the cultural philistines was the characteristic peril of commercial society, whose primary public area was the exchange market for goods and ideas. The disappearance of culture in a mass society, on the other hand, comes about when we have a consumers' society which, in so far as it produces only for consumption, does not need a public worldly space whose existence is independent of and outside the sphere of its life process. In other words, a consumers' society does not know how to take care of the world and the things which belong to it: the society's own chief attitude toward objects, the attitude of consumption, spells ruin to everything it touches. If we understand by culture what it originally meant (the Roman *cultura*—derived from *colere*, to take care of and preserve and cultivate) then we can say without any exaggeration that a society obsessed with consumption cannot at the same time be cultured or produce a culture.

For all their differences, however, one thing is common to both these anticultural processes: they arise when all the worldly objects produced by the present or the past have become "social," are related to society, and are seen in their merely functional aspect. In the one case, society uses and exchanges, evaluates and devaluates them; in the other, it devours and consumes them. This functionalization or "societization" of the world is by no means a matter of course; the notion that every object must be functional, fulfilling some needs of society or of the individual—the church a religious need, the painting the need for self-expression in the painter and the need of self-perfection in the onlooker, and so on—is historically so new that one is tempted to speak of a modern prejudice. The cathedrals were built *ad majorem gloriam Dei;* while they as buildings certainly served the needs of the community, their elaborate beauty can never be explained by these needs, which could have been served quite as well by any nondescript building.

An object is cultural to the extent that it can endure; this durability is the very opposite of its functionality, which is the quality which makes it disappear again from the phenomenal world by being used and used up. The "thingness" of an object appears in its shape and appearance, the proper criterion of which is beauty. If we wanted to judge an object by its use value alone, and not also by its appearance (that is, by whether it is beautiful or ugly or something in between), we would first have to pluck out our eyes.

Thus, the functionalization of the world which occurs in both society and mass society deprives the world of culture as well as beauty. Culture can be safe only with those who love the world for its own sake, who know that without the beauty of man-made, worldly things which we call works of art, without the radiant glory in which potential imperishability is made manifest to the world and in the world, all human life would be futile and no greatness could endure.

ERNEST VAN DEN HAAG

A Dissent from the Consensual Society

EDWARD SHILS replaces Van Wyck Brooks' high, middle, and lowbrow classification (lately elaborated fruitfully by Richard Chase[1]) with his own: "refined," "mediocre," and "brutal" culture. The old terminology was unsatisfactory; but the new one is much more so. The evaluative element inherent in both should be formulated independently.[2] It is stronger in the new notation. Further, this notation is misleading in its implications. "Refined" has a genteel connotation, which I find hard to apply to such highbrows as Joyce, Kafka, Dostoyevski, Céline, or Nathanael West. Nor are lowbrow and "brutal" equivalent; indeed, the belief that they are is a middlebrow cliché, a projection of ambivalent desire and fear that identifies vitality and brutality. Actually, much lowbrow culture is maudlin and sentimental rather than brutal.[3] Even the term "mediocre" culture, though less misleading than the others, is not satisfactory and provides a criterion that would be hard to apply.

In my opinion, emphasis on cultural objects misses the point. A sociologist (and to analyze mass culture is a sociological enterprise) must focus on the function of such objects in people's lives: he must study how they are used; who produces what for whom; why, and with what effects. To be sure, value judgments cannot be avoided, but the qualities of the product become relevant only when related to its social functions. Middlebrow culture objects are not necessarily "mediocre." To be a middlebrow is to *relate* to objects, any objects, in a certain way, to give them a specific function in the context of one's life. A middlebrow might, for example, use a phrase, whatever its origin, as a cliché—i.e., in such a way that it loses its emotional impact and specific, concrete meaning and no longer communicates but labels or stereotypes and thus avoids perception and communication. The phrase is not middlebrow (or "mediocre"); he is. Beethoven does not become "mediocre," even though he may be-

95

come a favored middlebrow composer and function as part of middlebrow culture. Mozart may "tinkle" for the middlebrow; it is not Mozart but the audience that is "mediocre." Indeed, it is characteristic of much middlebrow culture to overuse highbrow cultural objects of the past without understanding them and thus both to honor and debase them. Mr. Shils's terminology precludes the description of cultural dynamics in these terms and thus disregards one of the most important aspects of mass culture: the corruption and sterilization of the heritage of the past.

Mass culture is not the culture of a class or group throughout history. It is the culture of nearly everybody today, and of nearly nobody yesterday; and because of production, market, and social changes, it is quite a new phenomenon which cannot be reduced to quantitative changes nor identified with timeless categories. Mr. Shils dismisses the conditions under which mass culture is produced and consumed with some descriptive phrases but does not relate mass production to the qualities of the cultural objects he discusses. His categories remain ahistorical, even though garnished with familiar historical references. Thus, the problem of mass culture is defined away, instead of being analyzed.

Mr. Shils hopefully maintains that "refined" culture now has become available to more people than ever before. This is true, but it constitutes the problem—not the solution. What are people making of the cultural heritage that is becoming available to them? What impact does it have on them? What are they doing to it? Mass culture involves a change in the conditions in which objects are produced, consumed, and related to on all levels, a change in the role each level plays, and a change finally in the way people relate to each other. At times Mr. Shils seems to recognize this change; but his categories preclude analysis of it. The destruction of folk culture by mass culture is apparently denied and then explained by the hypothesis that the proportion of gifted people remains "fairly constant" in any population and that they are now "diverted into other spheres." This is, of course, what is meant by the destruction of folk culture, in addition to other effects of increased mobility and communication. It is remarkable that Shils also says that, if high culture has declined (which he denies) possibly "our neural equipment is poorer than that of our ancestors." Neither of the two inconsistent hypotheses—unchanged or changed "neural equipment"—can be proved. Does this mean that we can use both? Since we know so little about neurological change, would it not be sensible to look for social changes to explain cultural changes? Mr. Shils recognizes social changes but refuses to relate them to cultural changes, which he denies, asserts, deplores, and approves. He cannot be wrong since he has left all possibilities open.

Mr. Shils suggests that anyone critical of mass culture must be a *laudator temporis acti;* I see no basis for this, nor for his own temporal chauvinism. We have no measurements; and history is not a homogeneous stream; hence, comparisons with the past depend largely on the period selected as standard. Comparison of specific aspects and levels of culture may be instructive or, at least, illustrative; but wholesale judgments seem futile. [4]

The crucial issue is fully comprised in the question with which Rostovtzeff concludes his *magnum opus*: "Is it possible to extend a higher civilization to the lower classes without debasing its standard and diluting its quality to the vanishing point? Is not every civilization bound to decay as soon as it begins to penetrate the masses?"

Mr. Shils describes mass society as one in which there is "more sense of attachment to society as a whole . . . more sense of affinity with one's fellows." According to him, the mass stands in a closer relationship to the center; there is a "dispersion of charisma" with "greater stress on individual dignity"; "the value of sensation has come to be widely appreciated"; individuality has been "discovered and developed," as has the value of personal relationships; the masses begin to "become capable of more subtle perception and judgment" as their "moral responsiveness and sensibility are aroused."

The society which Mr. Shils describes is not the one in which I live. I am forced to conjecture that the generosity of his wishes has relaxed the customary strictness of his methods and blunted the accuracy of his perception. [5]

Progress toward the fulfillment of Mr. Shils's wishes is implied by the terms he uses. Yet there are some material doubts. Is "the value of sensation" more widely appreciated than it was in antiquity, the Renaissance, or even the nineteenth century? I find American society singularly antisensual: let me just mention the food served in restaurants, or preprandial cocktails intended—often charitable—to kill sensation. And the congested seating arrangements in restaurants, or the way cities, suburbs, exurbs, and resorts are built hardly support the hypothesis of increased value placed on privacy. Even sex is largely socialized and de-sensualized. Do we stand in closer relationship to the center—or are we alienated, suffering from what Wordsworth described as "perpetual emptiness, unceasing change" because in Yeats' words, "Things fall apart; the centre cannot hold"? Has there actually been a "dispersion of charisma"?[6] Or has there been a shift from real to Hollywood queens? Does our society foster "personal relationships," "individuality," and "privacy," or marketability, outer-directedness, and pseudo-personalizations parasitically devouring the genuine personalities of those who assume them? Could Jesus go into the desert today to contemplate? Wouldn't he be followed by a crew of *Life* photographers, cameramen, publishers' agents, etc? What of the gossip columns, of people's interest in other people's *private* lives and particularly their *personal* relations—don't these phenomena suggest a breakdown of reserve, vicarious living—indeed, pseudo-life and experience?

Statistical data reveal that there is now higher income, more education and leisure, more equally distributed, increased mobility, travel, and communication. Undoubtedly there is more material opportunity for more people than ever before. But if so many people are so much better off in so many respects, is culture better than ever? The lowered barriers, the greater wealth, the increased opportunities are material achievements but only cultural promises. Mr. Shils appears to have taken all the promises of the age and confused them with fulfillments. It is as though one were to take the data of the Kinsey report and conclude that since there seems to be so much intercourse, people must love each other more than ever. I have nothing against Mr. Kinsey's entomological enterprise (though it makes me feel waspish). But we must distinguish it from sociological enterprise even though it may furnish raw data for it.

If people address each other by their first names right away do they really love and respect each other more than people who do not? Or does equally easy familiarity with all suggest a lack of differentiation, the very opposite of personal relations, which are based on discriminating among perceived individualities? "In America," de Tocqueville wrote, "the bond of affection is extended but it is relaxed." Mr. Shils notes the extension but not the dilution. Yet extension can be bought at the price of lessened intensity, depth, and stability.

Of course we have more communication and mobility than ever before. But isn't it possible that less is communicated? We have all the opportunities in the world to see, hear, and read more than ever before. Is there any *independent* indication to show that we experience and understand more? Does the constant slick assault on our senses and minds not produce monotony and indifference and prevent experience? Does the discontinuity of most people's lives not unsettle, and sometimes undo them? We surely have more external contacts than ever before. But most people have less spontaneous and personal (internalized) relationships than they might with fewer contacts and opportunities.

We have more equality of opportunity. But the burden of relative deprivations is felt more acutely the smaller they are and the greater the opportunities. [7] People become resentful and clamor for a different kind of equality, equality at the end rather than the beginning, in short, invidious leveling. Does the comminution of society not alienate people from one another—as the discontinuity of their existence fragments them—and replace their sense of purpose with a sense of meaninglessness? Is the increased "conviviality" Mr. Shils hails more than the wish for "togetherness" which marks the lonely crowd?

Mr. Shils contends that we have more intellectuals, consumers, and producers of "refined" culture than before. In one sense, he is quite right. But these are intellectuals by position (university teachers, authors, et al.), and having more of them tells us nothing about the number of intellectuals by ability, interest, and cultivation. Mr. Shils almost concedes as much. But he remains on the phenomenal level, and never goes to the root: [8] the marginal role, the interstitial life, of intellectuals in a mass culture society. And I mean those who remain engaged in intellectual life and do not allow themselves to be reduced to the status of technicians or manufacturers of middlebrow entertainment.

Similarly, Mr. Shils mentions the possibility that intellectual and artistic creators may be seduced into more remunerative pseudo-creative activities only to dismiss it by pointing out that "the mere existence of opportunity will not seduce a man of strongly impelled creative capacities once he has found his direction." Of course, no one is impelled *only* by "creative capacities." The trouble is that the lure of mass media (and of foundation money and prestige) and the values that go with them are internalized long before the potential creator "has found his direction."

Mr. Shils declares that "the heart of the revolution of mass culture" is "the expanding radius of empathy and fellow feeling" which "have given to youth opportunities never available before." These opportunities, Mr. Shils concedes, are utilized mainly through "mediocre and brutal culture." But he does not point out (though noting the effect) that the appalling ignorance of educated youth is produced by reliance on the equally ignorant peer group which is endowed with "charisma"; by the belief, in short, that there is little to learn from the

past and its representatives. The loss of respect for learning and tradition, particularly in its less tangible aspects, is not independent of
the leveling dear to Mr. Shils; it is not unrelated to the widely held
view that obsolescence automatically overtakes aesthetic and moral
values, as it does technological invention. It should be evident that
this notion is generated by the pragmatic nature of mass culture and
by the high mobility that Mr. Shils extolls.[9]

To object to some of Mr. Shils's views is to agree with others. For
he starts by praising and ends by deploring mass culture. This nice
balance is achieved, I feel, at the expense of a coherent theory of
mass culture. Let me suggest a few prolegomena to such a theory.

The most general characteristics of mass culture are deducible
from premises on which there is no disagreement—they are concom-
itants of any industrial, mass production society. Among these are
increased income, mobility and leisure, more equally distributed;
increased egalitarianism, communication and education; [10] more
specialization and less scope for individuality in work. The consequences that I deduce from these premises are consistent and fit my
impressions. But there is no strict empirical proof, although I do believe it may be possible to test some of these hypotheses after appropriate reformulation. Further, other hypotheses may be consistent
with these premises, and the real question turns on their relative importance and relevance. With these qualifications, I submit that
this quasi-deductive method which relates the ascertainable to the
less tangible is the only one that can yield a theory of mass culture
deserving the name "theory."

(1) There is a separation of the manufacturers of culture from the
consumers, which is part of the general separation of production and
consumption and of work and play. Culture becomes largely a spectator sport, and life and experience become exogenous and largely
vicarious. (Nothing will dissuade me from seeing a difference between a young girl walking around with her pocket radio listening to
popular songs and one who sings herself; nor am I persuaded that the
tales collected by the brothers Grimm remain the same when enacted
on television or synthetically reproduced by Walt Disney.)

(2) Mass production aims at pleasing an average of tastes and
therefore, though catering to all to some extent, it cannot satisfy
any taste fully. Standardization is required and necessarily de-
individualizes—as do the techniques required by mass production
and marketing.

(3) Since culture, like everything else in a mass society, is mainly produced to please an average of consumer tastes, the producers become (and remain) an elite by catering to consumer tastes rather than developing or cultivating autonomous ones. Initiative, and power to bestow prestige and income, have shifted from the elite to the mass. The difference may be seen by comparing the development of ritual dogmatic beliefs and practices in the Protestant denominations and in the Roman Catholic church. The latter has minimized, the former maximized dependence on consumers. In the Protestant churches, there is, therefore, no body of religious (as distinguished from moral) beliefs left, except as an intellectual curiosity.

(4) The mass of men dislikes and always has disliked learning and art. It wishes to be distracted from life rather than to have it revealed; to be comforted by traditional (possibly happy and sentimental) tropes, rather than to be upset by new ones. It is true that it wishes to be thrilled, too. But irrational violence or vulgarity provides thrills, as well as release, just as sentimentality provides escape. What is new here is that, apart from the fact that irrelevant thrills and emotions are now prefabricated, the elite is no longer protected from the demands of the mass consumers.

(5) As a result of the high psychological and economic costs of individuality and privacy, gregariousness has become internalized. People fear solitude and unpopularity; popular approval becomes the only moral and aesthetic standard most people recognize. This tendency is reinforced by the shrinkage in the importance and size of primary groups, which have also become looser; by a corresponding increase in the size and importance of secondary groups and publics; and finally, by the shift of many of the functions of primary to secondary groups.

(6) The greatly increased lure of mass markets for both producers and consumers diverts potential talent from the creation of art. (Within the arts, the performing do better than the creative ones.) Here interesting empirical questions arise: to what extent is talent bent endogenously and exogenously? to what extent can it be?

(7) Excessive communication serves to isolate people from one another, from themselves, and from experience. It extends bonds by weakening them. People become indifferently and indiscriminately tolerant; their own life as well as everything else is trivialized, eclectic, and styleless.

(8) Mass media for inherent reasons must conform to prevailing

average canons of taste.[12] They cannot foster art; indeed, they replace it. When they take up classics, they usually reshape them to
meet expectations. But even when that is not the case, they cannot
hope to individualize and refine taste, though they may occasionally
supply an already formed taste for high culture. Half a loaf, in these
matters, spoils the appetite, even with vitamins added, and is not
better than none. The technical availability of good reproductions
and the paperback editions of noncondensed books are unlikely to
change this situation; they often add alien elements which merely
decorate lives styled by mass culture.[13]

(9) The total effect of mass culture is to distract people from lives
which are so boring that they generate obsession with escape. Yet
because mass culture creates addiction to prefabricated experience,
most people are deprived of the remaining possibilities of autonomous
growth and enrichment, and their lives become ever more boring and
unfulfilled.

This very brief sketch of the general features of mass culture should
make it clear that I do not agree with those optimists who favor and
believe possible the wide presentation of "refined" culture through the
mass media. I do not think this desirable or desired. Nor, for that
matter, practicable. People get what they wish and I see no way of
imposing anything else on them. I have to disagree with those who
appear to think that the issue is to improve the culture offered the
mass of men and to try to reach the masses in greater and greater
numbers. My conclusion is different: high or refined culture, in my
opinion, is best preserved and developed by avoiding mass media. I
should go further and give up some advantages of mass production
for the sake of greater individualization. This would reverse many
present policies. For instance, I should favor fairly high direct taxes
on most mass media, or a tax on advertising. Perhaps we are still
capable of replacing the noise that would be thus eliminated with
conversation.

REFERENCES

1 Richard Chase, *The Democratic Vista*, Garden City: Doubleday, 1958.
2 Unless it is contended that everything (and everybody) "refined" is morally
and aesthetically superior to everything (and everybody) "brutal" or "mediocre," etc. Yet the possibility of excellence *sui generis* must not be excluded
by definition—unless, instead of social and cultural, purely aesthetic categories are to be discussed. On this score—and in the whole taxonomic scheme
—Mr. Shils is confusing.

3 See *True Romances*, various soap operas, and lowbrow religious and familial piety. "Kitsch," which is part of low and of middle-lowbrow culture, means corny sentimentalization and, contrary to Mr. Shils, it does not "represent aesthetic sensibility and aesthetic aspiration, untutored . . ." but a synthetic, an *Ersatz* for both. Paper flowers, however real they look, will never grow.

4 Elsewhere Mr. Shils has suggested that critics of mass culture are sour ex-Marxists. Possibly. Ex-Marxists are likely to be critical minds. That is what made them first Marxists and then ex. But though ex-Marxists may incline to be critics of mass culture (and only some, by no means all), the converse certainly does not follow. At any rate, I am tempted to paraphrase advice attributed to Lincoln: abstemious sociologists might benefit by a draught of radical ex-Marxism.

5 John Stuart Mill (*On Liberty*, ch. 3) concludes his discussion of the power of public opinion in egalitarian societies by pointing out that as leveling proceeds, "there ceases to be any social support for nonconformity . . . any substantive power in society which . . . is interested in taking under its protection opinions and tendencies at variance with those of the public." From de Tocqueville to David Riesman, the dangers of "cultural democracy" have been considered. I do not believe that Mr. Shils comes seriously to grips with these dangers.

6 I am not convinced even that the greater inclusiveness of our society can quite be taken for granted. The fate of the Jews in Germany cannot be that easily dismissed. Nazism was political Kitsch as well as a rise of "brutal culture."

7 "The more complete this uniformity the more insupportable the sight of such a difference becomes," de Tocqueville notes.

8 Even on that level, one might quarrel with Mr. Shils. England is not yet as much imbued with mass culture as we are. The class system and selective education have not been entirely overcome; nor have the traditions of elite culture. With only a quarter of our population—not to speak of wealth—England publishes more books every year than we do. And it has at least as many economists, philosophers, and novelists of the first rank as we do.

9 The phenomenon is part of mass culture everywhere, but the ignorance and rejection of the past were particularly fostered in America because of the immigrant background of many parents, the melting-pot nature of the school system, and the rapid rate of change which makes the experience of the old seem old-fashioned and diminishes their authority.

10 Note that more has to be learned through formal instruction, partly because less culture is transmitted informally and individually. This is no advantage because our school system helps bring about the spread of a homogenized mass culture intentionally and unintentionally.

11 For a fuller exposition of my views, see Ralph Ross and Ernest van den Haag, *The Fabric of Society* (New York: Harcourt, Brace and Company, 1957), ch. 15.

12 In Frank Stanton's words, "Any mass medium will always have to cater to the middle grounds . . . the most widely held, or cease to be."

13 Joseph Bram has called my attention to the several distinct phases of mass culture. It often begins with a rather moving attempt of the uneducated to become seriously educated. One sees this in countries beginning their industrial development. The adulteration of, and disrespect for, education comes with full industrialization, when the mass culture market is created and supplied with goods manufactured for it.

OSCAR HANDLIN

Comments on Mass and Popular Culture

THE QUESTION of the uses of culture, raised in this discussion, offers a strategic point for analysis of the differences between those forms of expression communicated by the mass media and all other popular varieties of art. For, although no society has been devoid of culture, that which we now associate with the mass media appears to be unique in its relationship to the way of life of the people. A brief consideration of the function of culture will illuminate the character of that uniqueness.

Until the appearance of those phenomena which we now associate with the mass media, culture was always considered incidental to some social end. Men did not build architecture or compose music in the abstract. They constructed churches in which to worship or homes in which to live. They composed masses and cantatas as parts of a sacred service. The forms within which they built or composed were important in themselves, but they were also intimately related to the functions they served for those who used them.

Hence the significance of Miss Arendt's suggestive statement which pointed out that in the eighteenth and nineteenth centuries in Europe, culture acquired another kind of utility: that is, it became a means by which the bourgeoisie sought to identify itself with aristocratic society. I would add that an analogous development occurred in the United States in the last quarter of the nineteenth century, complicated by the fact that here the aristocracy was putative only and had to improvise its own standards. The difficulty of doing so brought the whole process to the surface and as a result it was much more open and visible in America than in Europe.

In any case, by 1900 almost everywhere in the Western world the term culture had acquired a distinctive connotation, just as the term Society had. Society no longer referred to the total order of the popu-

105

lace in a community, but only to a small self-defined segment of it. And culture no longer referred to the total complex of forms through which the community satisfied its wants, but only to certain narrowly defined modes of expression distinguished largely by their lack of practicality.

In the process of redefinition, culture lost all connection with function other than that of establishing an identification with that narrow society which had made itself the custodian of the values attached to the arts. The châteaux of Fifth Avenue were not erected to meet men's needs for homes, any more than the rare books of the tycoons were assembled to satisfy their desire for reading matter. Architecture, literature, art, and music, as defined by society and its intermediaries, became, rather, primarily the symbols of status.

That very fact, indeed, served Society as the justification of its aristocratic pretensions. "Changes in manners and customs," an influential manual explained, "no matter under what form of government, usually originate with the wealthy or aristocratic minority, and are thence transmitted to the other classes. . . . This rule naturally holds good of house-planning, and it is for this reason that the origin of modern house-planning should be sought rather in the prince's mezzanine than in the small middle-class dwelling."*

By the end of the nineteenth century, therefore, Americans could readily identify a miscellaneous congeries of artistic forms as their culture. The citizens of the Republic and foreign observers had no difficulty in recognizing what was American music, literature, or painting, for an elaborate apparatus of critical institutions—museums, orchestras, journals, and universities—existed to pass judgment on what belonged and what did not. These institutions and the impresarios who controlled them had the confidence and support of Society, that segment of the community which assumed that wealth or birth gave it leadership.

Outside the realm of the official culture as defined by Society there persisted other, but excluded, modes of action and expression. The peasants of Europe, the workers of the industrial cities, the ethnic enclaves of the United States did not share the forms of behavior, the tastes and attitudes of the would-be or genuine aristocracy, although they often acknowledged the primacy of the groups above them. But peasants, laborers, and foreigners did retain and employ in their own

* Edith Wharton and Ogden Codman, Jr., *The Decoration of Houses* (New York: Charles Scribner's Sons, 1897), p. 5.

lives a complex of meaningful forms of expression of their own. At the time these were commonly characterized as popular or folk culture. Thus in the early decades of this century, it was usual to refer to popular music, popular literature, and popular art, set off and distinct from *the* music, *the* literature, and *the* art of Society.

That designation was misleading, in so far as it carried the implication that popular culture was as coherent and uniform as the official culture. In actuality, popular culture, in America at least, was composed of a complex of sub-cultures. The mass of the population of the metropolitan cities, the Negroes, the farmers of the Great Plains, and other groups which together constituted the bulk of the American population had no taste for the music played by the Philharmonic or the novels approved by Thomas Bailey Aldrich or the paintings certified by Duveen. These people sang and danced, they read, and they were amused or edified by pictures. Only, what they sang or read or looked at was not music or literature or art in the sense defined by Society, and therefore was explained away by the general designation, popular.

Superficially, popular culture differed from the defined culture in the lack of an accepted set of canons or of a normative body of classics. A vaudeville song or a piece of embroidery or a dime novel was accepted or rejected by its audience without comparison with or reference to standards extraneous to itself. But this surface difference sprang from a deeper one. Popular, unlike defined, culture retained a functional quality in the sense that it was closely related to the felt needs and familiar modes of expression of the people it served. Popular songs were to be danced to, vaudeville to be laughed at, and embroidery to be worn or to cover a table.

The development of mass culture—or more properly speaking of the culture communicated through the mass media—has had a disturbing effect upon both popular and defined cultures. The consequences for the latter are the easier to distinguish, for it left not only vestiges but a record of its past which makes possible ready comparisons with the present.

It is far more difficult to make similar comparisons in the case of popular culture. Precisely because it lacked a canon, it also lacked a history. It was not only displaced by later forms; its very memory was all but obliterated. As a result we know very little about the culture that until recently served the people who now consume the products of the mass media. And that gap in our information has given rise to the misconception that the "mass culture" of the present is but an extension of the popular culture of the past.

Yet if that popular culture did not produce its own record, it can be pieced together from fragmentary historical materials which reveal that the mass media have had as deep an impact upon popular as upon official culture. The Ed Sullivan show is not vaudeville in another guise any more than "Omnibus" is a modernized Chautauqua. Television, the movies, and the mass-circulation magazines stand altogether apart from the older vehicles of both popular and defined culture.

An examination of the popular theater, of vaudeville, of the popular newspapers, especially in the Sunday supplements, and of the popular literature of the 1890's reveals four significant elements in the difference between the popular culture of that period and that communicated by the mass media of the present.

In the first place, popular culture, although unstructured and chaotic, dealt directly with the concrete world intensely familiar to its audience. There was no self-conscious realism in this preoccupation with the incidents and objects of the everyday world. Rather, this was the most accessible means of communication with a public that was innocent in its approach to culture, that is, one that looked or listened without ulterior motive or intent.

In the second place, and for similar reasons, popular culture had a continuing relevance to the situation of the audience that was exposed to it. That relevance was maintained by a direct rapport between those who created and those who consumed this culture. The very character of the popular theater, for instance, in which the spontaneous and the "ad lib" were tolerated, encouraged a continuous and highly intimate response across the footlights. So too, the journalism of the American ethnic sub-groups maintained an immediate awareness of the needs and problems of their readers. In general, furthermore, in all media, the writers and actors sprang from the identical milieu as their audience did, and maintained a firm sense of identification with it.

In the third place, popular culture was closely tied to the traditions of those who consumed it. A large part of it was ethnic in character, that is, arranged within the terms of a language and of habits and attitudes imported from Europe. But even that part of it which was native American and which reached back into the early nineteenth and eighteenth centuries, maintained a high degree of continuity with its own past.

Finally, popular culture had the capacity for arousing in its audience such sentiments as wonder and awe, and for expressing the sense of irony of their own situation which lent it enormous emotional power. Men and women shed real tears or rocked with laughter in the playhouses of the Bowery, as they could not in the opera or the theater uptown. The acrobats and the animals of the circus evoked wonder as the framed pictures of the museum could not. The difference was the product of the authenticity of the one type of culture and the artificiality of the other.

Out of American popular culture there emerged occasional bursts of creativity of high level. Instances may be found in the work of Charlie Chaplin, in some of the jazz music of the decade after 1900, and in that strain of literary realism developed by novelists and dramatists whose experience in journalism had brought them into direct contact with popular culture.

In total perspective, however, popular culture was not justified by such by-products so much as by the function it served. Millions of people found in this culture a means of communication among themselves and the answers to certain significant questions that they were asking about the world around them. Indeed, it was the perception of this function that attracted the avant-garde in the opening decades of the twentieth century. Those creative spirits, repelled by the inert pretensions of official culture, often found refreshing elements of authenticity in the popular culture of their times. Bohemia, too, was a kind of ghetto in which the artist, equally with the Italian or Negro laborer, was alien, cut off from respectable society. In fact some of the Bohemians were inclined to idealize popular culture in revulsion against the inability of the official culture to satisfy their own needs.

In the light of these considerations, it is possible to begin to assess the effects of the mass media on the character of popular culture. To some extent the impact of the new media is simply a product of their size. The enormous growth of these media has been of such an order as to involve immediate qualitative changes. The transformation of an audience, once numbered in the thousands, to one of millions profoundly altered all the relationships involved. More specifically, the impact of the mass media has altered the earlier forms of control; it has deprived the material communicated of much of its relevance; and it has opened a gulf between the artist and the audience.

A good deal of the familiar talk about the degree to which advertisers or bankers or interest groups control the mass media is irrelevant. There has been a genuine change in the character of the control of these media as contrasted with the situation of fifty or sixty years ago. But it has taken a more subtle form than is usually ascribed to it.

What is most characteristic of the mass media today is precisely the disappearance of the forms of control that existed in the popular culture of a half-century ago. No one can decide now (as Hearst or Pulitzer could in 1900) to use a newspaper as a personal organ. Nor could any TV or movie executive, advertiser, agent, or even a large sector of the audience dictate the content of what is transmitted through these media. The most they can do is prevent the inclusion of material distasteful to them.

The only accurate way of describing the situation of the mass media is to say they operate within a series of largely negative restraints. There are many things they cannot do. But within the boundaries of what they may do, there is an aimless quality, with no one in a position to establish a positive direction. In part this aimlessness is the product of the failure to establish coherent lines of internal organization; in part it flows from the frightening massiveness of the media themselves; but in part also it emanates from a lack of clarity as to the purposes they serve.

The inability to exercise positive control and the concomitant inability to locate responsibility heighten the general sense of irrelevance of the contents of the mass media. It would, in any case, be difficult for a writer or performer to be sensitive to the character of an unseen audience. But the problems are magnified when the audience is numbered in the millions, in other words, when it is so large that all the peculiarities of tastes and attitudes within it must be canceled out so that all that remains is an abstract least common denominator. And those problems become insoluble when no one has the power or the obligation to deal with them.

In the world of actuality, Americans are factory workers or farmers, Jews or Baptists, of German or Irish descent, old or young; they live in small towns or great cities, in the North or the South. But the medium which attempts to speak to all of them is compelled to discount these affiliations and pretend that the variety of tastes, values, and habits related to them do not exist. It can therefore only address itself to the empty outline of the residual American. What it has to say, therefore, is doomed to irrelevance in the lives of its audience; and the feedback from the consciousness of that irrelevance, without effective countermeasures, dooms the performer and writer to sterility.

The critics of the mass media are in error when they condemn its products out of hand. These media can tolerate good as well as bad contents, high as well as low art. Euripides and Shakespeare can perfectly well follow the Western or quiz show on TV, and the slick magazine can easily sandwich in cathedrals and madonnas among the pictures of athletes and movie queens.

What is significant, however, is that it does not matter. The mass media find space for politics and sports, for science and fiction, for art and music, all presented on an identical plateau of irrelevance. And the audience which receives this complex variety of wares accepts them passively as an undifferentiated but recognizable series of good things among which it has little capacity for choice, and with which it cannot establish any meaningful, direct relationship.

The way in which the contents of the mass media are communicated deprives the audience of any degree of selectivity, for those contents are marketed as any other commodities are. In our society it seems possible through the use of the proper marketing device to sell anybody anything, so that what is sold has very little relevance to the character of either the buyers or of the article sold. This is as true of culture as of refrigerators or fur coats. The contents of the magazine or the TV schedule or the newspaper have as little to do with their sales potential as the engine specifications with the marketability of an automobile. The popularity of quiz shows no more reflects the desires of the audience than the increase in circulation of *American Heritage* or *Gourmet* reflects a growing knowledge of American history or the development of gastronomic taste, or, for that matter, than the efflorescence of tail fins in 1957 reflected a yearning for them on the part of automobile buyers. All these were rather examples of excellent selling jobs.

The mass media have also diluted, if they have not altogether destroyed, the rapport that formerly existed between the creators of popular culture and its consumers. In this respect, the television playlet or variety performance is far different from the vaudeville turn, which is its lineal antecedent. The performer can no longer sense the mood of his audience and is, in any case, bound by the rigidity of his impersonal medium. The detachment in which he and they operate makes communication between them hazy and fragmentary. As a result, the culture communicated by the mass media cannot serve the function in the lives of those who consume it that the popular culture of the past did.

Yet the latter was no more able to withstand the impact of the mass media than was official culture. The loose, chaotic organization of popular culture, its appeal to limited audiences, its ties to an ethnic past attenuated with the passage of time, all prevented it from competing successfully against the superior resources of the mass media. Much of it was simply swallowed up in the new forms. What survived existed in isolated enclaves, without the old vitality.

The most important consequences of this change were the destruction of those older functional forms of popular culture, the separation of the audience from those who sought to communicate with it, and the paradoxical diminution of the effectiveness of communication with the improvement of the techniques for communication. Thus far the result has been a diffusion among the audience of a sense of apathy. The intense involvement of the masses with their culture at the turn of the century has given way to passive acquiescence. Concomitantly, the occasional creative artist who wishes to communicate with this audience has lost the means of doing so. At best his work will be received as one of the succession of curious or interesting images that flicker by without leaving an enduring impression upon anyone's consciousness.

Thus there is passing a great opportunity for communication between those who have something to say and the audiences who no longer know whether they would like to listen to what there is to be said.

LEO ROSTEN

The Intellectual and the Mass Media: Some Rigorously Random Remarks

MOST INTELLECTUALS do not understand the inherent nature of the mass media. They do not understand the process by which a newspaper or magazine, movie or television show is created. They project their own tastes, yearnings, and values upon the masses—who do not, unfortunately, share them. They attribute over-simplified motivations to those who own or operate the mass media. They assume that changes in ownership or control would necessarily improve the product. They presume the existence of a vast reservoir of talent, competence, and material which does not in fact exist.

A great deal of what appears in the mass media is dreadful tripe and treacle; inane in content, banal in style, muddy in reasoning, mawkish in sentiment, vulgar, naïve, and offensive to men of learning or refinement. I am both depressed and distressed by the bombardment of our eyes, our ears, and our brains by meretricious material designed for a populace whose paramount preferences involve the narcotic pursuit of "fun."

Why is this so? Are the media operated by cynical men motivated solely by profit? Are they controlled by debasers of culture—by ignorant, vulgar, irresponsible men?

Many intellectuals think so and say so. They think so and say so in the face of evidence they either do not examine or cannot bring themselves to accept: that when the public is free to choose among various products, it chooses—again and again and again—the frivolous as against the serious, "escape" as against reality, the lurid as against the tragic, the trivial as against the serious, fiction as against fact, the diverting as against the significant. To conclude otherwise is to deny the data: circulation figures for the press, box-office receipts

113

for the movies and the theater, audience measurement for radio and television programs.

The sad truth seems to be this: that relatively few people in any society, not excluding Periclean Athens, have reasonably good taste or care deeply about ideas. Fewer still seem equipped—by temperament and capacity, rather than education—to handle ideas with both skill and pleasure.

The deficiencies of mass media are a function, in part at least, of the deficiencies of the masses. Is it unfair to ask that responsibility for mental laziness and deplorable taste be distributed—to include the schools, the churches, the parents, the social institutions which produce those masses who persist in preferring pin-ball games to anything remotely resembling philosophy?

Intellectuals seem unable to reconcile themselves to the fact that their hunger for more news, better plays, more serious debate, deeper involvement in ideas is not a hunger characteristic of many. They cannot believe that the subjects dear to their hearts bore or repel or overtax the capacities of their fellow citizens. Why this is so I shall try to explore later. At this point, let me remark that the intellectual, who examines his society with unyielding and antiseptic detachment, must liberate himself from the myths (or, in Plato's term, the royal lies) by which any social system operates. It is ironic that intellectuals often destroy old myths to erect and reverence special myths of their own. A striking example is found in the clichés with which they both characterize and indict the mass media. Let us consider the principal particulars in that indictment.*

"The mass media lack originality."

They certainly do. Most of what appears in print, or on film, or on the air, lacks originality. But is there any area of human endeavor of which this is not true? Is not the original as rare in science or philosophy or painting as it is in magazines? Is not the original "original" precisely because it is rare? Is it not self-evident that the more that is produced of anything, the smaller the proportion of originality is likely to be? But is the absolute number of novel creative products thereby reduced? Are we dealing with Gresham's Law—or with imperfect observation?

---

* For the best general summary, and critical comment, see Chapter XV in *The Fabric of Society,* by Ralph Ross and Ernest van den Haag (Harcourt, Brace & Co., 1957), a work of remarkable lucidity and good sense.

The mass media are not characterized by endless inventiveness and variation. But they are considerably more varied and inventive, given their built-in limitations, than we give them credit for. Consider these limitations: neither life nor truth nor fiction offers infinite choices: there is only a limited number of plots or stories or themes; there is only a limited number of ways of communicating the limited body of material; audiences develop a cumulative awareness of resemblances and an augmented resistance to the stylized and the predictable; and even the freshest departures from routine soon become familiar and routine. Besides, originality is often achieved at the price of "balance" or proportion: the most arresting features in, say, *The New Yorker* or *Time* often incur the displeasure of scholars precisely because they prefer vitality to a judicious ordering of "all the facts."

The artist, of course, wrests freshness and new insight from the most familiar material; but true artists, in any field at any given time, are so rare that their singularity requires a special word— "genius."

The mass media are cursed by four deadly requirements: a gargantuan amount of space (in magazines and newspapers) and time (in television and radio) *has* to be filled; talent—on every level, in every technique—is scarce; the public votes, i.e., is free to decide what it prefers (and it is the deplorable results of this voting that intellectuals might spend more time confronting); and a magazine, paper, television or radio program is committed to periodic and unalterable publication. Content would be markedly improved if publications or programs appeared only when superior material was available. This applies to academic journals no less than to publications or programs with massive audiences.

"The mass media do not use the best brains or freshest talents."

Surely the burden of proof is on those who make this assertion. The evidence is quite clear that talent in the popular arts is searched for and courted in ways that do not apply in other fields: seniority is ignored, tenure is virtually nonexistent, youth is prized. In few areas is failure so swiftly and ruthlessly punished, or success so swiftly and extravagantly rewarded.

And still—talent is scarce. It is a woeful fact that despite several generations of free education, our land has produced relatively few first-rate minds; and of those with first-rate brains, fewer have imagination; of those with brains and imagination, fewer still possess judgment. If we ask, in addition, for the special skills and experience involved in the art of communicating, the total amount of talent available to the media is not impressive.

"The best brains" in the land do not gravitate to the media—if by brains we mean skill in analyzing complexities, or sustaining abstract propositions for prolonged intellectual operations. But the best brains would not necessarily make the best editors, or writers, or producers, or publishers—at least they would not long survive in a competitive market.

The media are enterprises, not IQ tests. They feed on inventiveness, not analytic discipline. They require creative skills and nonstandardized competences. Their content has, thus far at least, resisted the standardized and accumulative statement of propositions of a Euclid or an Adam Smith.

"The mass media do not print or broadcast the best material that is submitted to them."

To edit is to judge; to judge is, inevitably, to reward some and disappoint others.

The assumption that a vast flow of material pours into the editorial offices of the media—from which publishers or producers simply select the worst—is simply incorrect. A huge proportion of what finally appears in magazines, radio, and television was "dreamed up" inside the media offices, and ordered from the staff or from freelance writers. And as often as not, even when the best talent is employed, at the highest prices, and given complete freedom, the results disappoint expectations. Excellence is not necessarily achieved because it is sought.*

"The mass media cannot afford to step on anyone's toes."

The following recent articles in popular magazines most conspicuously stepped on quite powerful toes: What Protestants Fear About Catholics; Cigarettes and Lung Cancer; Birth Control; The Disgrace

---

* Yet consider that the mass media have recently presented to the public such indubitable highbrows as, say, Jacques Maritain, Reinhold Niebuhr, Robert Oppenheimer, Edith Hamilton, Aldous Huxley, Warren Weaver, Edith Sitwell, Jacques Barzun, James Bryant Conant, and Julian Huxley.

of Our Hospitals; Fee-Splitting by Doctors; Agnosticism; Financial Shenanigans and Stock Manipulations; A Mercy Killing; The Murder of Negroes in the South.

The movies and television recently offered all but the deaf and blind these scarcely soporific themes: miscegenation; adultery; dope addiction; white-Negro tensions; the venality of television; the vulgarity of movie executives; the cowardice of a minister, a banker; hypocrisy in business and advertising; big business and call girls; the degeneracy of Southern whites.

It was long assumed that the most sacred of sacred cows in a capitalist society is the Businessman or Big Business as an institution. But in recent years we have been exposed to a striking number of revelations about Business. Advertising men and methods, presumably too "powerful" to expose, much less deride, have been raked with coals of fire—in media which depend upon advertisers and advertising. "The Man in the Grey Flannel Suit" became a symbol of conformity to the masses, no less than the intellectual, through the mass media.

It is worth noticing that the sheer size of an audience crucially influences the content of what is communicated to it. Taboos, in movies or television, are not simply the fruit of cowardice among producers (though their anxiety is often disproportionate, and their candor unnecessarily hampered by pessimistic assumptions of what public reaction will be). Taboos are often functions of audience size, age-range, and heterogeneity. Things can be communicated to the few which cannot be communicated (at least not in the same way) to the many.

Books, magazines, and newspapers can discuss sex, homosexuality, masturbation, venereal disease, abortion, dope addiction, in ways not so easily undertaken on television or film. The reader reads alone— and this is a fact of great importance to those who write for him.

"The mass media do not give the public enough or adequate information about the serious problems of our time."

Never in history has the public been offered so much, so often, in such detail, for so little. I do not mean that Americans know as much as intellectuals think they ought to know, or wish they did know, about the problems which confront us. I do mean that the media already offer the public far more news, facts, information, and interpretations than the public takes the trouble to digest. I find it impossible to escape the conclusion that, apart from periods of acute crisis, most people do not want to be *involved*, in precisely those areas which the intellectual finds most absorbing and meaningful.

Consider these recent authors and subjects in popular journalism: Winston Churchill on the war; Harry S. Truman on the presidency; Geoffrey Crowther on United States-British relations; William O. Douglas on Russia; Dean Acheson on Berlin; Joseph Alsop on Suez; George Kennan on Europe; Henry Kissinger on nuclear weapons; Adlai Stevenson on nine different countries and their problems; Nehru on India and the West; Ben-Gurion on the Middle East.

I wonder how many academic journals have been more relevant or edifying.

Do intellectuals find it unnoteworthy that, year after year, four to five times as many citizens in New York City choose the *Daily News* as against the New York *Times* or *Herald Tribune*? Or that for decades the citizens of Chicago have preferred the Chicago *Tribune* to competitors closer to the intellectuals' heart? Or that for decades the people of Los Angeles have voted in favor of the Los Angeles *Times*, at the expense of less parochial competitors?

"The aesthetic level of the mass media is appalling: truth is sacrificed to the happy ending, escapism is exalted, romance, violence, melodrama prevail."

The mass media do not attempt to please intellectuals, on either the aesthetic or the conceptual plane. Some commentators believe that if the media offered the public less trivia, the taste of the public would perforce be improved. But if the media give the public too little of what they want, and too much of what they don't want (too soon), they would simply cease to be mass media—and would be replaced by either "massier" competitors or would drive the public to increased expenditures of time on sports, parlor games, gambling, and other familiar methods of protecting the self from the ardors of thought or the terrors of solitude.

The question of proportion (how much "light stuff" or staple insipidity to include as against how much heavy or "uplifting" material) is one of the more perplexing problems any editor faces. It is far from uncommon to hear an editor remark that he will run a feature which he knows will be read by "less than 5 per cent of our readers."

I suspect that intellectuals tend to judge the highbrow by its peaks and the nonhighbrow by its average. If we look at the peaks in both cases, how much do the mass media suffer by comparison? American movies, for instance, caught in staggering costs (and, therefore, risks), have produced, in a short span of time, such films as *The Bridge on the River Kwai, Marty, The African Queen, Twelve Angry Men, The Defiant Ones, High Noon, The Sheepman, Seven Brides for Seven Brothers*, etc.

Television, beset by the problem of a heterogeneous audience, and submitting to the disgraceful practice of advertisers permitted to exercise editorial censorship, has produced some extraordinary news and documentary programs, and such dramas as: *Middle of the Night, Patterns, Little Moon of Alban, Days of Wine and Roses, The Bridge of San Luis Rey, The Winslow Boy, Requiem for a Heavyweight*. CBS's "Camera Three" recently presented, with both skill and taste, three programs dramatizing Dostoevski's *Notes from the Underground, A File for Fathers* (scenes from Lord Chesterfield, Lewis Carroll, Oscar Wilde), *Père Goriot*, Chekhov's *The Proposal*.

In my opinion, some of the more insightful work of our time can be found in the mass media, for example, the comic strip *Peanuts*, which throws an original and enchanting light on children; the comic strip *Li'l Abner*, which is often both as illuminating and as savage as social satire should be; the movies of, say, William Wyler, George Stevens, Jules Dassin, John Huston, David Lean, Delbert Mann.

Intellectuals generally discover "artists" in the popular arts long after the public, with less rarefied aesthetic categories, has discovered them. Perhaps there is rooted in the character structure of intellectuals an aversion, or an inability, to participate in certain sectors of life; they do seem blind to the fact that the popular can be meritorious. This changes with time (e.g., consider the reputations of Twain, Dickens, Dumas, Balzac, Lardner). And a Jack Benny or Phil Silvers may yet achieve the classic dimension now permitted the Marx Brothers, who—once despised as broad vaudevillians—have become the eggheads' delight.

"The mass media corrupt and debase public taste; they create the kind of audience that enjoys cheap and trivial entertainment."

This implies that demand (public taste or preference) has become a spurious function of manipulated supply. Here the evidence from

Great Britain is illuminating: for years the government-owned BBC and the admirable Third Program offered the British public superior fare: excellent music, learned talks, literate discussions. For years, the noncommercial radio defended the bastions of culture. Yet when the British public was offered choices on television, it dismayed Anglophiles by taking to its heart the same silly quiz shows, panel shows, Westerns, melodramas, and "situation comedies" which the critics of daily newspapers deplore both in London and New York.

Or consider what happened in March 1959 when the Granada TV network, a British commercial chain, presented *The Skin of Our Teeth* with no less a star than Vivien Leigh—and in her first appearance on television. The noncommercial BBC ran, opposite the Wilder play and Lady Vivien, a twenty-five-year-old American movie, *Follow the Fleet*, with Ginger Rogers and Fred Astaire. The English critics sang rare hosannahs for Thornton Wilder's play, its glamorous star, the script, the direction, the production. But for every seventeen homes in London that chose the Pulitzer Prize play, sixty-six preferred the twenty-five-year-old musical. Outside of London, the ratio was even more depressing. Viewers by the millions, reported Reuters, switched their dials away from Wilder and Leigh to Fred and Ginger. The head of the Granada network even castigated the BBC in the press, urging that it be "ashamed of itself" for seducing a public that might have adored Art by offering it Entertainment. (A similar *contretemps* occurred on American television when the magnificent production of *Green Pastures* lost viewers by the millions to the ghastly *Mike Todd Party* in Madison Square Garden.) The final and crushing irony lies in the fact that *Follow the Fleet* put a BBC program among the first ten, in popularity, for the first time in the year.

Doubtless the mass media can do more, much more, to elevate what the public reads, sees, and hears. But the media cannot do this as easily or as rapidly as is often assumed. Indeed, they cannot get too far in front of their audiences without suffering the fate of predecessors who tried just that. There is considerable evidence to support the deflating view that the media, on the whole, are considerably *ahead* of the masses—in intelligence, in taste, in values, e.g., the vocabulary in almost any popular journal, not excluding fan magazines, is often too "highbrow" for its readers.

It seems to me a fair question to ask whether the intelligence or taste of the public is really worse today than it was before the mass media came along.

"The mass media are what they are because they are operated solely as money-making enterprises."

Publishers and producers are undoubtedly motivated by a desire for profits. But this is not *all* that motivates them. Publishers and producers are no less responsive than intellectuals to "ego values"; they are no less eager to win respect and respectability from their peers; they respond to both internalized and external "reference groups"; they seek esteem—from the self and from others.

Besides, producers know that a significant percentage of what they present in the mass media will not be as popular as what might be substituted—but it is presented nonetheless. Why? Partly because of nonpecuniary values, and partly because of what critics of the crass profit-motive seem blind to: the fact that part of the competitive process involves a continuous search for products which can win favor with audiences not attracted to, or satisfied by, the prevailing output. New and minority audiences are constantly courted by the media, e.g., the strictly "egghead" programs on television, the new magazines which arise, and flourish, because they fill a need, as *Scientific American, American Heritage.*

Whenever profits, used as either a carrot or a stick, are criticized, it is tacitly assumed that reliance on other human impulses would serve man better. Is this so? Do virtue, probity, self-sacrifice guarantee excellence? It seems to me that most of the horrors of human history have been the work not of skeptical or cynical or realistic men, but of those persuaded of their superior virtue.

To replace publication for profit by publication via subsidy would of course be to exchange one set of imperfections for another.* The postal system offers scant support to those who assume that non-profit enterprise is necessarily better than private competition (I hasten to add that in some fields, e.g., public health, it clearly is).

It should be noted, parenthetically, that anyone who enters the magazine or newspaper field in the expectation of high profits is either singularly naïve, extremely optimistic, or poorly informed: few

---

* It is unthinkable, for instance, that any open competitive system would have barred from the air someone like Winston Churchill—who was not given access to BBC, for his then-maverick opinions, from 1934 to 1939. Nor is it likely that a government-controlled network would be able to withstand the furore that followed CBS's initial interview with Nikita Khrushchev. Nor would a governmentally supervised program dare to present a show such as *The Plot to Kill Stalin.*

areas of American business show so high a mortality rate, are plagued by such unpredictabilities, promise so many headaches, and return so low a net profit. Successful magazines earn as modest a profit as three percent on invested capital. To the purely profit-minded, business has long offered innumerable opportunities outside of publishing which far surpass it in profitability, security, or potential.

"The mass media are dominated—or too much influenced —by advertisers."

The influence of advertising is often too great—even if that influence is one-tenth as potent as many assume it to be. The editorial function should be as entirely free of non-editorial influences as possible.

But publishers, producers, and editors would respond to power or influence *even if all advertising were abolished.* It is an inescapable fact of human organization that men adjust to power (that, indeed, is one of power's attributes); that men consider, or try to anticipate, the effect of their acts on those who hold most of whatever is most prized in a society.

There is a reverse and paradoxical angle to advertising: when a newspaper or magazine, a radio or television station becomes successful, the advertiser needs it as much as the other way around. Revenues from many advertisers increase the capacity to resist pressure from individual advertisers. Organs which can be "bought" nearly always decline in prosperity and influence.

Purely professional calculations often override vested interest. Some news or stories are so significant that it is impossible to prevent their publication.

The instance of the cigarette industry, mentioned above, is worth notice. Tobacco companies represent one of the largest and most consistent sources of national advertising revenue. Yet within an hour after medical reports appeared linking cigarette smoking to lung cancer, they were fully and dramatically presented to the public— not only on the front pages of newspapers but in radio and television reporting as well. The news was simply too big, too "newsworthy" to be suppressed (even though several discussion programs shied away from the subject). The deficiencies of automobiles, where safety is concerned, have been analyzed in magazines which receive huge advertising revenues from automobile companies.

This is not to say that all truths which threaten power—in business, in the arts, even in the groves of academe—always gain as swift and public an airing as they deserve. They often do not. They do not because men, even men in power, are often timid, or weak, or frightened, or avaricious, or opportunistic, or unwise, or short-sighted. Some media operators, like some politicians, some clergymen, some labor leaders, some economists, are overly sensitive to the side on which their bread is buttered.

There is another and telling body of evidence about advertising on which no one, so far as I know, has commented: motion pictures accept no advertisements, never did, never depended on it, and were never "at the mercy of advertisers."* Yet of all the mass media, it is the movies which have been most parochial and timorous. Is it because movies do depend entirely on box-office receipts, and have no advertising revenues to subsidize independence?

Advertisers seem to me to exercise their most pernicious influence in television. For in television, advertisers are permitted to decide what shall or shall not appear in the programs they sponsor. This seems to me insupportable. An advertiser in a newspaper or magazine buys a piece of space in which to advertise his product. He does not buy a voice on the news desk or at the editorial table. But the television advertiser buys time both for his commercials and for *the time between commercials*; he becomes a producer and publisher himself. I am convinced that this is bad for the public, bad for television, and (ultimately) bad for the sponsors.†

"The mass media do not provide an adequate forum for minority views—the dissident and unorthodox."

Producers and publishers give more space and time to minority views (which include the *avant-garde*) than numerical proportions require. They feel that it is the function of specialized journals to carry specialized content. The popular media carry far more material of this kind than anyone would have predicted two decades ago.

The democratic society must insure a viable public forum for the dissenter—in politics, morals, arts. That forum will never be as large as the dissenters themselves want. But I know of no perfect way to determine who shall have what access to how many—at the expense

---

* Some movie theaters show advertisements on their screens before and after a feature, but advertising is not to be found *in* movies.

† When I wrote a similar criticism in *Harper's Magazine* in 1958, certain television executives hotly denied this. That was eighteen months before the recent and sensational revelations of advertiser-control over quiz shows.

of whom else—except to keep pressing for as free a market as we can achieve.

It may seem to some readers that I have substituted an indictment of the masses for an indictment of the mass media; that I have assigned the role of villain to the masses in a social drama in which human welfare and public enlightenment are hamstrung by the mediocrity, laziness, and indifference of the populace. I hope that detachment will not be mistaken for cynicism.

I should be the first to stress the immensity of the social gains which public education and literacy alone have made possible. The rising public appreciation of music, painting, ballet; the growth of libraries; the fantastic sales of paperback books (however much they are skewed by *Peyton Place* or the works of Mickey Spillane), the striking diffusion of "cultural activities" in communities throughout the land, the momentous fact that popular magazines *can* offer the public the ruminations of such nonpopular minds as Paul Tillich or Sir George Thomson—the dimensions of these changes are a tribute to the achievements of that society which has removed from men the chains of caste and class that hampered human achievement through the centuries. I, for one, do not lament the passing of epochs in which "high culture" flourished while the majority of mankind lived in ignorance and indignity.

What I have been emphasizing here is the inevitable gap between the common and the superior. More particularly, I have been embroidering the theme of the intellectual's curious reluctance to accept evidence. Modern intellectuals seem *guilty* about reaching conclusions that were once the *a priori* convictions of the aristocrat. It is understandable that twentieth-century intellectuals should dread snobbery, at one end of the social scale, as much as they shun mob favor at the other. But the intellectual's snobbery is of another order, and involves a tantalizing paradox: a contempt for what *hoi polloi* enjoy, and a kind of proletarian ethos that tacitly denies inequalities of talent and taste.

The recognition of facts has little bearing on motivations and should surely not impute preferences. The validity of an idea has nothing to do with who propounds it—or whom it outrages. The author is aware that he is inviting charges of Brahminism, misanthropy, a reactionary "unconscious," or heaven knows what else. But is it really heresy to the democratic credo for intellectuals to admit, if only in the privacy of professional confessionals, that they are, in fact, more literate and more skillful—in diagnosis, induction, and generalization, if in nothing else—than their fellow-passengers on the ship of state?

Perhaps the intellectual's guilt, when he senses incipient snobbery within himself, stems from his uneasiness at being part of an elite, moreover, a new elite which is not shored up by ancient and historic sanctions. For intellectualism has been divorced from its traditional *cachet* and from the majesty with which earlier societies invested their elites: a classical education, Latin or Greek (in any case, a language not comprehensible to the untutored), a carefully cultivated accent, the inflection of the well born, the well bred, or the priestly. One of the painful experiences spared intellectuals in the past was hearing Ideas discussed—with profundity or insight—in accents which attest to birth on "the other side of the tracks."

It may be difficult for shopkeepers' sons to admit their manifest superiority over the world they left: parents, siblings, comrades. But the intellectual who struggles with a sinful sense of superiority, and who feels admirable sentiments of loyalty to his non-U origins, must still explain why it was that his playmates and classmates did not join him in the noble dedication to learning and the hallowed pursuit of truth. The triumph of mass education is to be found not simply in the increment of those who can read, write, add, and subtract. It is to be found in a much more profound and enduring revolution: the provision of opportunities to express the self, and pursue the self's values, opportunities not limited to the children of a leisure class, or an aristocracy, or a landed gentry, or a well-heeled bourgeoisie. The true miracle of public education is that no elite can decide where the next intellectual will come from.

Each generation creates its own devils, and meets its own Waterloo on the heartless field of reality. The Christian Fathers blamed the Prince of Darkness for preventing perfectible man from reaching Paradise. Anarchists blamed the state. Marxists blame the class system. Pacifists blame the militarists. And our latter-day intellectuals seem to blame the mass media for the lamentable failure of more people to attain the bliss of intellectual grace. This is a rank disservice to intellectuals themselves, for it dismisses those attributes of character and ability—discipline, curiosity, persistence, the renunciation of worldly rewards—which make intellectuals possible at all. The compulsive egalitarianism of eggheads even seems to lure them into a conspicuous disinterest in the possible determinism of heredity.

Responsibility increases with capacity, and should be demanded of those in positions of power. Just as I hold the intellectual more responsible than others for the rigorous exploration of phenomena and the courageous enunciation of truths, so, too, do I ask for better and still better performance from those who have the awesome power to shape men's minds.

FRANK STANTON

Parallel Paths

THE MASS MEDIA are tempting targets: they are big, they are conspicuous, they are easily distorted, they invite bright and brittle condemnations—and they do have built-in limitations of their virtues. They have shown themselves inefficient warriors, and on the whole have tended to be too little concerned with what the intellectuals have had to say.

On the other side, the fondest attachment of the intellectuals is to theory not to practice; more importantly, there is among many intellectuals an uncongeniality with some of the basic ingredients of a democratic society and, in many cases, a real distrust of them. Democratic procedures, to some extent even democratic values, necessarily involve quantitative considerations, about which intellectuals are always uneasy. This uneasiness is not restricted to cultural matters. For example, it influences their view of the legislative processes and of economic interplays in our society. The intellectual is highly impatient of much that is imperfect but also inevitable in democracies. But despite these differences between intellectuals and the mass media, I think that they have something in common, that their efforts are fundamentally going toward the same general goal but along different paths.

I take it to be the distinguishing characteristic of civilized man that he is concerned with the environment and destiny of himself and his kind. The end of all scholarship, all art, all science, is the increase of knowledge and of understanding. The rubrics of scholarship have no inherent importance except in making the expansion of knowledge easier by creating system and order and catholicity. The freedom of the arts has no inherent value except in its admitting unlimited comments upon life and the materials of life. There is no *mystique* about science; its sole wonder exists in its continuous

127

expansion of both the area and the detail of man's comprehension of his physical being and his surroundings.

The ultimate use of all man's knowledge and his art and his science cannot be locked up into little compartments to which only the initiate hold the keys. It cannot be contemplated solely by closeted groups, or imposed from above. If vitality is to be a force in the general life of mankind, it must sooner or later reach all men and enter into the general body of awarenesses. The advancement of the human lot consists in more people being aware of more, knowing more, understanding more.

The mass media believe in the broad dissemination of as much as can be comprehended by as many as possible. They employ techniques to arrest attention, to recruit interest, to lead their audiences into new fields. Often they must sacrifice detail or annotation for the sake of the general idea.

Although it may be presumptuous, perhaps I can suggest a general contrast in the position of the professional intellectual: he feels that knowledge, art, and understanding are all precious commodities that ought not to be diluted. He believes that if things were left to him this dilution would not happen, because the doors of influence would be closed to the inadequately educated until they had earned the right to open them, just as he did. His view is that if standards remain beyond the reach of the many, the general level will gradually rise.

In this respect, I dissent from Mr. Rosten's conclusion that the intellectuals "project their own tastes, yearnings, and values upon the masses."* I do not believe there is such an irreducible gap between the tastes, yearnings, and values of the intellectuals and those of the masses. The difficulty is that the intellectuals do not project at all to the uninitiated. Their hope is to attract them, providing that it is not too many, too fast. They would wait for more and more people to qualify to the higher group, although they themselves want to stay a little ahead of the new arrivals.

This accounts, I believe, for the intellectuals' fear of popularization. The history of the Book-of-the-Month Club illustrates this point. Intellectuals have repeatedly made statements (not entirely characterized by a disciplined array of evidence), that the book club would bring about an "emasculation of the human mind whereby everyone

*Leo Rosten, see page 71.

loses the power of his determination in reading,"[1] and that the club's selections were "in many cases, not even an approximation to what the average intelligent reader wants."[2] Yet a study by a Columbia University researcher found that over an eighteen-year span the reaction of reviewers, critics, and professors to the Book-of-the-Month Club selections was far higher in terms of approval than their reaction to random samples of nonselections.[3]

By comparing the two heaviest book selections of the club in 1927 to their two lightest ones in 1949 (without other evidence) Stanley Edgar Hyman suggests that the standards of selection are deteriorating.* Yet he makes no mention of the fact that in 1949 the Book-of-the-Month Club for the first time in its history distributed a serious contemporary play, *Death of a Salesman*, that it distributed a serious discussion of a vital issue in Vannevar Bush's *Modern Arms and Free Men*, that it put into hundreds of thousands of homes William Edward Langer's *Encyclopedia of World History*, that it brought to its subscribers George Orwell's *Nineteen Eighty-four*, Winston Churchill's *Their Finest Hour*, and A. B. Guthrie's Pulitzer-Prize novel, *The Way West*.

Let me press what Mr. Hyman regards as evidence of "deterioration" of the Book-of-the-Month Club selections to the conclusion at which he himself arrived, that in the decade since 1949 "the selections seem to have continued to deteriorate." Even a glance at the evidence would refute this slashing generality. Indeed, the books distributed by the club throughout the 1950's suggest some high levels of excellence: in fiction there have been three books by William Faulkner, three by James Gould Cozzens, two by John Hersey, seven plays by Shaw, six by Thornton Wilder, Eugene O'Neill's *Long Day's Journey into Night*, novels by Feuchtwanger, Salinger, Thomas Mann, Hemingway, John Cheever, and James Agee; there have been eight historical works by Churchill, two by Schlesinger, two by Van Wyck Brooks, others by Morison and Nevins, Dumas Malone, Bernard DeVoto, Catherine Drinker Bowen's life of John Adams, Toynbee's *Study of History*, two of Edith Hamilton's studies of ancient Greece, and Max Lerner's *American Civilization*; in poetry, Stephen Vincent Benet, and *The Oxford Book of American Verse*; from the classics, Bulfinch's *The Age of Fable*, Frazer's *The Golden Bough*, the Hart edition of Shakespeare, a new translation of *The Odyssey*, works by

*Stanley E. Hyman, see page 132.

Dostoevsky, Gustave Flaubert, and Mark Twain; in art, Francis Henry Taylor's *Fifty Centuries of Art*, John Walker's *Masterpieces of Painting from the National Gallery*, and *Art Treasures of the Louvre*; in reference works, Fowler's *Modern English Usage*, Palmer's *Atlas of World History*, Audubon's *Birds*, and Evans' *Dictionary of Contemporary American Usage*.[4]

To turn to television, I hear over and over such generalities as, "There is nothing but Westerns on television," or "Television is all mysteries and blood and thunder." Such charges usually come from people who do not look at television, but that does not modify their position. As in the case just cited, there is no uncertainty about this exaggeration; one can look at the actual record.

Let us take by way of example the week of February 15 to 21, 1959, on the CBS Television Network, because that week had nothing exceptional about it. During the preceding week, there were such outstanding broadcasts as Tolstoy's *Family Happiness* and a repetition of the distinguished documentary, *The Face of Red China*. In the following week, the programs included the New York Philharmonic and the Old Vic Company's *Hamlet*. Returning to the unexceptional week of February 15, about 4½ hours, or ⅟₁₈ of CBS Television's total program content of 75½ hours, were devoted to Westerns; about 5 hours, or ⅟₁₅, were taken up by mysteries. On the other hand, 7¾ hours, or about ⅟₁₀ of the total number of hours, were devoted to news and public affairs. Altogether, some 78 percent of the evening programing was occupied by drama, fairly evenly divided among serious, comedy, mystery, Westerns, and romance-adventure.

Looking at the record for the first five months of 1959, I find on the CBS Television Network alone four Philharmonic concerts; 90-minute-long productions of plays by Shakespeare, Barrie, and Saroyan, adaptations of Shaw and Ibsen, full-length productions of *The Browning Version*, Melville's *Billy Budd*, Henry James' *Wings of the Dove*, Hemingway's *For Whom the Bell Tolls*, and many distinguished original dramas; thirteen conversations with people of such diverse minds and talents as James Conant, Sir Thomas Beecham, and James Thurber; nine historic surveys of great personalities or developments of the twentieth century; and nine specially scheduled programs inquiring into major issues in public affairs, such as the Cuban revolution, the closing of integrated high schools, statehood for Hawaii, and the Geneva Conference.

I am citing these for two purposes. One is to show how, by using selected examples, it can be as easily proved that television is exclusively instructive as that it is exclusively diverting. My other purpose is by way of considering a practical response to the complaints that the intellectuals voice about all the mass media.

What do the intellectuals really want? Do they want us to do *only* serious programing, only programs of profound cultural value? Or do they just want us to do more? And if so, what is more? Do they want the Book-of-the-Month Club to distribute only heavy reading, or just more? Does the club do harm because it has included books of humor among the thirty to forty selections, alternates, and dividends it distributes each year? Is there any serious belief anywhere that among the paperback books we ought to censor what we consider culturally insignificant and allow only what we consider culturally enriching? Or do not the intellectuals really want to stake out reserves, admission to which would be granted only on their terms, in their way, at their pleasure?

Television occupies the air waves under the franchise of the American people. It has a threefold function: the dissemination of information, culture, and entertainment. There are different levels and different areas of interest at which these are sought by a hundred and fifty million people. It is our purpose—and our endlessly tantalizing task—to make certain that we have enough of every area at every level of interest to hold the attention of significant segments of the public at one time on another. Therefore we do have programs more likely to be of interest to the intellectuals than to others. We can try to include everybody somewhere in our program planning, but we cannot possibly aim all the time only at the largest possible audience.

The practice of sound television programing is the same as the practice of any sound editorial operation. It involves always anticipating (if you can) and occasionally leading your subscribers or readers or audience. The "mass of consumers" does not decide, in the sense that it initiates programs, but it does respond to our decisions. A mass medium survives when it maintains a satisfactory batting average on affirmative responses, and it goes down when negative responses are too numerous or too frequent. But so also does the magazine with a circulation of five thousand—as the high mortality rate of the "little magazines" testifies. Success in editing, whether a mass medium or an esoteric quarterly, consists in so respecting the audience that one labors to bring to it something that meets an interest, a desire, or a need that has still to be completely filled. Obviously, the narrower and the more intellectually homogeneous your audience, the easier this is to do; and conversely, the larger it is and the more heterogeneous, the more difficult.

I must dissent from the unqualified charge that "advertisers today . . . exercise their most pernicious influence in television." The basis of this charge is that, while an advertiser buys space in a magazine with no power of choice as to the editorial content of the magazine, on television he allegedly controls both the commercials and what program goes into the time space. The matter is not so simple.

In the first place I categorically assert that no news or public-affairs program at CBS, however expensive to the sponsor, has ever been subject to his control, influence, or approval. There is a total and absolute independence in this respect.

An advertiser in magazines does have the power to associate his advertising with editorial content by his choice of a magazine. If he makes a household detergent, he can choose a magazine whose appeal is to housewives. In television, he can achieve this association only by seeking out kinds of programs, or, more properly, the kinds of audience to which specific programs appeal. This is of course why a razor blade company wants to sponsor sports programs. But this does not mean that the company is going to referee the game or coach the team. In television, for the most part, advertisers are sold programs by networks or by independent producers, somewhat in the sense that space in the magazines is sold by sales efforts based on the kind of audience the magazine reaches. At the same time, we are perfectly aware that in the rapid growth of television the problem of the advertiser's relationship with program content has not yet been satisfactorily solved. It is an area to which we are going to have to devote more thought and evolve new approaches.

I return to a central point: that some sort of hostility on the part of the intellectuals toward the mass media is inevitable, because the intellectuals are a minority, one not really reconciled to some basic features of democratic life. They are an articulate and cantankerous minority, not readily given to examining evidence about the mass media and then arriving at conclusions, but more likely to come to conclusions and then select the evidence to support them. But they are an invaluable minority. We all do care what they think because they are a historic force on which our society must always rely for self-examination and advancement. They constitute the outposts of our intellectual life as a people, they probe around frontiers in their splendid sparsity, looking around occasionally to see where—how far behind—the rest of us are. We are never going to catch up, but at least we shall always have somewhere to go.

As for the mass media, they are always in the process of trying, and they never really find the answers. They also are the victims of their pressing preoccupations, and can undoubtedly improve their performances, better understand their own roles, learn more rapidly. I feel that intellectuals and the media could really serve one another better if both parties informed themselves more fully, brought somewhat more sympathy to each other's examinations, and stopped once in a while to redefine their common goals. We in the mass media have probably been negligent in not drawing the intellectuals more intimately into our counsels, and the intellectuals, by and large, have not studied the evidence carefully enough before discussing the mass media. The mass media need the enlightened criticism, the thorough examination, of the intellectuals. When the latter are willing to promise these, we shall all make progress faster and steadier.

REFERENCES

1 Edward F. Stevens, cited in Charles Lee, *The Hidden Public* (Garden City: Doubleday, 1958), p. 51.

2 *Ibid.*

3 Joseph W. Kappel, "Book Clubs and the Evaluation of Books," *Public Opinion Quarterly*, 1948, *12*: 243-252.

4 For complete selections for 1926-1957, see Lee, *op. cit.*, pp. 161-194.

JAMES JOHNSON SWEENEY

The Artist and the Museum
in a Mass Society

ONE SHOULD PUT ASIDE at the outset the notion that there is any essential threat in the mass media to the genuinely creative artist or to genuine art. The artist, qua artist, is an individualist, and the quality of his art lies in its individuality. A work of art is the concrete record of an artist's discovery of himself, first to himself, then at a second remove to the world around him. In this sense, what may from one point of view be seen as a "monologue" may also be regarded as a hypothetical duologue or conversation.

The true artist does not feel the need to address a mass meeting to have the sense of conversing with his fellow man. He speaks to an ideal audience, but what speaker succeeds in envisaging his audience otherwise? Consequently, for the advantages of audience the mass media may offer, the true artist will not be tempted, nor will the true artist's work suffer, in a culture given its broad color by those advantages. Only the current equivalents of pseudo-artists who in the past have sacrificed their individuality to other temptations will suffer from the seductions of mass media.

Any suggested threat to the creative artist through mass culture does, however, serve very frequently to obscure the true issue. For the real present danger is not to the creative artist or to creative art, but to the conditioning of the public in its response to creative art, particularly in the field of painting and sculpture. As S. E. Hyman has pointed out: "The technological revolution does not yet seem to have brought the plastic arts into mass culture. . . . Mass-produced copies of pictures and sculptures have been around for a long time and make all but the most contemporary work cheaply available in

134

reproduction, but they seem to have had little of the impact on taste of paperbacks and long-playing records."*

Whether or not long-playing records have had any profound effect on musical discrimination, if the test is not merely one of recognizing accepted works, is difficult to say. It seems evident that an ear educated only by long-playing records would be as far from the real experience of a musical work as any eye trained by color reproductions would be from the sensuous experience of actual painting. In Hyman's linking the influences of paperbacks and long-playing records, it seems to me he has slightly mixed his categories of reproduction. The paperback is merely a less luxurious form of book, for the text is, or should be, the same; but between a long-playing record and a live rendition there is a difference in sense stimuli, just as there is between a painting and a printed reproduction of a painting—perhaps not a wide difference, but an essential one.

What both long-playing records and color reproductions basically provide is "information" about the works of art in question, not an immediate experience of either the music as played or the actual painting. In painting and sculpture the danger lies in the confusion which can so readily develop between information about a work of art and the experience an immediate sensuous contact with a work of art provides. And a true appreciation of works of art in these fields can only come through direct experience.

Reproductions of painting and sculpture speak to the eye of the observer through materials different from those of the original. The material in which an artist works is an essential element of his expression. Materials different from those employed in the original must provide different relationships in the result. At best, the reproduction can only resemble or suggest the original, although at times it misleads the uncritical observer by its pretension to do more.

Reproduction in the mass media will never supply a truly adequate equivalent for the immediate experience of a painting or a sculpture. What might be achieved is an equivalent expression within the limitations of the medium, much as one had hoped (and still hopes) for a color cinema which would set out, not to reproduce effects, but to exploit the potentialities of creating new forms through color and light effects—fresh expressions of visual order rather than the imitation of already existent expressions. But because the technological

* Stanley E. Hyman, from an earlier draft of his article, as delivered to the participants of this symposium.

revolution has not yet found a way either to bring the pictorial and sculptural arts into mass culture, or to create a fresh expression within the various media which might be analogous, information is offered as a substitute, and the indolent public is readily led to accepting it, with the resultant danger of eventual confusion between the two.

The general educational approach to the appreciation of painting and sculpture is in part a consequence of mass culture and the influence of mass media; in part, it is a result of indolence. I refer to a general emphasis on the informational approach in schools and even in museums where there is so little excuse for it. It is easier to approach painting or sculpture through the ears than through the eyes: our temptation today is to lean on the accepted authority, rather than to look for ourselves and respond directly to the sensory stimuli of the work of art. Yet when we speak of accepted authority with regard to a work of art, this can only refer to a work of the past. The viewer who leans on accepted authority can never depend on such a crutch in the case of a truly fresh work, nor can he ever experience a direct communication between a work of art and himself: it must always be at second hand.

The indolent approach to the visual arts is now generally encouraged as a result of the hasty democratization of education of the past century. Everyone has a right to know and appreciate all; therefore, everyone ought to know and appreciate all, and if one does not, it is cause for shame, and one should pretend to be a connoisseur. Art is long; time is short; therefore, any means toward creating this impression of familiarity is welcome, whether it actually interferes with a true, direct appreciation of a work or not.

Museums and educational institutions in general for the past three or four decades (those in which mass media have been developing apace) have fallen deep into this betrayal of the public in the field of the visual arts. Perhaps museums, as looked upon by certain museum trustees, are primarily intended as instruments of popular education along mass media lines. The interest of museum trustees in popular attendance would point this way. Attendance statistics would readily show them that an exhibition of painting or sculpture in an idiom familiar to the public and by an artist or artists whose name it knows will draw crowds. By contrast, the attendance at an exhibition of work by a less known or less publicized artist, or artists, even though more interesting in quality and freshness to the exploring gallery-goer or connoisseur, will suffer. To catch and hold the attention of the indolent visitor, elaborate biographical, critical, explanatory labels, even canned lectures over earphones, are provided, like aesthetic water wings, so one may dabble about without getting too deep into the water. Art should never be spoon-fed nor offered in capsule, digested form. Yet this is what is being essayed in our museums today, simply because museum trustees or perhaps even museum directors are ambitious to embrace the broadest possible public and, in our democratic age, have not the courage to face the fact that the highest experiences of art are only for the elite who "have earned in order to possess."

In the case of a commercial television station, one can adopt a degree of leniency toward this attitude: profits are involved. To a certain extent, the public is bound to dictate the editorial policies if the station is to succeed financially. But in the case of a museum there is no such ground for exculpation. A museum is a nonprofit organization which should be responsible only to its own standards. There is no comparison between the freedom which a museum or a publication like *Partisan Review* should enjoy in maintaining these standards and the responsibility of a television network to its consumers.

The function of a museum is the encouragement of the enjoyment of art and through this the indirect encouragement of the creative artist. Visual art is basically a sensory experience, one of relationships of form, of colors, and of associations, physical, unconscious, or representational. Therefore, the first step in a museum's educational process is the confrontation of the spectator with the actual work of art, so that the artist can speak directly to the spectator. The immediate sensory experience of a work of art is the only direct approach to the artist's communication. Mass media cannot provide this experience, but the museum can and should. On this foundation of a direct sensory acquaintance, the experience of a work of art may be soundly enriched by its peripheral associations. It is the responsibility of the museum to stimulate the indolent public to approach art directly through aesthetic experience, pleasurable and enjoyable, and to incite the visitor to make the effort, always more or less arduous, which is necessary for him to enter into communication with the artist through the artist's personal expression. For it is this interaction between the observer and the creative artist that makes it possible to maintain or raise standards of judgment and appreciation.

A lowering of standards would appear inevitable when all or most energies are expended toward raising the lowest or broadest common denominator. In turn, this will encourage a broadening and a dilution of culture, as indeed has been the case over the past thirty years, not only in our own country, but in others where the mass media have developed.

If the general trend lies in this direction, and if even such non-profit institutions as museums widen their embrace to attract the broadest possible number (fit or unfit as the case may be), where are we to look for standards of aesthetic quality in this new culture? Here is where the creative artist must play his part. For if the mass media have no influence on the true artist, who by his essential nature is a seeker, an explorer, always apart and in advance of his fellows, it is he who provides what the mass media fail to give: standards of quality and integrity for our culture as a whole.

RANDALL JARRELL

A Sad Heart at the Supermarket

THE EMPEROR AUGUSTUS would sometimes say to his Senate: "Words fail me, my Lords; nothing I can say could possibly indicate the depth of my feelings in this matter." But I am speaking about this matter of mass culture, the mass media, not as an Emperor but as a fool, as a suffering, complaining, helplessly nonconforming poet-or-artist-of-a-sort, far off at the obsolescent rear of things: what I say will indicate the depth of my feelings and the shallowness and one-sidedness of my thoughts. If those English lyric poets who went mad during the eighteenth century had told you why the Age of Enlightement was driving them crazy, it would have had a kind of documentary interest: what I say may have a kind of documentary interest.

> The toad beneath the harrow knows
> Exactly where each tooth-point goes;

if you tell me that the field is being harrowed to grow grain for bread, and to create a world in which there will be no more famines, or toads either, I will say, "I know"—but let me tell you where the tooth-points go, and what the harrow looks like from below.

Advertising men, businessmen, speak continually of "media" or "the media" or "the mass media"—one of their trade journals is named, simply, *Media*. It is an impressive word: one imagines Mephistopheles offering Faust media that no man has ever known; one feels, while the word is in one's ear, that abstract, overmastering powers, of a scale and intensity unimagined yesterday, are being offered one by the technicians who discovered and control them— offered, and at a price. The word, like others, has the clear fatal ring of that new world whose space we occupy so luxuriously and precariously; the world that produces mink stoles, rockabilly records, and tactical nuclear weapons by the million; the world that Attila, Galileo, Hansel and Gretel never knew.

And yet, it's only the plural of "medium." "Medium," says the dictionary, "that which lies in the middle; hence, middle condition or degree. . . . A substance through which a force acts or an effect is transmitted. . . . That through or by which anything is accomplished; as, an advertising *medium*. . . . *Biol.* A nutritive mixture or substance, as broth, gelatin, agar, for cultivating bacteria, fungi, etc." Let us name *our* trade journal *The Medium*. For all these media (television, radio, movies, popular magazines, and the rest) are a single medium, in whose depths we are all being cultivated. This medium is of middle condition or degree, mediocre; it lies in the middle of everything, between a man and his neighbor, his wife, his child, his self; it, more than anything else, is the substance through which the forces of our society act upon us, make us into what our society needs.

And what does it need? For us to need . . . Oh, it needs for us to do or be many things—to be workers, technicians, executives, soldiers, housewives. But first of all, last of all, it needs for us to be buyers; consumers; beings who want much and will want more —who want consistently and insatiably. Find some spell to make us no longer want the stoles, the records, and the weapons, and our world will change into something to us unimaginable. Find some spell to make us realize that the product or service which seemed yesterday an unthinkable luxury is today an inexorable necessity, and our world will go on. It is the Medium which casts this spell— which is this spell. As we look at the television set, listen to the radio, read the magazines, the frontier of necessity is always being pushed forward. The Medium shows us what our new needs are—how often, without it, we should not have known!—and it shows us how they can be satisfied: they can be satisfied by buying something. The act of buying something is at the root of our world: if anyone wishes to paint the beginning of things in our society, he will paint a picture of God holding out to Adam a checkbook or credit card or Charge-A-Plate.

But how quickly our poor naked Adam is turned into a consumer, is linked to others by the great chain of buying!

> No outcast he, bewildered and depressed:
> Along his infant veins are interfused
> The gravitation and the filial bond
> Of nature that connect him with the world.

Children of three or four can ask for a brand of cereal, sing some soap's commercial; by the time that they are twelve they are not children but teen-age consumers, interviewed, graphed, analyzed. They are on their way to becoming that ideal figure of our culture, the knowledgeable consumer. I'll define him: the knowledgeable consumer is someone who, when he goes to Weimar, knows how to buy a Weimaraner. He has learned to understand life as a series of choices among the things and services of this world; because of being an executive, or executive's wife, or performer, or celebrity, or someone who has inherited money, he is able to afford the choices that he makes, with knowing familiarity, among restaurants, resorts, clothes, cars, liners, hits or best-sellers of every kind. We may still go to Methodist or Baptist or Presbyterian churches on Sunday, but the Protestant ethic of frugal industry, of production for its own sake, is gone. Production has come to seem to our society not much more than a condition prior to consumption: "The challenge of today," writes a great advertising agency, "is to make the consumer raise his level of demand." This challenge has been met: the Medium has found it easy to make its people feel the continually increasing lacks, the many specialized dissatisfactions (merging into one great dissatisfaction, temporarily assuaged by new purchases) that it needs for them to feel. When, in some magazine, we see the Medium at its most nearly perfect, we hardly know which half is entertaining and distracting us, which half making us buy: some advertisement may be more ingeniously entertaining than the text beside it, but it is the text which has made us long for a product more passionately. When one finishes *Holiday* or *Harper's Bazaar* or *House and Garden* or *The New Yorker* or *High Fidelity* or *Road and Track* or—but make your own list—buying something, going somewhere seems a necessary completion to the act of reading the magazine. Reader, isn't buying or fantasy-buying an important part of your and my emotional life? (If you reply, *No*, I'll think of you with bitter envy as more than merely human; as deeply un-American.) It is a standard joke of our culture that when a woman is bored or sad she buys something to make herself feel better; but in this respect we are all women together, and can hear complacently the reminder of how feminine this consumer-world of ours is. One imagines as a characteristic dialogue of our time an interview in which someone is asking of a vague gracious figure, a kind of Mrs. America: "But while you waited for the Intercontinental Ballistic Missiles what did you *do*?" She answers: "I bought things."

She reminds one of the sentinel at Pompeii—a space among ashes, now, but at his post: she too did what she was supposed to do. . . . Our society has delivered us—most of us—from the bonds of necessity, so that we no longer need worry about having food enough to keep from starving, clothing and shelter enough to keep from freezing; yet if the ends for which we work, of which we dream, are restaurants and clothes and houses, consumption, possessions, how have we escaped? We have merely exchanged man's old bondage for a new voluntary one. But *voluntary* is wrong: the consumer is trained for his job of consuming as the factory worker is trained for his job of producing; and the first is a longer, more complicated training, since it is easier to teach a man to handle a tool, to read a dial, than it is to teach him to ask, always, for a name-brand aspirin—to want, someday, a stand-by generator. What is that? You don't know? I used not to know, but the readers of *House Beautiful* all know, and now I know: it is the electrical generator that stands in the basement of the suburban houseowner, shining, silent, until at last one night the lights go out, the freezer's food begins to—

Ah, but it's frozen for good, the lights are on forever; the owner has switched on the stand-by generator.

But you don't see that he really needs the generator, you'd rather have seen him buy a second car? He has two. A second bathroom? He has four. He long ago doubled everything, when the People of the Medium doubled everything; and now that he's gone twice round he will have to wait three years, or four, till both are obsolescent—but while he waits there are so many new needs that he can satisfy, so many things a man can buy.

> Man wants but little here below
> Nor wants that little long,

said the poet; what a lie! Man wants almost unlimited quantities of almost everything, and he wants it till the day he dies.

We sometimes see in *Life* or *Look* a double-page photograph of some family standing on the lawn among its possessions: station wagon, swimming pool, power cruiser, sports car, tape recorder, television sets, radios, cameras, power lawn mower, garden tractor, lathe, barbecue set, sporting equipment, domestic appliances—all the gleaming, grotesquely imaginative paraphernalia of its existence. It was hard to get them on two pages, soon they will need four. It is like a dream, a child's dream before Christmas; yet if the members of the family doubt that they are awake, they have only to reach out and pinch something. The family seems pale and small, a negligible appendage, beside its possessions; only a human being would need to ask, "Which owns which?" We are fond of saying that something-or-other is not just something-or-other but "a way of life"; this too is a way of life—our way, the way.

Emerson, in his spare stony New England, a few miles from Walden, could write:

> Things are in the saddle
> And ride mankind.

He could say more now: that they are in the theater and studio, and entertain mankind; are in the pulpit and preach to mankind. The values of business, in an overwhelmingly successful business society like our own, are reflected in every sphere: values which agree with them are reinforced, values which disagree are cancelled out or have lip-service paid to them. In business what sells is good, and that's the end of it—that is what *good* means; if the world doesn't beat a path to your door, your mousetrap wasn't better. The values of the Medium (which is both a popular business itself and the cause of popularity in other businesses) are business values: money, success, celebrity. If we are representative members of our society, the Medium's values are ours; even when we are unrepresentative, non-conforming, our hands are (too often) subdued to the element they work in, and our unconscious expectations are all that we consciously reject. (Darwin said that he always immediately wrote down evidence against a theory because otherwise, he'd noticed, he would forget it; in the same way we keep forgetting the existence of those poor and unknown failures whom we might rebelliously love and admire.) *If you're so smart why aren't you rich?* is the ground-bass of our society, a grumbling and quite unanswerable criticism, since the society's nonmonetary values *are* directly convertible into money. (Celebrity turns into testimonials, lectures, directorships, presidencies, the capital gains of an autobiography *Told To* some professional ghost who photographs the man's life as Bachrach photographs his body.) When Liberace said that his critics' unfavorable reviews hurt him so much that he cried all the way to the bank, one had to admire the correctness and penetration of his press-agent's wit: in another age, what mightn't such a man have become!

Our culture is essentially periodical: we believe that all that is deserves to perish and to have something else put in its place. We speak of "planned obsolescence," but it is more than planned, it is felt

—is an assumption about the nature of the world. The present is better and more interesting, more real, than the past; the future will be better and more interesting, more real, than the present. (But, consciously, we do not hold against the present its prospective obsolescence.) Our standards have become, to an astonishing degree, those of what is called "the world of fashion," where mere timeliness—being orange in orange's year, violet in violet's—is the value to which all other values are reducible. In our society "old-fashioned" is so final a condemnation that a man like Norman Vincent Peale can say about atheism or agnosticism simply that it is old-fashioned; the homely recommendation of "Give me that good old-time religion" has become after a few decades the conclusive rejection of "old-fashioned" atheism.

All this is, at bottom, the opposite of the world of the arts, where commercial and scientific progress do not exist; where the bone of Homer and Mozart and Donatello is there, always, under the mere blush of fashion; where the past—the remote past, even—is responsible for the way that we understand, value, and act in, the present. (When one reads an abstract expressionist's remark that Washington studios are "eighteen months behind" those of his colleagues in New York, one realizes something of the terrible power of business and fashion over those most overtly hostile to them.) An artist's work and life presuppose continuing standards, values stretched out over centuries or millennia, a future that is the continuation and modification of the past, not its contradiction or irrelevant replacement. He is working for the time that wants the best that he can do: the present, he hopes—but if not that, the future. If he sees that fewer and fewer people are any real audience for the serious artists of the past, he will feel that still fewer are going to be an audience for the serious artists of the present, for those who, willingly or unwillingly, sacrifice extrinsic values to intrinsic ones, immediate effectiveness to that steady attraction which, the artist hopes, true excellence will always exert. The past's relation to the artist or man of culture is almost the opposite of its relation to the rest of our society. To him the present is no more than the last ring on the trunk, understandable and valuable only in terms of all the earlier rings. The rest of our society sees only that great last ring, the enveloping surface of the trunk; what's underneath is a disregarded, almost hypothetical foundation. When Northrop Frye writes that "the preoccupation of the humanities with the past is sometimes made a reproach against them by those who forget that we face the past: it may be shadowy, but it is all that is there," he is saying what for the artist or man of culture is self-evidently true; yet for the Medium and the People of the Medium it is as self-evidently false—for them the present (or a past so recent, so quick-changing, so soon-disappearing, that it might be called the specious present) is all that is there.

In the past our culture's frame of reference, its body of common knowledge (its possibility of comprehensible allusion) changed slowly and superficially; the amount added to it or taken away from it in any ten years was a small proportion of the whole. Now in any ten years a surprisingly large proportion of the whole is replaced. Most of the information people have in common is something that four or five years from now they will not even remember having known. A newspaper story remarks in astonishment that television quiz programs have "proved that ordinary citizens can be conversant with such esoterica as jazz, opera, the Bible, Shakespeare, poetry and fisticuffs." You may exclaim, "Esoterica! If the Bible and Shakespeare are esoterica, what is there that's common knowledge?" The answer, I suppose, is that Elfrida von Nardoff and Teddy Nadler (the ordinary citizens on the quiz programs) are common knowledge; though not for long. Songs disappear in two or three months, celebrities in two or three years; most of the Medium is lightly felt and soon forgotten. What is as dead as day-before-yesterday's newspaper, the next-to-the-last number on the roulette wheel? and most of the knowledge we have in common is knowledge of such newspapers, such numbers. But the novelist or poet or dramatist, when he moves a great audience, depends upon the deep feelings, the live unforgotten knowledge, that the people of his culture share; if these have become contingent, superficial, ephemeral, it is disastrous for him.

New products and fashions replace the old, and the fact that they replace them is proof enough of their superiority. Similarly, the Medium does not need to show that the subjects that fill it are timely or interesting or important—the fact that they are its subjects makes them so. If *Time, Life,* and the television shows are full of Tom Fool this month, he's no fool. And when he has been gone from them a while, we do not think him a fool—we do not think of him at all. He no longer exists, in the fullest sense of the word "exist": to be is to be perceived, to be a part of the Medium of our perception. Our celebrities are not kings, romantic in exile, but Representatives who, defeated, are forgotten; they had always only the qualities that we delegated to them.

After driving for four or five minutes along the road outside my door, I come to a long row of one-room shacks about the size of kitchens, made out of used boards, metal signs, old tin roofs. To the people who live in them an electric dishwasher of one's own is as much a fantasy as an ocean liner of one's own. But since the Medium (and those whose thought is molded by it) does not perceive them, these people are themselves a fantasy: no matter how many millions of such exceptions to the general rule there are, they do not really exist, but have a kind of anomalous, statistical subsistence; our moral and imaginative view of the world is no more affected by them than by the occupants of some home for the mentally deficient a little farther along the road. If, some night, one of these outmoded, economically deficient ghosts should scratch at my window, I could say only, "Come back twenty years ago." And if I, as an old-fashioned, one-room poet, a friend of "quiet culture," a "meek lover of the good," should go out some night to scratch at another window, shouldn't I hear someone's indifferent or regretful, "Come back a century or two ago"?

When those whose existence the Medium recognizes ring the chimes of the writer's doorbell, fall through his letter slot, float out onto his television screen, what is he to say to them? A man's unsuccessful struggle to get his family food is material for a work of art—for tragedy, almost; his unsuccessful struggle to get his family a stand-by generator is material for what? Comedy? Farce? Comedy on such a scale, at such a level, that our society and its standards seem, almost, farce? And yet it is the People of the Medium, those who long for and get, or long for and don't get, the generator, whom our culture finds representative, who are there to be treated first of all. And the Medium itself—one of the ends of life, something essential to people's understanding and valuing of their existence, something many of their waking hours are spent listening to or looking at— how is *it* to be treated as subject matter for art? The writer cannot just reproduce it; should he satirize or parody it? But often parody or satire is impossible, since it is already its own parody; and by the time the writer's work is published, the part of the Medium which is satirized will already have been forgotten. Yet isn't the Medium by now an essential part of its watchers? Those whom Mohammedans speak of as the People of the Book are inexplicable, surely, in any terms that omit it; we are people of the magazine, the television set, the radio, and are inexplicable in any terms that omit them.

Oscar Wilde's wittily paradoxical statement about Nature's imitation of Art is literally true when the Nature is human nature and the

Art that of television, radio, motion pictures, popular magazines. Life is so, people are so, the Medium shows its audience, and most of the audience believe it, expect people to be so, try to be so themselves. For them the People of the Medium are reality, what human beings normally, primarily are: and mere local or personal variations are not real in the same sense. The Medium mediates between us and raw reality, and the mediation more and more replaces reality for us. In many homes either the television set or the radio is turned on most of the time the family is awake. (Many radio stations have a news broadcast every half hour, and many people like and need to hear it.) It is as if the people longed to be established in reality, to be reminded continually of the "real," the "objective" world—the created world of the Medium—rather than be left at the mercy of actuality, of the helpless contingency of the world in which the radio receiver or television set is sitting. (And surely we can sympathize: which of us hasn't found a similar refuge in the "real," created world of Cézanne or Goethe or Verdi? Yet Dostoievsky's world is too different from Wordsworth's, Piero della Francesca's from Goya's, Bach's from Hugo Wolf's, for us to be able to substitute one homogeneous mediated reality for everyday reality in the belief that it *is* everyday reality.) The world of events and celebrities and performers, the Great World, has become for many listeners, lookers, readers, the world of primary reality: how many times they have sighed at the colorless unreality of their own lives and families, sighed for the bright reality of, say, Lucille Ball's—of some shadow dyed, gowned, directed, produced, and agented into a being as equivocal as that of the square root of minus one. The watchers call the celebrities by their first names, approve or disapprove of "who they're dating," handle them with a mixture of love, identification, envy, and contempt—for the Medium has given its people so terrible a familiarity with everyone that it takes great magnanimity of spirit not to be affected by it. These celebrities are not heroes to us, their valets.

Better to have these real ones play themselves, and not sacrifice too much of their reality to art; better to have the watcher play himself, and not lose too much of himself in art. Usually the watcher is halfway between two worlds, paying full attention to neither: half distracted from, half distracted by, this distraction—and able for the moment not to be affected too greatly, have too great demands made upon him, by either world. For in the Medium, which we escape to from work, nothing is ever *work*, nothing ever makes intellectual or emotional or imaginative demands which we might find it difficult to satisfy. Here in the half-world everything is homogeneous —is, as much as possible, the same as everything else: each familiar novelty, novel familiarity, has the same texture on top and the same attitude and conclusion at bottom; only the middle, the particular subject of the particular program or article, is different. (If it *is* different: everyone is given the same automatic "human interest" treatment, so that it is hard for us to remember, unnecessary for us to remember, which particular celebrity we're reading about this time—often it's the same one, we've just moved to a different magazine.) Heine said that the English have a hundred religions and one sauce; so do we; and we are so accustomed to this sauce or dye or style, the aesthetic equivalent of Standard Brands, that a very simple thing can seem perverse, obscure, without it. And, too, we find it hard to have to shift from one art form to another, to vary our attitudes and expectations, to use our unexercised imaginations. Poetry disappeared long ago, even for most intellectuals; each year fiction is a little less important. Our age is an age of nonfiction; of gossip columns, interviews, photographic essays, documentaries; of articles, condensed or book length, spoken or written; of real facts about real people. Art lies to us to tell us the (sometimes disquieting) truth; the Medium tells us truths, facts, in order to make us believe some reassuring or entertaining lie or half truth. These actually existing celebrities, of universally admitted importance, about whom we are told directly authoritative facts—how can fictional characters compete with them? These *are* our fictional characters, our Lears and Clytemnestras. (This is ironically appropriate, since many of their doings and sayings are fictional, made up by public relations officers, columnists, agents, or other affable familiar ghosts.) And the Medium gives us such facts, such photographs, such tape recordings, such clinical reports not only about the great, but also about (representative samples of) the small; when we have been shown so much about so many—*can* be shown, we feel, anything about anybody—does fiction seem so essential as it once seemed? Shakespeare or Tolstoy can show us all about someone, but so can *Life;* and when *Life* does, it's someone real.

The Medium is half life and half art, and competes with both life and art. It spoils its audience for both; spoils both for its audience. For the People of the Medium life isn't sufficiently a matter of success and glamor and celebrity, isn't entertaining enough, distracting enough, *mediated* enough; and art is too difficult or individual or novel, too restrained or indirect, too much a matter of tradition and the past, of special attitudes and aptitudes: its mediation sometimes is queer or excessive, and sometimes is not even recognizable as mediation. The Medium's mixture of rhetoric and reality, which gives people what we know they want in the form we know they like, is something more efficient and irresistible, more habit-forming, than any art. If a man all his life has been fed a sort of combination of marzipan and ethyl alcohol—if eating, to him, is a matter of being knocked unconscious by an ice cream soda—can he, by taking thought, come to prefer a diet of bread and wine, apples and well-water? Will a man who has spent his life watching gladiatorial games come to prefer listening to chamber music? And those who produce the bread and wine and quartets for him—won't they be tempted either to give up producing them, or else to produce a bread that's half sugar, half alcohol, a quartet that ends with the cellist at the violist's bleeding throat?

The Medium represents to the artist all that he has learned not to do: its sure-fire stereotypes seem to him what any true art, true spirit, has had to struggle past on its way to the truth. The artist sees the values and textures of this art substitute replacing those of his art with most of society, conditioning the expectations of what audience he has kept. Any outsider who has worked for the Medium will have noticed that the one thing which seems to its managers most unnatural is for someone to do something naturally, to speak or write as an individual speaking or writing to other individuals, and not as a subcontractor supplying a standardized product to the Medium. It is as if producers, editors, supervisors were particles forming a screen between maker and public, one that will let through only particles of their own size and weight (or, as they say, the public's); as you look into their bland faces, their big horn-rimmed eyes, you despair of Creation itself, which seems for the instant made in their own owl-eyed image. There are so many extrinsic considerations about everything in the work, the maker finds, that by the time it is finished all intrinsic considerations have come to seem secondary. It is no wonder that the professional who writes the ordinary commercial success, the ordinary script, scenario, or article, resembles imaginative writers less than he resembles advertising agents, columnists, editors, and producers. He is a technician who can supply a standard product, a rhetorician who can furnish a regular stimulus for a regular response, what has always made the dog salivate in this situation. He is the opposite of the imaginative artist: instead of stubbornly or helplessly sticking to what he sees and feels, to what seems right for him, true to reality, regardless of what the others think and want, he gives the others what they think and want, regardless of what he himself sees and feels.

Mass culture either corrupts or isolates the writer. His old feeling of oneness, of speaking naturally to an audience with essentially similar standards, is gone; and writers do not any longer have much of the consolatory feeling that took its place, the feeling of writing for the happy few, the kindred spirits whose standards are those of the future. (Today they feel: the future, should there be one, will be worse.) True works of art are more and more produced away from, in opposition to, society. And yet the artist needs society as much as society needs him: as our cultural enclaves get smaller and drier, more hysterical or academic, one mourns for the artists inside them and the public outside. An incomparable historian of mass culture, Ernest van den Haag, has expressed this with laconic force: "The artist who, by refusing to work for the mass market, becomes marginal, cannot create what he might have created had there been no mass market. One may prefer a monologue to addressing a mass meeting. But it is still not a conversation."

Even if the rebellious artist's rebellion is whole-hearted, it can never be whole-stomached, whole-Unconscious'd. Part of him wants to be like his kind, is like his kind; longs to be loved and admired and successful. Our society (and the artist, in so far as he is truly a part of it) has no place set aside for the different and poor and obscure, the fools for Christ's sake: they all go willy-nilly into Limbo. The artist is tempted, consciously, to give his society what it wants, or if he won't or can't, to give it nothing at all; is tempted, unconsciously, to give it superficially independent or contradictory works which are at heart works of the Medium. (Tennessee Williams' *Sweet Bird of Youth* is far less like Chekhov than it is like Mickey Spillane.) It is hard to go on serving both God and Mammon when God is so really ill-, Mammon so really well-organized. Shakespeare wrote for the Medium of his day; if Shakespeare were alive now he'd be writing *My Fair Lady*; isn't *My Fair Lady*, then, our *Hamlet*? shouldn't you be writing *Hamlet* instead of sitting there worrying about your superego? I need my *Hamlet*! So society speaks to the artist; but after he has written it its *Hamlet*, it tries to make sure that he will never do it again. There are more urgent needs that it wants him to satisfy: to lecture to it; to make public appearances, to be interviewed; to be on television shows; to give testimonials; to make trips abroad for the State Department; to judge books for contests or Book Clubs; to read for publishers, judge for publishers, be a publisher for publishers; to be an editor; to teach writing at colleges or writers' conferences; to write scenarios or scripts or articles, articles about his home town for *Holiday*, about cats or clothes or Christmas for *Vogue*, about "How I Wrote *Hamlet*" for anything; to . . .

But why go on? I once heard a composer, lecturing, say to a poet, lecturing: "They'll pay us to do *anything*, so long as it isn't writing music or writing poems." I knew the reply that, as a member of my society, I should have made: "So long as they pay you, what do you care?" But I didn't make it—it was plain that they cared. . . . But how many more learn not to care, love what they once endured! It is a whole so comprehensive that any alternative seems impossible, any opposition irrelevant; in the end a man says in a small voice, "I accept the Medium." The Enemy of the People winds up as the People—but where there is no Enemy, the people perish.

The climate of our culture is changing. Under these new rains, new suns, small things grow great, and what was great grows small; whole species disappear and are replaced. The American present is very different from the American past: so different that our awareness of the extent of the changes has been repressed, and we regard as ordinary what is extraordinary (ominous perhaps) both for us and the rest of the world. For the American present is many other peoples' future: our cultural and economic example is, to much of the world, mesmeric, and it is only its weakness and poverty that prevent it from hurrying with us into the Roman future. Yet at this moment of our greatest power and success, our thought and art are full of troubled gloom, of the conviction of our own decline. When the President of Yale University writes that "the ideal of the good life has faded from the educational process, leaving only miscellaneous prospects of jobs and joyless hedonism," are we likely to find it unfaded among our entertainers and executives? Is the influence of what I have called the Medium likely to make us lead any good life? to make us love and try to attain any real excellence, beauty, magnanimity? or to make us understand these as obligatory but transparent rationalizations, behind which the realities of money and power are waiting?

Matthew Arnold once spoke about our green culture in terms that have an altered relevance (but are not yet irrelevant) to our ripe one. He said: "What really dissatisfies in American civilization is the want of the *interesting*, a want due chiefly to the want of those two great elements of the interesting, which are elevation and beauty." This use of *interesting* (and, perhaps, this tone of a curator pointing out what is plain and culpable) shows how far along in the decline of the West Arnold came; it is only in the latter days that we ask to be interested. He had found the word in Carlyle. Carlyle is writing to a friend to persuade him not to emigrate to the United States; he asks, "Could you banish yourself from all that is interesting to your mind, forget the history, the glorious institutions, the noble principles of old Scotland—that you might eat a better dinner, perhaps?" We smile, and feel like reminding Carlyle of the history, the glorious institutions, the noble principles of new America, that New World which is, after all, the heir of the Old. And yet . . . Can we smile as comfortably, today, as we could have smiled yesterday? listen as unconcernedly, if on taking leave of us some tourist should say, with the penetration and obtuseness of his kind:

I remember reading somewhere: that which you inherit from your fathers you must earn in order to possess. I have been so much impressed with your power and possessions that I have neglected, perhaps, your principles. The elevation or beauty of your spirit did not equal, always, that of your mountains and skyscrapers: it seems to me that your society provides you with "all that is interesting to your mind" only exceptionally, at odd hours, in little reservations like those of your Indians. But as for your dinners, I've never seen anything like them: your daily bread comes *flambé*. And yet—wouldn't you say?—the more dinners a man eats, the more comfort he possesses, the hungrier and more uncomfortable some part of him becomes: inside every fat man there is a man who is starving. Part of you is being starved to death, and the rest of you is being stuffed to death. . . . But this will change: no one goes on being stuffed to death or starved to death forever.

This is a gloomy, an equivocal conclusion? Oh yes, I come from an older culture, where things are accustomed to coming to such conclusions; where there is no last-paragraph fairy to bring one, always, a happy ending—or that happiest of all endings, no ending at all. And have I no advice to give you, as I go? None. You are too successful to need advice, or to be able to take it if it were offered; but if ever you should fail, it is there waiting for you, the advice or consolation of all the other failures.

The South East Essex
College of Arts & Technology

ARTHUR BERGER

Notes on the Plight of the American Composer

IN RECENT YEARS there has been much rejoicing over the phenomenal improvement in American taste for "serious" or "concert" music. As far back as 1951, *The Wall Street Journal* reported that Americans leave more money at the concert-hall box-office than at the gates of professional baseball games. In 1920 there were some hundred symphony orchestras in the United States; today there are over a thousand (including those of colleges, communities and youth groups)—about half the current total of all symphony orchestras in the world.

Domestic cultivation of serious music also shows progress on many other levels. A much larger percentage of the American population now hears more and better music than ever heard it before, thanks to radio and—especially since the launching of the economical long-playing record in 1948—the phonograph. Early fears that "canned" music would deplete audiences for "live" concerts have been unwarranted. The loudspeaker cultivates interest in serious music and brings recruits to concerts and opera houses.

It seems to follow that the state of music in America could scarcely be more flourishing. Unlike most other arts—isolated from the public and practiced by esoteric groups—good music, at least, seems to have won a firm place for itself within the media of American mass culture. Technology has made products of this art more economical for the consumer and, thus, more easily accessible.

This conclusion is, however, tenable only if we disregard the very important native musical creativity. I am inclined to take the extreme view that precisely because the outlets upon which our advanced composer must depend (symphony orchestras, recordings, opera

153

companies, and organized networks for touring artists and chamber groups) have become successful mass media, the efflorescence of vital new American music is seriously hampered. A mass medium is not favorable to the problematic. Yet a composer, unlike a poet or a painter, cannot realize his works without an intermediary. The musical symbols rely on performers for their fulfillment. Only by hearing his music can a composer be sure he has achieved what he has conceived, and only faithful reproduction can suggest further development of new ideas for his next work. Charles Ives, whose innovations were spurned as incompetent and unfeasible by instrumentalists, resigned himself to a professional life as a Connecticut insurance man, with music as an avocation.[1] His career offers a revealing contrast to that of his contemporary, Wallace Stevens, also an insurance man, whose avocation was poetry. Stevens was the more finished artist, while Ives typified the artist whose remarkable gifts were unrealized. Given the technological developments in the field of recording and playing music, Ives would presumably have greater opportunities to fulfill himself today. I shall try to show later the extent to which these opportunities are illusory.

Aaron Copland has always conscientiously sought to preserve a balance between his creative aims and the new public's demands.[2] Yet even he has admitted that the artist "must never give up the right to be wrong, for the creator must forever be instinctive and spontaneous in his impulses, which means that he may learn as much from his miscalculations as from his successful achievements."[3] But the colossal arena that is supposed to serve as a proving-ground for new American music is scarcely the place for a composer to risk making mistakes or attempting techniques that may seem monstrous and arbitrary until they are later revealed—as so often happens in the life-span of a masterpiece—to be epoch-making and inspired. Purveyors of serious music, bent on reaping financial gain from public interest in this music, cannot take chances. Their need for prompt success restricts them to the narrow path of repertory already approved: the "fifty pieces" that, according to Virgil Thomson, dominate orchestral fare. For the most part, new works are ventured only if they are so conventional that they do not repel listeners frankly disposed toward the eighteenth and nineteenth centuries and only if they are so simple in conception that they do not require much intellectual effort.

A mass audience that has grown up to be comfortable listening to

Bach, Mozart, Beethoven, and Brahms does not feel at home with Anton Webern, Elliott Carter, or Karlheinz Stockhausen. Gabriel Marcel once observed that many people were indifferent to revelation. It takes time for what is revealed by vital new art to be interpreted to the public through watered-down imitations and propaganda from the experts. It has always been so. Why expect it to be otherwise now? The new factor is a reversal in the attitude toward traditional music. Traditional music has become the object of public devotion; formerly it was contemporary music that was played while earlier composers went out of fashion and their music was forgotten. Thus after his death in 1750, Bach fell into oblivion for the better part of a century until Mendelssohn and Schumann revived him. Before long, current fashion caught up with Bach, who was re-arranged to sound like Brahms. By 1900 the *Bach Gesellschaft* had completed its sixty-volume edition after working for half a century on the scholarly restoration of the authentic texts.

In our century the development of musicology has made faithful reproduction of the classics a major objective. The public has undeniably come a long way in its regard for good music, and no one should resent or deprecate our musical awakening. Indeed few would have predicted it four or five decades ago. But, because we are intoxicated with the progress of public interest in serious music, we are apparently blind to the fact that in some areas the situation of the musician and the condition of music are still poor—perhaps worse than they were before. By 1950, for example, the avant garde groups, which had been organized in the opulent twenties to perform new music before select audiences, had pretty much ceased concert activity. These were snobbish coteries, attended by some people just to be seen and thus numbered among the "select." But the ends justified snobbery. Dissolution of these groups resulted when the composers who were their leading spirits began to have their music disseminated by radio and phonograph, either because their manner was suitable to a mass medium or because they adapted their language to it. As a highly deplorable corollary to this development, the official organ of the League of Composers, *Modern Music*—for years the only domestic periodical devoted to expert and literate commentary on new music —was abandoned, leaving no substitute.

The need for specialized listening groups grows rather than decreases. Since public-supported concerts as we now know them have become common (not much more than a century ago), the cleavage between the public and the composer has widened considerably in some realms. Milton Babbitt presents the most uncompromising view of this condition:

> "The unprecedented divergence between contemporary serious music and its listeners, on the one hand, and traditional music and its following, on the other, is not accidental and—most probably—not transitory. Rather, it is a result of a half-century revolution in musical thought, a revolution whose nature and consequences can be compared only with, and in many respects are closely analogous to, those of the mid-nineteenth century revolution in mathematics and the twentieth century revolution in theoretical physics." [4]

Babbitt suggests that musicians who are occupied with advanced techniques be subsidized as scientists are, so that compositional research and test-performances of new works may be carried on within professional groups and for professional audiences.

Many people find this idea shocking since music is considered a social art. But let us recall a few landmarks from epochs when music was far less complex than it is now. No musical genre has more popular appeal than opera. Yet it was a small *Camerata* of savants and noblemen, meeting at the Florentine home of Count Bardi around 1600, whose lucubrations over a revival of Greek drama yielded a new fusion of music, poetry, and spectacle. In the eighteenth century the Esterhazys required the most menial servant in their employment to be qualified to play an instrument in an orchestra placed at Haydn's disposal. Still later, Wagner had grandiose aspirations that might never have been carried out without support from King Ludwig II of Bavaria.

The old system of private patronage, according to Mr. Shils, imposed "misery and humiliation" and was "capricious and irregular." I do not quarrel with this, but the public can be capricious, too, and more selfish. We still depend on patronage—foundation patronage—of a perhaps less capricious kind than that from vainglorious noblemen. But experts who determine foundation policy often seek to cut down those whom they benefit to their own size. Only a small part of foundation aid to music has gone to advanced causes: the Rockefeller Foundation subsidy of a Columbia-Princeton project for research in electronic music, for example, or the commissions of the gratifyingly unbureaucratic Fromm Music Foundation.

One may ask why expert performers cannot be assembled without subsidy to try out new works before the public is exposed to them. After all, the courageous innovations of atonality and twelve-tone music had the laboratory of the *Verein Für Musikalische Privataufführungen,* the private Viennese concerts after World War I, at which a handful of dedicated performers played the music of Schoenberg and his school for interested audiences.

The answer is that a strong American union has established good fees for the instrumentalist, while radio and recording lure him with more work than he has time to accept. The performance of advanced music requires more hours for its preparation, but the players have fewer to spare. The performer is normally more anxious to take advantage of the opportunities to earn a living than to donate his services. Private concerts are an ideal to be pursued. But in the climate of American prosperity, even if they are exclusively restricted to chamber music, private concerts must be heavily endowed.

The increased cost of preparing advanced music makes it difficult to include such music on programs of a major American orchestra whose annual budget runs as high as two or three million dollars. One such orchestra has only about twelve hours to rehearse its weekly program. Performances of some highly demanding new works have been cancelled because funds for an extra rehearsal were unavailable. It is difficult to justify an increase in the orchestra's deficit by around $1,500 (the cost of an added three-hour rehearsal) when most subscribers will find the new work objectionable anyway. But even if this were not the case, a conductor must spend most of his time re-polishing standard works on his program, for the public and critics will be alert to the slightest mishap in their performance. A new work is fortunate if it receives a few hours of rehearsal, scarcely enough time for the orchestra to grasp it, with no time at all for polishing. Mishaps in execution will be attributed to the composer.

The extent to which long-playing records redeem new American composers is easily exaggerated. Soaring LP and paper-back sales are often viewed as symptoms of a cultural upswing. However, the American composers recorded are usually those who have already made some impression at concerts. This is almost entirely true in symphonic and operatic music. Record companies spare huge costs by taking advantage of preparations for public performances. The normal procedure is to assemble the orchestra in the studio soon after the concert. Recording engineers can proceed directly to tape the results.

True, record catalogues today contain a much wider range of offerings than they did two or three decades ago. In anticipation of its hundredth issue (April 1958), which roughly coincided with the launching of stereo and the tenth anniversary of LP, the *Schwann Long Playing Catalog* contained some interesting statistics. For example, the March issue of the Catalog listed 303 labels in contrast to eleven in the first issue (Oct. 1949).[5] Since LP records are cheaper to make and mail than the old 78 rpm's, small record manufacturing companies have sprung up in profusion in recent years. Incapable of competing with the major companies, for which high-priced celebrities make multiple versions of the same standard works, new companies promote themselves with contemporary and pre-classical works previously absent from the catalogue. In a hundred issues of *Schwann*, the number of serious American composers listed rose from four to over one hundred and fifty. [6]

Statistics of this order have led some observers to conclude that recordings offer more opportunity to American composers than do concerts. But the correlation of record and concert repertory is a knotty statistical problem that has yet to be solved. Annual surveys of American concert programs count orchestral works which, because of the costs involved, comprise a small portion of recorded American music. Most American composers in the catalogue are credited with chamber music or brief choral pieces. A more convincing comparison between concert and recording gains would have to be made by collating, genre by genre and year by year, the American works publicly performed with those added to the record catalogue.

Even so, numerical results would not be altogether reliable. The amount of truly advanced American music on records is small—smaller, I suspect, than the amount heard at concerts. To be sure, the advantages of hearing this music over and over when it is recorded are incalculable. But except in occasional cases of special subsidy, the record industry takes its cue from concert life, and eighteenth and nineteenth century music far outweighs all other music played on records or in the concert hall. The *Schwann Catalogue* of March 1958 had 868 listings for Mozart, which is almost twice the number of listings for all living serious American composers. [7]

Advanced European music fares somewhat better on domestic records, as exemplified by the very welcome album of Webern's complete works. We pay lip-service to the claim that American music has "come of age," but we still bow to European initiative. The fact that Elliott Carter's commanding String Quartet (1951) won first prize in a Belgian competition of 1953 played no small role in catapulting him into a well-earned position of eminent musical statesman. Firmly established as one of a handful of the most recognized American composers of intellectual distinction, he now commands infinite respect from young men in the universities, who have become consecrated exegetes of his complex scores.

Yet Carter remains a musician's composer. The larger public is scarcely aware of him. American symphony orchestras have played little of his music, although they doubtless will play him before long. Meanwhile, however, his prestige among the informed demonstrates that an American composer can still make a solid reputation without the benediction of a mass audience. But, since it becomes increasingly difficult for him to do so on his own, the environment within which he carries on his advanced work must be subsidized.

In *Conversations with Igor Stravinsky*, the interviewer, Robert Craft, asks: "While composing do you ever think of an audience? Is there such a thing as a problem of communication?" Stravinsky responds (italics mine):

> "When I compose something, I cannot conceive that it should fail to be recognized for what it is, and understood. I use the language of music, and my statement in my grammar will be clear to the musician *who has followed music up to where my contemporaries and I have brought it.*" [8]

Stravinsky has adapted his methods lately to advanced serial techniques as developed, in particular, by Webern. If concert and radio programs as well as sales of advanced music on records are taken as indices, a very small percentage of the mass public (measured in six or seven figures) follows this kind of music. Even Schoenberg's half-century old "Five Pieces for Orchestra" which antedates twelve-tone practice is rarely played. When it is, the average listener still finds it very "far out."

The argument that the artist is obliged to communicate directly to the public fails to recognize that the sources for renewal of the popular arts have always been the discoveries of serious art. Without these sources the popular arts languish. The results of research in advanced music frequently seep down into wider channels of communication. We may observe this process in the use of atonal music as background for TV mysteries and the occasional exploitation of twelve-tone devices in jazz. If practical justification for subsidy of this research is necessary, here is certainly a cogent one.

Subsidy is not likely to come from any of the three most important groups involved in the mass commnication of music: audience, managers, and performers. The audience is content with its traditional music and with the accessible contemporary works that will continue to be written even if advanced music is more extensively subsidized. Profits of the managers are predicated on audience preference. The most problematic figure in the triumvirate is the performer. Even if he is offered compensation for preparing difficult new music, he may prefer to earn a living taxing his abilities less by playing music with which he is familiar. It is the rare performer, usually a youthful one, who will sacrifice himself for the advanced composer. The word "sacrifice" does not refer to technical difficulty alone. The increased determinacy in much advanced music, where every nuance is prescribed, limits the interpreter's capacity to convey his individuality.

The gap between performance technique and the precise requirements of this music has been one of the motivations for developing electronic music. A machine for synthesizing sounds directly from sound wave formations allows a composer to realize his conception completely, without the intermediary of human interpreters. It will be some time before any but a few composers are equipped to cope with the electronic machine, but its possibilities are limitless. To many people they are also frightening—especially the prospect of a machine replacing human musicians. However, photography did not replace painting, and it is likely that mechanical and humanly performed music will exist side by side, somewhat as those two arts do. [9]

As a matter of fact, some of the very musicians who compose with the precise values of the electronic machine have developed a related style based on indeterminacy. Indeterminacy, among other things, allows performers to complete the composer's process of creation by making their own choices. It is distantly related to jazz improvisation or to pre-nineteenth century improvisation in the execution of serious music.

From these examples it may be gathered that the avant garde is developing trends virtually unknown to the American mass public, since even recording has not caught up with them. One new trend, which may be added to those mentioned, will not even lend itself to reasonably faithful reproduction until multiple speakers (not simply two, as in stereo) become common in the home. I refer to the use of several small orchestras or instrumental groups (*Gruppen*) placed around the audience and playing at once from all directions.

Because of government subsidy of the arts, these trends receive more encouragement in Europe than they do here; and erudite journals abroad analyze them carefully. In America the prospect of government subsidy for the arts carries an aura of totalitarianism, while foundation subsidy is considered more democratic. [10] However this may be, it is urgent that the disparity between the substantial subsidies allocated for specialized study in the sciences and the insignificant amounts granted advanced musical composition be eliminated. The unexpected success of serious music (some of it contemporary) in America should not be taken as an assurance that all levels can prosper on their own. If American musical creativity is to avoid stagnation, we must examine this success more closely and ask, as Joseph Wood Krutch has, "Is the Good always the friend of the Best or is it sometimes and somehow its enemy?"[11]

REFERENCES

1 See *Charles Ives and His Music*, Henry and Sidney Cowell (New York; Oxford University Press, 1955).

2 See *Aaron Copland*, Arthur Berger, New York, 1953, pp. 26-33 and 57 ff.

3 From "Creativity in America," the Blashfield Address, delivered May 28, 1952 before the American Academy of Arts and Letters and the National Institute of Arts and Letters.

4 "Who Cares If You Listen?" *High Fidelity Magazine*, February, 1958, p. 38 ff.

5 Statistics from 1958 are used here to present the most generous picture. Since publication of the hundredth issue of *Schwann*, record companies have dropped numerous monaural listings as a result of the advent of stereo. Naturally, esoteric music has been the first to suffer.

6 An approximate figure is given because what precisely constitutes a "serious American composer" is open to interpretation.

7 A "listing" is not necessarily one record, since some records may be listed more than once.

8 *Conversations with Igor Stravinsky*, New York, 1959, p. 14.

9 Allen Forte "Composing with Electronics in Cologne" *High Fidelity Magazine*, October 1956, p. 64 ff.

10 I have touched briefly upon a House committee's attitude toward federal aid to the arts on p. 70 of *The Atlantic*, July, 1958, in an article ("Music for Nothing: The Cost of Composing") that relates the composer's large expenditures for preparing orchestral materials to the poor returns from performance.

11 "Is Our Common Man Too Common?" *The Saturday Review*, January 11, 1953, p. 9.

Mass Culture and the Creative Artist

Some Personal Notes

SOMEONE once said to me that the people in general cannot bear very much reality. He meant by this that they prefer fantasy to a truthful re-creation of their experience. The Italians, for example, during the time that De Sica and Rossellini were revitalizing the Italian cinema industry, showed a marked preference for Rita Hayworth vehicles; the world in which she moved across the screen was like a fairy tale, whereas the world De Sica was describing was one with which they were only too familiar. (And it can be suggested perhaps that the Americans who stood in line for *Shoe Shine* and *Open City* were also responding to images which they found exotic, to a reality by which they were not threatened. What passes for the appreciation of serious effort in this country is very often nothing more than an inability to take anything very seriously.)

Now, of course the people cannot bear very much reality, if by this one means their ability to respond to high intellectual or artistic endeavor. I have never in the least understood why they should be expected to. There is a division of labor in the world—as I see it— and the people have quite enough reality to bear, simply getting through their lives, raising their children, dealing with the eternal conundrums of birth, taxes, and death. They do not do this with all the wisdom, foresight, or charity one might wish; nevertheless, this is what they are always doing and it is what the writer is always describing. There is literally nothing else to describe. This effort at description is itself extraordinarily arduous, and those who are driven to make this effort are by virtue of this fact somewhat removed from the people. It happens, by no means infrequently, that the people hound or stone them to death. They then build

162

statues to them, which does not mean that the next artist will have it any easier.

I am not sure that the cultural level of the people is subject to a steady rise: in fact, quite unpredictable things happen when the bulk of the population attains what we think of as a high cultural level, i.e., pre-World War II Germany, or present-day Sweden. And this, I think, is because the effort of a Schönberg or a Picasso (or a William Faulkner or an Albert Camus) has nothing to do, at bottom, with physical comfort, or indeed with comfort of any other kind. But the aim of the people who rise to this high cultural level—who rise, that is, into the middle class—is precisely comfort for the body and the mind. The artistic objects by which they are surrounded cannot possibly fulfill their original function of disturbing the peace —which is still the only method by which the mind can be improved —they bear witness instead to the attainment of a certain level of economic stability and a certain thin measure of sophistication. But art and ideas come out of the passion and torment of experience; it is impossible to have a real relationship to the first if one's aim is to be protected from the second.

We cannot possibly expect, and should not desire, that the great bulk of the populace embark on a mental and spiritual voyage for which very few people are equipped and which even fewer have survived. They have, after all, their indispensable work to do, even as you and I. What we are distressed about, and should be, when we speak of the state of mass culture in this country, is the over-whelming torpor and bewilderment of the people. The people who run the mass media are not all villains and they are not all cowards —though I agree, I must say, with Dwight Macdonald's forceful sug-gestion that many of them are not very bright. (Why should they be? They, too, have risen from the streets to a high level of cultural attainment. They, too, are positively afflicted by the world's highest standard of living and what is probably the world's most bewilder-ingly empty way of life.) But even those who are bright are handi-capped by their audience: I am less appalled by the fact that *Gunsmoke* is produced than I am by the fact that so many people want to see it. In the same way, I must add, that a thrill of terror runs through me when I hear that the favorite author of our Presi-dent is Zane Grey.

But one must make a living. The people who run the mass media and those who consume it are really in the same boat. They must continue to produce things they do not really admire, still less, love,

College of Arts & Technology
The South East Essex

in order to continue buying things they do not really want, still less, need. If we were dealing only with fintails, two-tone cars, or programs like *Gunsmoke*, the situation would not be so grave. The trouble is that serious things are handled (and received) with the same essential lack of seriousness.

For example: neither *The Bridge On the River Kwai* nor *The Defiant Ones*, two definitely superior movies, can really be called serious. They are extraordinarily interesting and deft: but their principal effort is to keep the audience at a safe remove from the experience which these films are not therefore really prepared to convey. The kind of madness sketched in *Kwai* is far more dangerous and widespread than the movie would have us believe. As for *The Defiant Ones*, its suggestion that Negroes and whites can learn to love each other if they are only chained together long enough runs so madly counter to the facts that it must be dismissed as one of the latest, and sickest, of the liberal fantasies, even if one does not quarrel with the notion that love on such terms is desirable. These movies are designed not to trouble, but to reassure; they do not reflect reality, they merely rearrange its elements into something we can bear. They also weaken our ability to deal with the world as it is, ourselves as we are.

What the mass culture really reflects (as is the case with a "serious" play like *J.B.*) is the American bewilderment in the face of the world we live in. We do not seem to want to know that we are *in* the world, that we are subject to the same catastrophes, vices, joys, and follies which have baffled and afflicted mankind for ages. And this has everything to do, of course, with what was expected of America: which expectation, so generally disappointed, reveals something we do not want to know about sad human nature, reveals something we do not want to know about the intricacies and inequities of any social structure, reveals, in sum, something we do not want to know about ourselves. The American way of life has failed—to make people happier or to make them better. We do not want to admit this, and we do not admit it. We persist in believing that the empty and criminal among our children are the result of some miscalculation in the formula (which can be corrected), that the bottomless and aimless hostility which makes our cities among the most dangerous in the world is created, and felt, by a handful of aberrants, that the lack, yawning everywhere in this country, of passionate conviction, of personal authority, proves only our rather appealing tendency to be gregarious and democratic. We are very cruelly trapped between what we would like to be, and what we actually are. And we cannot possibly become what we would like to be until we are willing to ask ourselves just why the lives we lead on this continent are mainly so empty, so tame and so ugly.

This is a job for the creative artist—who does not really have much to do with mass culture, no matter how many of us may be interviewed on TV. Perhaps life is not the black, unutterably beautiful, mysterious, and lonely thing the creative artist tends to think of it as being; but it is certainly not the sunlit playpen in which so many Americans lose first their identities and then their minds.

I feel very strongly, though, that this amorphous people are in desperate search for something which will help them to re-establish their connection with themselves, and with one another. This can only begin to happen as the truth begins to be told. We are in the middle of an immense metamorphosis here, a metamorphosis which will, it is devoutly to be hoped, rob us of our myths and give us our history, which will destroy our attitudes and give us back our personalities. The mass culture, in the meantime, can only reflect our chaos: and perhaps we had better remember that this chaos contains life—and a great transforming energy.

STANLEY EDGAR HYMAN

Ideals, Dangers, and Limitations of Mass Culture

THE TERM "CULTURE" creates initial difficulties, I think. For Matthew Arnold it meant "the study of harmonious perfection" through the arts and the humanities. A character in a recent dialogue on the subject defines it as "the realm of art, manners, and morals." For the Soviet Russians and some of our own middle class, it appears to mean restrained public behavior, so that a noisy drunk in Moscow or Scarsdale is "uncultured." All of these uses, including the present one (which I think we get from the sociologists), are invidious, suggesting that culture is a good thing to have and that not everyone has it. For this reason, among others, some of us now try to confine the term to its usage in modern anthropology, where it means the whole of the non-biological inheritance, and is not invidious at all, since everyone partakes of it. For the subject of our present discussion, I should prefer "the popular arts" or "the mass arts." Since terms have agreed-on rather than innate meanings, however, there is no reason why we cannot agree to use "culture" here in the more limited sense of the popular arts and entertainments, use it consistently, and know what we mean when we say it.

Since I am in the position of proposing some tentative evaluations, I rely on earlier participants in the discussion to deal with the origins, nature, and functions of mass culture, to explore the problems of its producers and consumers, and to analyze the ingredients. I shall confine myself to a hasty survey of some current trends in the mass arts, choosing examples simply as they come to mind, following it with an attempt at some conclusions and a suggested role, or roles, for the critic.

In my own experience, the technological revolution is most visible, and perhaps most hopeful, in two areas, books and records. In books,

166

it is dramatically the rise of the paperback in the past two decades. At present some six thousand titles from about ninety companies are available, in fairly attractive and readable form, at prices ranging from twenty-five cents to two-ninety-five and averaging about a dollar. Among them are such coterie books as *Finnegans Wake* and Jane Harrison's *Prolegomena to the Study of Greek Religion.* According to figures Clifton Fadiman recently published in the *Herald-Tribune,* *Waiting for Godot* has sold almost 100,000 copies, *The Lonely Crowd* over 300,000, *Patterns of Culture* over three-quarters of a million, *Catcher in the Rye* over a million. Not all of them sell that well, however. I understand that the selected poetry and prose of one of America's foremost living poets has sold fewer than ten thousand copies in paperback. Salacity apparently sells best, as in hardcover publishing, and *Peyton Place* and *God's Little Acre,* books of very different degrees of seriousness but equal salaciousness, share the paperback sales record at eight million each. Still, the audience for books, many of them good ones, has increased enormously, and with it the income of writers, along with the income of composers of science fiction and historical novels.

The other striking trend in current publishing is the mass marketing of remainders, and the related transformation of book clubs into discount houses, less interested in sponsoring a monthly selection than in furnishing almost any book at a reduction. Remainders are sold at prices comparable to those of paperbacks, with many under a dollar, and the clubs supply something like two books for the retail price of one. Readers priced out of the market by the high retail cost of books are thus priced back in again, at the expense of the author, whose royalty ranges from none, in the case of remainders, to a smaller percentage in the case of the book clubs. He is allowed to console himself with a greater public for his art, and can buy copies to give to his friends very cheaply. Other trends in publishing are less dramatic. I have written elsewhere about what it is convenient to call "pseudo-fictions," the increasing number of non-fictions disguised as works of the imagination and published as novels. The absence of any market whatsoever for most volumes of new poetry published in our time seems to me the single most depressing feature of current publishing, although now as always there are brave and ingenious efforts to remedy it, ranging from binding poets in bunches like carrots to a revival of pamphlet publishing. Almost equally depressing has been the progessive debasement of The Modern Library under Bennett Cerf. No one who remembers the early list, where one first discovered de Gourmont, Andreyev, or George Moore, can welcome without writhing such current classics as Damon Runyon, Daphne du Maurier, James A. Michener, or Kaufman and Hart. Even Everyman's Library, which one would have thought immune to such stock-watering, recently replaced Sir Arthur Keith's scholarly introduction to its edition of *The Origin of Species* with an incoherent and spiteful introduction by a Canadian biological control official. He rejects the book, its arguments, and the whole theory of evolution by natural selection, on grounds that at first pretend to be scientific but soon emerge as supernaturalist.

The invention of tape-recording and long-playing records, with their booming production and sales, may turn out to be an even greater cultural revolution than paperbacks, and tapes and LPs have certainly done more for poetry than any form of publishing. Here literally hundreds of companies, some no larger than a label, produce countless thousands of records, making a wide variety of music available everywhere, and stimulating a growing demand for live music outside its familiar centers. Technically, in high-fidelity and stereophonic sound, the reproduced sound is of a quality and range unimaginable two decades ago. About the classic repertoire I am not competent to speak, although I am familiar with complaints that such favorites as Beethoven's Fifth Symphony are available in two dozen versions while relatively obscure music is still not available in one. About folk music and jazz I can speak with somewhat more authority. A single company, Folkways, has issued several hundred records of folk music, some of it as exotic and unlikely as *Eskimo Music of Alaska and the Hudson Bay* or *Temiar Dream Songs from Malaya*, and it is possible for anyone with the price to have a collection that could not have been matched by any of the world's great archives a generation ago. To take the example of an individual singer: Cynthia Gooding, who seems to me the most talented and exciting of American folk singers, if certainly not the best-known, has in a few years' time recorded almost a hundred songs, from a dozen different national traditions, on seven long-playing records. Not long ago, a lucky world traveler with an interest in such matters could hear that many folksongs in a busy lifetime.

The case of jazz is a more complex one because of its status as America's contribution to the world's arts, and its international-relations aspects, with jazz conventions in Melbourne, combos in every Swedish high school, and jazz magazines published in Tokyo and Reykjavik. In the indescribable welter of jazz records, to my taste the great single contribution, rivaling that of Folkways in folk music, is the achievement of Riverside in reissuing old Paramount and Gennett "race" records on LPs, restoring to the world such obscure masterpieces as Jabo Williams playing and singing *Fat Mama Blues*. The future of jazz is endlessly debated by the archaizers, who argue that the way King Oliver played in 1922 is the way jazz must be played, and the progressivists, who believe the comparable fallacy that arts improve as they develop, and that the latest is thus necessarily the best.

It would be pointless to enter into this controversy, but it should be noted that the Negro folk form from which jazz derived, the vocal blues, seems to be far from extinct. In the raucous and travestied form of rock 'n' roll, it is again a mass art, and along with its uneducated white audience has an uneducated Negro audience singularly uninterested in Dixieland jazz (the educated Negro audience seems largely to have turned to modern jazz). The case of the singer who calls herself Odetta is a significant one, and she is a phenomenon some of us have been predicting for many years. Her voice is in the great line of Negro blues voices stretching from "Ma" Rainey and Bessie Smith to Mahalia Jackson, but she belongs to the first Negro generation so cut off from its folk roots as to be unfamiliar with the blues tradition, and she sings blues as though she had learned them at a German conservatory. Odetta may herald the eventual death of the blues, but the example of Jimmy Rushing, who after many years as an unexceptional vocalist for the Basie band has suddenly emerged, in a handful of recent records, as a blues singer as pure and powerful as any of the great pioneers, suggests that the death may be a long time coming.

After books and records, I speak more tentatively about other mass arts. Where the vulgarity of radio takes the form of the familiar soap operas and the endless monotonous popular tunes, the vulgarity of television takes new and amazing forms: blindfolded contestants taking lobsters out of a pail with their bare feet, learned panels competing in discovering which of three high school girls wrote an inane song hit, a popular program testing the broadmindedness of wives by giving a married man a young actress to take home with him. Where the value of radio lies in the good music and in such public services as Edward R. Murrow's famous investigation of the call girl as an industrial consultant, the achievements of television seem harder to characterize, and perhaps I should leave the problem to better-informed discussants. In a decade it has given this observer a chance to see: the great clown A. Robins before his death, the hands of gangsters during the Kefauver investigation, some memorable sporting events and old films, and Mort Sahl saying things that seemed to me more often true and disconcerting than funny. The commercials are hard on the ears but appear to be of considerable cultural interest. One in which Lestoil emulsifies villainous Dirt is probably the only survivor of the *agitprop* drama of the twenties, in which the characters were called Worker and Capitalist. I know several people who found the events of the last World Series less interesting than a commercial they waited for in which a portly batter or golfer, on behalf of a ball-point pen reputed not to skip, swung impotently at the ball and cursed in engaging doubletalk.

I suspect that the art film and the documentary are past their peak, at least in this country, and that if the American film has a future apart from television it continues to lie with Hollywood. I get my look at the New Hollywood mostly from such reporting as Dwight Mac-Donald's in *Esquire*, from which I quote:

> Jerry Wald, a dark, plump, baldish, cigar-chewing type who talks rapidly and freely on any topic, was also full of cultural optimism. His walls were lined with Roualt prints and other O.K. modern art products, and he was just beginning a major production of Faulkner's *The Sound and the Fury*. "Mass audiences are hep now," he said. "There are twenty-five million college graduates. There's no such thing as highbrow and lowbrow any more. They get the best TV and radio shows. They can appreciate quality. I'm gonna do Lawrence's *Sons and Lovers* next and I just bought *Winesburg*." I suggested that *Ulysses* would make a splendid movie. "I got an option on it!" he replied instantly, adding: "It's basically just a father searching for a son. Universal theme!"

My own experience with the New Hollywood as a moviegoer suggests that the principal new boldness is a more pervasive homosexual imagery, whether used to add resonances to serious meaning, as in the ending of *The Defiant Ones*, or played for laughs, as in the transvestite comedy *Some Like It Hot*. Certainly the eye-catching deformity of such stars as Jayne Mansfield seems the same sort of satire on heterosexuality that Mae West used to represent.

The encouraging renaissance of the drama, off-Broadway and throughout the country, probably does not have the proportions of mass culture, and perhaps the living drama no longer can. These matters are relative, however, and the enormous widening of the audience for such coterie playwrights as Beckett, Genêt, and Ionesco is surely relevant to a discussion of mass culture. Off-Broadway is analogous to paperbacks and remainders as a device for again getting the product to an audience that had been priced out of the market, while Broadway, like hardcover publishing, finds costs so high that it must aim at surefire hits. This formula theatre produces something like Lindsay and Crouse's *Tall Story* from Howard Nemerov's superior novel *The Homecoming Game*, and in the realm of the musical, the world of decline and fall between Rodgers and Hart and Rogers and Hammerstein.

Our older mass arts, the newspaper and magazine, do not seem to be thriving. A. J. Liebling in *The New Yorker* and Francis Williams in *The New Statesman* and *Nation* echo and reinforce each other's plaints about the shrinkage of newspaper competition and the increasing substitution of syndicated boilerplate for independent and regional journalism. The genuine new art form that American newspapers produced, the comic strip, has mostly given way to adventure serials in outer space, and the few archaic survivors simply rehash their stock jokes. The audience for little magazines and literary quarterlies must be substantial, judging by their number, but no single magazine is apparently able to tap enough of it to be economically viable (perhaps the same few thousand people buy all the magazines). For the rest, each of the commercial magazines that has survived the competition of television seems to have found its formula, its precise stratum of intelligence and taste (or status and buying-power), and to be hewing to it far more rigorously than magazines did a generation ago. I for one find the resolute middlebrow coloration of the journals of liberal opinion like *The Nation* and *The New Republic,* or of such cultural journals as *Harper's* and *Saturday Review,* worse than the slicks, and there is a distastefulness to the semi-commitment of people like Maxwell Geismar and John Ciardi that the non-commitment or wrong-commitment of the *Time-Life-Fortune* writers cannot equal. Below this level, on the newsstands, there is an infernal world one can hardly enter: magazines with one-syllable names full of comic drawings designed to give the purchaser a headache; magazines with two-syllable names consisting of naked girls and filler, like burlesque in its decline, when it ran movies to get the audiences out; magazines and comic books with no fixed names where you can live vicariously as a teen-age pusher or let a giant Martian have it right in the belly.

The technological revolution does not yet seem to have brought the plastic and pictorial arts into mass culture, except for the art of design, which has taken us all from tubular steel and plush to molded plywood and plastic in my short lifetime. Mass-produced copies of pictures and sculpture have been around for a long time, and make all but the most contemporary work cheaply available in reproduction, but they seem to have had little of the impact on taste of paperbacks and long-playing records. I know some high thinkers who will not have copies of pictures or sculpture in their houses, although they have plenty of paperbacks and records, and I think it has something to do with the fact that there is a better original around somewhere, as there is not, in any realistic sense, with books and records. If the people who paint by numbers buy Braque and Klee reproductions, what they paint continues to be traditional landscapes and vases of flowers. An unlikely collaboration between the Metropolitan Museum and the Book-of-the-Month Club, formerly engaged in marketing tiny reproductions, is now engaged in marketing "Art Seminars in the Home," which will delve into such dangerous matters as the Expressionism of van Gogh and the abstraction of Picasso, but the lag seems enormous. Perhaps the true effect of modern painting and architecture, at least, on mass culture is in their filtering down into design, so that people who would not live in a house by Le Corbusier now have a blendor that looks just like one, and their place mats might be Pollocks.

I lack space to deal with those aspects of mass culture that are more properly entertainments than arts, among them sport, religion, hobbies, education, and politics. Some of them are very closely involved with the communication arts. If television has helped in the sordid commercialization of baseball and has largely killed boxing, it has done wonders for the entertainment value of politics and may remake education, if you can get up that early. As for the sort of religion that competes with sport on Sunday, no mass art is alien to it: it writes the best-sellers, blesses the song hits, and tops any secular showmanship. The new soft slogans of peace rather than a sword, and works without faith, have been sold to America like a detergent. *This Week* recently conducted a poll on "Pick the Sermon You'd Like to Hear," and the six leading choices, in order, were:

How Can I Make Prayer More Effective?
How to Increase Religious Faith
How Can I Make the Greatest Contribution in Life?
Happier Families Through Religion
How Can Religion Eliminate Worry and Tension?
What Can the Individual Do for World Peace?
Perhaps mass culture's final answer to its own importunities is the

do-it-yourself hobby, or turn off everything, go down into the cellar alone, and build a catboat.

If these are some of the visible trends of mass culture, what do they suggest of its ideals, dangers, and limitations? In my opinion, the most important ideal is pluralism, making a wide variety of aesthetic goods available, rather than lifting us all half an inch by the great collective bootstrap. That is why paperbacks and long-playing records seem so hopeful a tendency despite their defects; *Marjorie Morningstar* and *Witch Doctor* are available in their millions, but *The Philosophy of Literary Form* and *Don Giovanni* (not to speak of *Fat Mama Blues*) are available in their thousands. Even the magazine situation is dreary and discouraging but still triumphantly pluralist; there is a magazine, however tiny, subsidized, or absurd, to publish every kind of writing, to furnish any sort of reading or looking (within the limits of the law) that any few readers or lookers want. One has only to compare the situation with England, which has one little magazine to every fifty of ours, or with Russia, which has not had one since Mayakovsky's day, to see the virtues of pluralism. It is only when the expenses of production become prohibitive, with a newspaper or film company, a radio or television station, that a wide variety of aesthetic goods becomes impossible, and only ventures that will satisfy many thousands or millions are feasible. Then it is necessary to talk of improving standards, raising levels, educating public taste, taking the initiative for better quality, and such functions more proper to a benign tyranny than to our anarchic cultural democracy.

The second ideal, about which I am somewhat more dubious but still hopeful, is the natural evolution of taste, given a variety of possibilities. (In other words, it depends on pluralism, although pluralism, as a good in itself, would make sense even if taste were known to be static.) This is the assumption that a certain number of those who read and enjoy *The Subterraneans* will go to read, and prefer, *The Possessed;* that some will comparably graduate from rock 'n' roll to traditional blues. This naturally happens at school age (although not in every case), and the ideal assumes its happening at every age. Here the evidence is rather mixed. William Phillips, in an article in *Partisan Review* (Winter 1959) describes the question as "the old senseless argument about whether a man who listens to popular tunes has taken the first step to Schönberg." This may, however, be a very important question for the future of our culture.

A decade ago the Book-of-the-Month Club sent around a circular listing its selections from 1926, the year of its founding, to 1949. The circular clearly made the point (which I do not think it was designed to make) that these had worsened annually, from books like Sylvia Townsend Warner's *Lolly Willowes* and Elinor Wylie's *Orphan Angel* in 1926 to Frances Gaither's *Double Muscadine* and the Gilbreths' *Cheaper by the Dozen* in 1949. Over the decade since, despite (or because of) the presence of such learned fellows as Gilbert Highet on the board of judges, the selections seem to have continued to deteriorate. If someone had subscribed and taken the selections over the past thirty years, *his* taste would not have evolved onward and upward. But the turnover is very high; how could we find out about those who learned to read books for pleasure as subscribers, then resigned from the club to read better books on their own?

The BBC radio, with its three programs designed for three levels of taste, would seem a perfect device for encouraging this sort of cultural mobility. Yet I wonder what percentage of listeners of mature years graduated from family comedy on the Light to sea chanteys on the Home to translations of Bulgarian poetry on the Third? How many slid slowly downward? Now, unfortunately, the Third has been curtailed, and with the increased cost of television production and a competing commercial channel, it has not been possible for the BBC to set up anything of the sort for television. Here for the first time some planned range of availability was created in a mass medium, but we know too little about its cultural results.

The third ideal of mass culture I take from a letter Patrick D. Hazard wrote to me in 1958 in connection with some remarks I had published about the ironic mode. He wrote: "Now it seems to me that a great many intellectuals in America have achieved a viable irony, but I wonder how the great mass who are no longer folk and not yet people can find a footing for their ironic stance. Do any of the following seem to you footholds?" He then proceeded to list such newer comic performers as Mort Sahl and Jonathan Winters, such older comic performers as Groucho Marx and Fred Allen, and such miscellaneous phenomena as Al Capp, *The Threepenny Opera*, and *Humbug* magazine. His comment on the list was: "These things seem to question in one way or another some aspect of flatulence in popular culture, its sentimentality, fake elegance, phony egalitarianism, or its perennial playpen atmosphere."

I did not know the answer to the question then and do not know it now, but I present Hazard's question and comment to raise the possibility of a third ideal. This is that mass culture throws up its own criticism, in performers of insight, wit, and talent, and in forms of irony and satire, to enable some of the audience to break through it into a broader or deeper set of aesthetic values. Again, I much prefer this sort of evolutionary possibility to types of patronizing enlightenment. We do well to be wary when a *Time* editor like Thomas Griffith writes *The Waist-High Culture* to ask whether we haven't sold our souls "for a mess of pottage that goes snap, crackle, and pop," or television producer David Susskind tells *Life*:

> I'm an intellectual who cares about television. There are some good things on it, tiny atolls in the oceans of junk. . . . You get mad at what you really care about—like your wife. I'm mad at TV because I really love it and it's lousy. It's a very beautiful woman who looks abominable. The only way to fix it is to clean out the pack who are running it and put in some brainy guys.

We assume that if Griffith ran *Time* it would crackle less, that Susskind is the sort of brainy lover TV needs. I would sooner rest my hopes in Groucho Marx, who does not describe himself as an intellectual, or the late Fred Allen, who had a cleansing bitterness and despair about the media themselves, and wasn't campaigning for David Sarnoff's job. If there are such footings as Hazard suggests for an ironic stance in mass culture, let them not crusade under our feet.

The dangers of mass culture are much easier to define than the ideas. The foremost one, which may negate all the ideals, is an overpowering narcotic effect, relaxing the tired mind and tranquilizing the anxious. Genuine art is demanding and difficult, often unpleasant, nagging at the mind and stretching the nerves taut. So much of mass culture envelops the audience in a warm bath, making no demands except that we all glow with pleasure and comfort. It is this that may negate the range of possibility (the bath is pleasanter at the shallow end), keep taste static or even deteriorate it a little, muffle the few critical and ironic sounds being made. That premature cultural critic Homer knew all about this effect, at various times calling it Lotus Eaters, Calypso, Circe, and the Sirens, and he just barely got our hero through intact.

An obvious source of danger is the cults. In one direction we have the cult of the folk. Some ten years ago I published an article called "The American Folksy" in *Theatre Arts* (April 1949), protesting that we were being overwhelmed by an avalanche of pseudo-folk corn. I turn out not to have been very prophetic. What I then took to be the height of something like the great tulip craze can now be seen to have been only the first tentative beginnings of something so vast and offensive that it dwarfs historical parallels. I named half a dozen folksy singers of the time, but could not have guessed that a decade later there would be hundreds if not thousands, that magazines would be devoted to guitar and banjo styles, that the production of washtub basses would be an American industry. I certainly could not have predicted Elvis Presley. I mention this failure of imagination now only to explain why the ramifying vertical combine that lives by falsifying America's cultural past seems to me a major deterrent to any of the hopes for mass culture.

Opposed to the cult of the folk, which identifies (however falsely) with a tradition, and blows hot, or passionate, is the cult of the hip which denies (however falsely) having any tradition, and blows cool. (At the juvenile end it tells sick jokes, glorying in the impassivity of: "Mrs. Brown, can Johnny come out and play ball?" "But you children know he has no arms or legs." "That's O.K. We want to use him for second base.") At higher levels it admits wryly to Jules Feiffer's truths, professes Zen, or joins Norman Mailer in making what he called in *Dissent*,* "the imaginative journey into the tortured marijuana-racked mind and genitalia of a hipster daring to live on the edge of the most dangerous of the Negro worlds." At this point, obviously, cool has become pretty hot, an outlaw folk tradition has been established, and perhaps both these polar cults are recognizable as the same sort of fantasy identification. To the extent that mass culture permits, encourages, and thrives on these adolescent gratifications, it is as spurious and mendacious as its harshest critics claim.

One more danger inherent in mass culture, and perhaps the most menacing one, is the existence of a captive audience with no escape. In regard to art, it is not much of a problem; many will sit through worse than they expected, and a few will sit through better than they desire. As a machinery for selling us consumer goods, using all the resources of a prostituted psychology and sociology, it becomes more menacing, although here too mass culture seems to throw up its counterstatements. Against a million voices stridently shouting "Buy!" the tiny neo-Thoreauvian voice of J. K. Galbraith whispers, "Reduce your wants," and is immediately amplified by a book club

* "The White Negro (Superficial Reflections on the Hipster)," *Dissent*, Summer 1957, 4:276-293.

and blurbs from a number of magazines that would not last a week if his advice were heeded. It is when the same technique is used to sell us politics that our status as a captive audience to mass media becomes menacing, an Eisenhower or a Nixon today but a Big Brother or a Big Daddy tomorrow.

At this point we are informed that the fashionable cult of New Conservatism, with its scorn for our worship of the mob and the mob's brittle toys, will save us, if only we elect to follow Burke and Calhoun instead of those demagogues Jefferson and Paine. The corrective here is reading the tribute to Roy Campbell that Russell Kirk published in *The Sewanee Review* (Winter 1956) and discovering that Kirk's heart's vision is not Edmund Burke orating nobly in the House of Commons, but Roy Campbell spanking a small, effeminate Marxist poet on a public lecture platform. In short, New Conservatism yearns masochistically for its fantasy storm troopers, and Kirk and his fellows are less the doctor than the disease.

Some of the limitations of mass culture have already been suggested. One absolute limitation is the Law of Raspberry Jam, that the wider you spread it the thinner it is. Another is the nature of art itself. As genuine art, advancing sensibility, stretching the limits of form, purifying the language of the tribe, it is always for an elite of education (which does not mean a formal education), sensibility, and taste. When its freshness has grown somewhat stale, diluted by imitators and popularizers, its audience widens, although if it is true art it will always continue to demand more than a mass audience cares to give it.

A special limitation, not inevitable and not universal, is the timidity of those in positions of authority in the mass media. Jerry Lewis, of all people, wrote in the *New York Times Magazine* for December 7, 1958:

Unfortunately, TV fell into the well-manicured hands of the Madison Avenue bully boys, who, awed by the enormousness of the monster, began to "run scared." They were easy prey for the new American weapon —the pressure group.

Steve Allen's reply in the same symposium suggests that we confront no simple matter of pressure or censorship, that here horses break themselves with alacrity and great civic responsibility. Allen writes:

There are, frankly, a few things I joke about in private that I do not touch upon on the air, but this implies no feeling of frustration. I realize that some tenets of my personal philosophy would antagonize the majority without educating them; hence, no good could come of experimenting with such subjects.

Matching the timidity of the producers is the ignorance of the consumers. Who knows what they might want if they knew what there was to want, if they knew what they didn't know? This again is a special and perhaps transitory limitation. As education spreads and leisure increases, some of our mass audiences may acquire, if not what we call "taste," at least a wider knowledge of cultural possibility. The well poisoner is an unlovely figure, but the responsibility of those poisoning *these* reservoirs from which millions drink is comparably greater. What defense has an ignorant and eager reader, buying *The Origin of Species* in the Everyman edition, against its introductory assurance that authoritative scientists no longer believe these things? He has scarcely heard of Darwin, how is he to know that W. R. Thompson is not the voice of modern science? If he happens to read T. H. Robsjohn-Gibbings' book attacking modern architecture and design, it is the confession of a contemporary designer to what he has always rather suspected; he is not apt to have encountered Mr. Robsjohn-Gibbings' hi-fi unit with Doric columns in a decorator's studio. Because it knows no better, in short, the mass audience is condemned to the fate of never knowing any better.

The final limitation of mass culture I would suggest is its tendency to sanctify the old, safe, and official. In his eighties, Robert Frost becomes poetry consultant to the Library of Congress and all America throbs to his absurd views about American painting and other matters. In his eighties, Carl Sandburg enthralls a joint session of Congress with a slushy eulogy to Lincoln. I quote what I take to be an innocent irony in the *Times* correspondent's account of the latter event:

> In its kindest of moods, Congress has little patience for poets, and normally it can scarcely sit still for Presidents or heads of foreign states. Mr. Sandburg, however, held them as they have not been held since General of the Army Douglas MacArthur's address to a joint session on April 19, 1951.

Any serious young American artist who could pack his audience into a closet (like young Robert Frost, who could not get his first book of verse published in this country), has the consolation of knowing that if he has the good fortune to live long enough he can become a Grand Old Man, and just at the time when he has nothing left to say a thicket of microphones and cameras will enable him to say it to the world.

We come finally to the matter of taking a stand or stands. Each of us confronts mass culture in a number of roles. My own include customer, parent, journalist, critic, teacher of literature. The role of teacher seems the best one from which to tackle the problem, since the college teacher of literature is not only assumed to be a custodian of traditional values, but must deal with the new values in his day-to-day contact with what students read and write. He cannot entirely ignore them or wash his hands of them. I would propose that there are at least six different things he must do about mass culture, varying with the quality and promise of the specimen involved, the differing needs of students, and his own needs and perhaps moods. I list them by the operative verbs, using literary examples as much as possible.

Reject. This is a traditional function of the critic of mass culture, and it can be performed in a variety of moods, from the high good fun of H. L. Mencken whacking one or another fatuosity of the boo-boisie to the owlish pomposity of recent *American Mercury* pundits. The best current example of rejection is Leslie Fiedler, who told a symposium at Columbia not long ago that the writer's proper role is a nay-saying and destructive one, that he should not hesitate to bite the hand which feeds him. Fiedler's slogan for Hollywood and TV was, "We must destroy their destructiveness." As a teacher, I would reserve this rejection for the real junk, Mickey Spillane and *Peyton Place.* Here, it seems to me, any sort of undercutting or resistance is legitimate, short of actually snatching the book out of the student's hands and pitching it into the garbage. Let the teacher rant and rave, appeal to his authority, the student's shame, or the ghost of Henry James. Let him expose and deride this pernicious trash in every way possible. The really hopeless is only a small percentage of the total output of mass culture, however, which allows the teacher to save some of his energy for other operations, and to contribute a small sum to a subscription to replace Leslie Fiedler's teeth when they wear out.

Embrace. This too is a traditional function, and we have had intellectual cults of the popular arts, of Chaplin or Keaton, Krazy Kat or Donald Duck, since there were popular arts. Reuel Denney's article on Pogo, reprinted in his book, *The Astonished Muse,* is a fine example of the passionate professorial embrace. Denney shows learnedly that the strip is "a study in the disintegration of the New Deal phase of the Democratic party," that "if the political stance of the strip is Democratic and Steffens-like, the literary stance is post-

Joycean, and the psychological stance is post-Freudian." Poor Albert Alligator becomes a parataxis of oral aggression, although at this point I begin to suspect that Denney is having a pull at the reader's leg. It was very shrewd of George P. Elliott to make his impossible sociologist in *Parktilden Village* the creator, as the result of his researches, of a cartoon strip that appealed to every cultural level. George Orwell was in something of this position, studying boys' books with loving attention, then himself writing a superior boys' book in *1984*, which sold its million copies in paperback. The products of mass culture one can wholeheartedly welcome and embrace are probably as small a percentage as those one ought wholeheartedly to reject. I would suggest such rare best-sellers as *Catcher in the Rye*, hovering on the edge of serious literature, such sparkling musical comedies as *Guys and Dolls* and *Pajama Game*, and comedians and comic strips to taste.

Ignore. This is perhaps more a teacher's dodge than any other. Several years ago at Bennington, David Riesman made some remarks (which I dare say he has since published) about the tyranny of the curricular. When he was an undergraduate, he said, his intellectual solace was that he could read Marx and Freud, which *they* (his teachers) didn't know about or didn't approve, and thus have an area of his mind and life that Harvard could not regiment. At a place like Bennington, he said, Marx and Freud would immediately be made the subject of courses, as would anything else in which the students showed interest.

I sat in the audience trying to get the arrow out of my throat, since that year I was teaching a course in Marx and Freud (along with Darwin and Frazer), and I had just organized a lively faculty seminar on rock 'n' roll, at which we told the students what it was all about. The only comfort I had was that however tyrannous the curricular, there was always *something* the students could block off privately; if they were being taught Marx and "Fats" Domino, perhaps they were pursuing Racine and Mozart on the sly. In any case, they had *some* underground culture the faculty would do best not to know about. I find this tactic of ignoring very useful in regard to West Coast poetry (I suspect that that book of verse called *Howl* circulates surreptitiously at Bennington, but I have never made any attempt to find out), in regard to the intricacies of modern cool jazz ("He doesn't dig *Mulligan!*"), and most particularly in regard to any combination of the two. Probably I would be better off, we would all be better off, ignoring more, letting them keep private whatever current work speaks to their condition, letting education grow up without daily watering and all those infernal sunlamps.

Improve. Here we have the traditional pedagogic tactic of using what the student likes as a guidepost to something better. Ah, one can sigh in relief, at last some *constructive* criticism, not that irresponsible ignoring. It is this attitude of exploring mass culture for signs of hope and maturity that has distinguished *Commentary* over the years. I think of such articles as Robert Warshow's "Paul, the Horror Comics, and Dr. Wertham," reprinted in Rosenberg and White's *Mass Culture,* and Norman Podhoretz's "Our Changing Ideals, as Seen on TV," reprinted in Brossard's *The Scene before You.* A sign of the awareness of the problem by a group of English teachers is the recent organization of a new section of the Modern Language Association, dealing with Literature and General Culture. An organizing statement that was circulated before the meeting expressed the hope that by studying mass culture "we may come to learn what clearly separates the best-seller from the work of distinction, and, if our aims become in part educational, offer our students the necessary exercises in discrimination." Again, I am wary of the big battalions. Teaching this sort of discrimination has always been the teacher's function, as it has always been the critic's. The works that call for it are those mixed bundles that cannot be rejected or embraced and should not be ignored, works of genuine imagination flawed by crassness, hokum, or sheer want of craft. I think of the novels of Jack Kerouac and the plays of Tennessee Williams. What attracts the student or reader to them is better available in Dostoevsky and Chekhov, in Fielding and Shakespeare, but they may be precisely the bridges to get there, and in any case are worth study in their own terms.

Replace. Beyond all this, the college teacher of literature as a custodian of traditional value has to remember what he has in his custody. John Crowe Ransom, in his 1958 Phi Beta Kappa address, "Our Age among the Ages," reprinted in the *Kenyon Review* (Winter 1959), came to a civilized and pluralist but deeply pessimistic conclusion. He wrote:

At any rate, the old ways of life have been disappearing much too rapidly for comfort, and we are in a great cultural confusion. Many millions of underprivileged persons now have income and leisure which they did not have before. They have the means to achieve the best properties of a culture, if they know how to spend their money wisely. And it is a fact that they spend handsomely on education. Now, I am in the education business, and I can report my own observations on that. It is as if a sudden invasion of barbarians had overrun the educational institution; except that the barbarians in this case are our neighbors and friends, and sometimes they are our own children, or they are ourselves, they are some of us gathered here on this very fine occasion. We should not fear them; they are not foreigners, nor our enemies. But in the last resort education is a democratic process, in which the courses are subject to the election of the applicants, and a course even when it has been elected can never rise above the intellectual passion of its pupils, or their comparative indifference. So, with the new generation of students, Milton declines in the curriculum; even Shakespeare has lost heavily; Homer and Virgil are practically gone. The literary interest of the students today is ninety percent in the literature of their own age; more often than not it is found in books which do not find entry into the curriculum, and are beneath the standard which your humble servants, the teachers of literature, are trying to maintain. Chaucer and Spenser and Milton, with their respective contemporaries, will have their secure existence henceforth in the library, and of course in the love and intimate acquaintance of a certain academic community, and there they will stay except for possible periods when there is a revival of the literature of our own antiquity. Our literary culture for a long time is going to exist in a sprawling fashion, with minority pockets of old-style culture, and some sort of a majority culture of a new and indeterminate style. It is a free society, and I should expect that the rights of minorities will be as secure as the rights of individuals.

Ransom's prediction may be exactly accurate, yet the teacher cannot reconcile himself to a minority status for his values in his own classroom, however reconciled he is to it everywhere else. He must ceaselessly bring to the attention of his students the greatest literature he knows. It is not easy for an ill-educated man to teach Homer and Virgil, Greek drama and the Bible, Milton and Shakespeare, as I can testify, but it is essential, and in our curricula Darwin and Marx, ballads and blues, must have a place, but not the primary place. "The best that has been thought and known," as Arnold somewhat pompously put it, is even more vital for college students these days when they seem to come already knowing the worst.

Warn. Here the teacher as critic of mass culture needs a good stout voice, along with the prescience of Ortega y Gasset and the bitterness of Randolph Bourne. The evidence, from Q. D. Leavis' *Fiction and the Reading Public* in 1939 to Margaret Dalziel's *Popular Fiction 100 Years Ago* in 1959, suggests that in some significant respects the standards of mass culture are deteriorating over the centuries, and that instead of flying the kites of our hopes for evolution and awakening, we had better dig in and try to keep things from getting worse than the Victorian penny dreadful. The notable voice here is Randall Jarrell's, and in "The Appalling Taste of Our Age" in the *Saturday Evening Post's* Adventures of the Mind series, he warned us in the most violent terms that the digest and the revised simplified version menace not only high literary culture but the art of reading itself, the use of the written word. In the most terrifying chapter of *Das Kapital*, "The Working Day," Marx told us of English laboring children so brutalized and degraded by working twelve and sixteen hours a day in the mills that they did not know the name of the Queen, or the story of Noah, or where London was. Now Jarrell tells us of our own children, raised in comfort and love, getting the most expensive education in the world, who do not know who Charlemagne was, or the story of Jonah, or what comes before E in the alphabet. Warn? One should bellow and curse and call down doom, like the prophet Jeremiah.

Yes, but of course also reject and embrace, ignore, improve, and replace. The teacher and the critic of mass culture cannot simply reduce himself to one attitude, but must keep varying the attack, like a young pitcher learning to supplement his high-school fast ball with a curve and a change of pace. Among the dangers of mass culture is the danger to the critic of atrophy, not to call it *rigor mortis*, of hardening in one fixed position. The comparable danger to the writer or artist is being squeezed dry too fast, like a television comedian, or brought up into the big time too soon, like a young fighter. The defense in both cases is wariness, and periodic rites of withdrawal. The ultimate ideal of mass culture is the ideal of the whole culture (to return to the anthropologists' term), something nearer the good life for all mankind. Here Homer and the Athenian tragic dramatists are useful in reminding us of basic limitation, of man's flawed, blind, and mortal nature, and of the ironies of hope and expectation.

We are not the good society, but we do have a vision of it, and that vision is a pluralist one, in which many different forms of satisfaction, including clearly spurious ones, can coexist peacefully. Mass culture is here to stay, but so, I hope, are those of us who want another sort of culture for ourselves and for anyone else who wants it, or who can be educated, led, or cajoled into wanting it. In so far as all of mass culture represents someone's organization of experience into what he intends as meaningful and pleasurable patterns, it is all a kind of shabby poetry, but we dare not forget that there are other kinds of poetry too.

Mass Culture and Social Criticism

CONTEMPORARY CRITICS of mass culture have gotten themselves into inextricable difficulties by refusing to admit to their own "snobbery." The original critics of the phenomenon, from de Tocqueville to Ortega y Gasset and Irving Babbitt, were frankly aristocrats who never thought of apologizing for the special and exclusive nature of their own standards. Indeed, it was precisely the fastidious distaste of the well born and the carefully educated that prompted the identification of mass culture at all. Culturally privileged elites have always resisted the invasion of the vulgar; there was no particular novelty in the fact that in the late nineteenth and early twentieth centuries people of humanistic education reacted so sharply against the unfamiliar standards of the "half-educated." The novelty appeared only when (as Edward Shils[1] has explained) the intellectual leaders began to identify themselves with democracy or socialism and sought virtue in the cultural pursuits of the common man. From this latter point of departure, a bewildered disappointment could be the only result.

For our contemporary critics have been trying to apply two incompatible standards at the same time. They have clung to the special cultural definitions of a narrow elite—the insistence on a common core of "humanist" reading or artistic enjoyment, on the importance of foreign languages, ancient or modern, and on the elegant manipulation of one's own—maintaining all the while that these things are perfectly capable of mass dissemination. They have tried to combine elitism and democracy—things compatible perhaps in a Periclean or Jeffersonian sense of popular government led by "the best," but, under contemporary conditions, radical opposites.

In a word, I believe that contemporary democracy and contemporary mass culture are two sides of the same coin, and that our discussions of the latter phenomenon, now and in the future, will get nowhere until we recognize this simple equation and the corollaries that stem from it. Few of us, I think, would be prepared to jettison democracy and to substitute some sort of aristocratic regime in its place. All sorts of reasons, both moral and technical, spring to our minds as counter-arguments. Hence, if we want to live in our world with some degree of equanimity, it is incumbent on us to make our peace with mass culture in at least a few of its more bearable manifestations.

By now it should be obvious that I agree with Messrs. Rosten and Shils that the mass media cannot be held responsible for "corrupting" popular taste. The taste of the masses, I believe, has always appeared more or less "corrupt" to the better educated, and I see no reason why this situation should change. I am also impressed with Mr. Rosten's argument that the media frequently produce or print things that are over the heads of their audience, and that the most serious limitation on them is the absence of talent to cope with the totally unprecedented demand for copy. At the same time (even under the most favorable conditions) I do not believe the media capable of performing the task of general education that their would-be reformers want to entrust to them. Or, more precisely, I think that only certain cultural values are susceptible of large-scale dissemination, and that certain other values, traditionally regarded as distinguishing features of the educated man, when subjected to such a process simply become diluted beyond recognition.

About twenty years ago I was first struck by Henry Adams' observation that the United States in 1800 possessed a cultural equipment that was almost exclusively restricted to theology, literature, and oratory. While these were frequently cultivated with intensity and finesse, the realm of the visual arts and music (the more sensuous gratifications of old Europe) were practically nonexistent.[2] As the years have passed since I first read those lines—and as our country has undergone the most profound social and cultural change in its history—I have watched Adams' words turn into their very opposite. Today it is the arts of language that have passed into disrespect: even the man of reasonable education can no longer handle English with any sureness of touch; we have become a nation of nongrammarians admirably represented by the curious syntax of our chief executive. At the same time, the enjoyment of music, the semiprofessional theater, and even painting has become diffused in a fashion almost nobody anticipated a generation ago. The arts of sensuous consumption are prospering everywhere. In the sphere of traditional music and the less difficult forms of the drama and the visual arts, popular taste has never been so well developed.

Now what the arts of sensuous consumption have in common (as opposed to reading, speaking, logical argument, or the more intellectualized forms of painting or music) is, of course, the passivity of their reception. This passive quality has been lamented again and again by the critics of our contemporary culture; they have repeatedly called for a return to the strenuous effort that they find characteristic of all true artistic or intellectual attainment. Here, I think, the critics have become impractical visionaries. For it is precisely the active, acute, finely perceptive elements of traditional culture that, *under contemporary conditions*, are incapable of mass dissemination. If spread too widely, they become unrecognizable. Or, perhaps more commonly, they produce boredom and a weary sensation of irrelevance.

Why is it that so much of what to us may seem the best parts of our cultural heritage strikes the majority of our countrymen, and even our students, as supremely irrelevant? The question is not as foolish as it sounds. And it is not to be answered merely by angry assertions of the greatness of a Virgil or a Milton. If almost no one cares to read Milton today, it is not just because we have lost our feeling for traditional culture. It is because most of what an author like Milton has to say has in simple truth become irrelevant to our contemporary lives.

The passivity of our cultural response mirrors the passivity of the society in which we live. Ours is a world without issues—or rather with one issue, so vast and so frightening that people prefer not to talk about it at all. If our students yawn over the classics, it is not just that they are boorish and obtuse; on the contrary, many of them may be acute enough to realize that the subject matter of these great works has very little to do with their own lives. Heroic endeavor, "purity" and chastity, poverty and pestilence, the fine distinctions of theology, the duties of kingship, the perfect society—all these noble old subjects seem muted and remote to contemporary Americans. The hardest task of the historian of ideas is to convince his students or his readers that at one time people cared, even to the point of dying for them, about notions that today seem hopelessly arid and scholastic.

And so we have come to social criticism. Without it, I maintain, any analysis of mass culture is shallow and unprofitable. For I think that there is in fact a qualitative difference between the cultural attitude of the ordinary man today and the plebeian standards within an earlier society. Both, of course, have been concerned primarily with sensual enjoyment. But in past ages the more perceptive and sensitive of the plebs had an uneasy awareness that their lives and standards were far from perfect: their consciences were not clear— at the very least, they felt excluded from the great stage where the major dramas of their time were being enacted. Today the ordinary man does not have the same sense of exclusion. Indeed, he is given a front-row seat: the media see to that. The only trouble is that nothing particularly exciting is going on, on the stage.

Hence there is no incentive to learn the fine points of the drama. If the audience is basically convinced that the great traditional issues of human life, both social and private, no longer have much meaning, if the public senses (as well it may) that the actors themselves are playing their roles mechanically and without putting much conviction into their lines, then its reception of the play will quite naturally be that of lazy-minded and passive spectators. How different things were a couple of generations ago! One has only to conjure up the image of half-literate European workers patiently listening to the exegesis of Marxian texts for hours at a stretch (a common scene around 1900) to realize the difference in cultural climate. These workers were obviously more poorly educated than their American counterparts of today: they had less capacity to follow a closely reasoned argument. But their inclination to do so was greater. For they were convinced that the lengthy and largely incomprehensible speeches of their leaders and teachers were of moment to them. The complex reasoning of these people from a loftier cultural sphere really mattered to their listeners: at some point (perhaps a very far-distant point), their auditors believed, it would make a difference in their own lives, or at least in the lives of their descendants.

Today most people have lost this conviction. They do not think that their own lives will get much better or even that their children will be happier than they are. Indeed, they suspect that the contrary may be true. At the conscious level, they repeat to themselves that they are already living in the promised land. Deeper down, they fear that the vision of such a land has vanished forever.

Unless we realize the full import of this loss of the vision of utopia, we shall never be able to understand properly our country and its culture—and along with these, the more general characteristics of twentieth-century society in the Western world. Without such a realization, we shall not be able to express what it is about mass culture that we find so peculiarly depressing. For, as so many of our contributors have asserted, it is not its *mass* character as such that is novel and threatening: it is rather its slackness and meaninglessness. And this flaccid quality springs precisely from the wider nature of the society of which mass culture is simply the most obvious and flamboyant manifestation.

Let me reiterate that I do not think this to be exclusively an American question. The same socio-cultural complex has recently begun to appear in Western and Central Europe, perhaps with a certain time lag, but still with unmistakably familiar features. And this not through what the defenders of the old culture angrily attack as "Americanization": rather than being primarily an importation from outside, the vast social and cultural change that Europe has been undergoing since the Second World War gives every evidence of indigenous and spontaneous origin; the direct copying from America seems to be relatively superficial.

As I look over the social and ideological scene today, I am impressed with the great similarity among the dominant views in the major Western nations—with the possible exception of Britain, which shows remnants of an earlier pattern of clearly marked and significant differences of opinion. Elsewhere one encounters a kind of gray uniformity. The ideologies that call themselves Christian Democracy in Germany and Italy, Gaullism in France, and the bipartisan consensus in our own country, on closer inspection, turn out to be very much the same thing. They stand for an ideology that is the negation of ideology—and of utopia also. In name and in formal organization they are liberal and democratic, but in fact they seem dedicated to draining liberal democracy of its content. No longer do they have any particular enthusiasm behind them. They rest, rather, on material prosperity, and beyond that, and more important than that, on weariness, on apathy, on passive acceptance, on a tacit agreement not to discuss potentially "divisive" issues—on what still needs to be called "conformity," despite the excessive use of that term during the past half-decade of post-McCarthy breast-beating.

I am not surprised, then, that Mr. Shils has referred to this situation as a "culture of consensus." That is exactly what it is—with all the virtues and all the defects that the term implies. I do not want to be misunderstood: I find this culture more tolerant, gentler, and more humane than anything that the Western world knew before; it provides a setting in which the artist, however marginal and irrelevant he may feel himself to be, is seldom mistreated, and almost never starves. One of our contributors has referred to the price we pay for democracy. I think that is a good expression—provided we recognize both that the price is worth paying and that it is a heavy price indeed.

A generation ago Karl Mannheim warned us of what it would mean to live without utopia—without any notion of transcendence in social and cultural pursuits.[3] He held up to us the vision of a cold, bleak world, a world drained of meaning. More recently writers like Lewis Mumford and Erich Fromm have echoed the warning. I do not agree with Mr. Hyman that we still have a vision of the good society. In fact, I could scarcely disagree more strongly. I believe we have lost that vision: most of us are quite satisfied with the ugliness of our cities, the waste in our economy, the cheerful incompetence of our leaders, the meaninglessness of public discourse, the general insensibility to the overwhelming danger that threatens us. Along with our vision, we have lost our capacity for indignation, our ability to feel a cosmic anger with what we see going on around us. And until we regain this vision, these capacities, our culture will continue to be what it is today—"weary, flat, stale, and unprofitable."

REFERENCES

1 "Daydreams and Nightmares: Reflections on the Criticism of Mass Culture." *The Sewanee Review*, LXV (1957).
2 *History of the United States during the Administrations of Jefferson and Madison*, I (New York, 1889), Chapters 3, 4, 5.
3 *Ideology and Utopia* (London and New York, 1936), pp. 230, 236.

ARTHUR SCHLESINGER, JR.

Notes on a National Cultural Policy

Too much discussion of the problems of mass culture takes the form of handwringing. The point to be understood, I would think, is that these problems, while complicated and often discouraging, are by no means insuperable, unless we ourselves make them so. Things can be done in all sorts of ways to counteract the more depressing tendencies in our mass civilization. I would like in this brief note to call particular attention to possibilities in the field of public policy.

Let me begin with something both important and specific—that is, the problem of television. There are now over 50 million television sets in the country, covering almost 90 percent of American households. From its inception, television has been in a downward spiral as an artistic medium; but it has taken recent disclosures of fraud in quiz programs to awaken the nation to the potentialities locked up in the tiny screen. The question is: what, if anything, can be done to improve the honesty and the quality of our television programing?

The first point is that television is an area in which there can be no question concerning the direct interest of the national government. No one has a divine right to a television channel. The air belongs to the public; and private operators can use the air only under public license. Why therefore should the national government stand helplessly by while private individuals, making vast sums of money out of public licenses, employ public facilities to debase the public taste? Obviously there seems no reason in law or prudence why this should be so. Government has not only the power but the obligation to help establish standards in media, like television and radio, which exist by public sufferance.

It has this obligation, among other reasons, because there seems no other way to rescue television from the downward spiral of competitive debasement. There are responsible and enlightened men managing television networks and stations; but they are trapped in a competitive situation. The man who gives his audience soap opera and give-away shows will make more money for his stockholders than the man who gives his audience news and Shakespeare. In consequence, the tendency is almost irresistible for television programs to vie with each other, not in elevating the taste of their audiences, but in catering to the worst side of the existing taste. As *Fortune* recently summed up the situation, it seems "that television has reached a kind of ceiling, that mediocrity is increasing, and that only *through some drastic change in the medium's evolution* will the excitement and aspiration of, say, 1954 return to our TV screens" (my italics). *Fortune*'s analysis was, as usual, better than its solution, which was Pay TV. Pay-as-you-see TV would be no more exempt from the passion to maximize its audiences than is free TV; and, in due course, it would doubtless undergo the same evolution. (See *Fortune*, December 1958.)

Still "some drastic change in the medium's evolution" remains necessary. But what? Actually there is nothing new about the situation of responsible TV people; they are in precisely the position that responsible businessmen were in twenty-five years ago when they wanted, for example, to treat their workers better but could not afford to do so because of the "competitive situation." Thus many employers disliked sweatshops and child labor but knew that raising wages and improving working conditions would increase their costs and thereby handicap them as against their more callous competitors. Private initiative was impotent to deal with this situation: gentlemen's agreements within an industry always broke down under pressure. There was only one answer—public action to establish and enforce standards through the industry. Finally the Wages and Hours Act required all employers in interstate commerce to meet certain specifications and thus abolished the economic risks of decency.

What television needs is some comparable means of equalizing the alleged competitive disadvantages of enlightened programing. Fortunately the machinery for this is already at hand. According to the Communications Act of 1934, the Federal Communications Commission is to grant licenses to serve the "public convenience, interest, or necessity." A television channel is an immensely lucrative thing; and those lucky enough to secure an FCC license ought to be regarded, not as owners of private property with which they can do anything they want, but as trustees of public property under the obligation to prove their continuing right to the public trust.

It is up to the FCC, in short, to spell out the equivalent of minimum wages and maximum hours for television. What would this imply? It would surely imply the following:

1. A licensing system which would cover networks as well as individual stations.

2. The writing into each license of a series of stipulations which the grantee pledges himself to fulfill in order to retain the license.

3. A major stipulation would be the assumption by the networks and stations of full control over their programing—which means that sponsors and advertising agencies would no longer influence the content of programs. Other media live off advertisements without letting advertising agencies and sponsors dictate and censor content as they do in television. So long as television permits this, it will be fourth-rate. We should go over to the British and Canadian systems, in which the advertiser purchases time on the air as he purchases space in a newspaper, and has to leave editorial matters alone.

4. Other stipulations might include the allocation of stated portions of broadcast time to cultural and educational programs, to programs dealing with public issues, to local live programs; the limitation of advertising (the House of Commons has currently under consideration a bill prohibiting advertising on British TV for more than six minutes in any hour); the allocation of free time during presidential campaigns to all parties polling more than 10 percent of the vote in the previous election.

5. Licenses should come up for annual renewal; and stations which have not met their obligations should expect to have their licenses revoked (the FCC has not refused a request for license renewal since 1932).

6. All this implies, of course, a revitalization of the FCC, which once had chairmen and commissioners of the caliber of Paul Porter, James Lawrence Fly, and Clifford Durr, but has become in recent years the preserve of complaisant political hacks.

Back in 1946, the FCC proposed in its famous Blue Book doing much this sort of thing for radio; but the industry issued the standard lamentations about governmental control, the public remained indifferent, and nothing came of it. One can expect to hear the same wail of "censorship" raised now against proposals for the establishment of federal standards. The fact is that we already have censorship of the worst kind in television. As John Crosby has written, "So long as the advertiser has direct personal control over programs, or direct ownership of programs, it's silly to talk about [government] censorship. The censorship is already stifling. The government should step in not to censor broadcasting but to free it."

The setting of federal standards does not mean government domination of the medium, any more than the Wages and Hours Act meant (as businessmen cried at the time) government domination of business. But the rejection of the Blue Book in 1946 emphasizes the difficulty of the problem. The FCC, even reconstituted as it would have to be in another administration, could not tighten up federal standards by itself. If the FCC proposes to buck the industry, it will require organized public support; it is perhaps a mistake that public energy which might have gone into establishing general standards was diverted into setting up separate facilities for educational television. And the FCC would also probably require some form of administration supplementation—perhaps a National Citizens' Advisory Board, of the kind proposed some years ago by William Benton,[1] or a National Broadcasting Authority, financed by rentals on the licenses, of the sort recently suggested by John Fischer in *Harper's*.[2]

The measures proposed above represent a minimum program. Walter Lippmann and others have recently argued for the establishment of a public network to be "run as a public service with its criterion not what will be most popular but what is good." Lippmann does not suppose that such a network would attract the largest mass audience. "But if it enlisted the great talents which are available in the industry, but are now throttled and frustrated, it might well attract an audience which made up in influence what it lacked in numbers. The force of a good example is a great force, and should not be underrated." Proposals of this sort still horrify many Americans, though fewer now than in the days when Charles Van Doren was a community hero. But clearly, if television cannot clean its own house and develop a sense of responsibility commensurate with its influence, we are bound to come to a government network. If, as Dr. Frank Stanton of the Columbia Broadcasting System insists (*his* italics), *"The strongest sustained attention of Americans is now, daily and nightly, bestowed on television as it is bestowed on nothing* *else,"*³ then television is surely a proper subject for public concern. If the industry will not undertake to do itself what is necessary to stop the drift into hopeless mediocrity (and, far from showing any signs of so doing, its leaders deny the reality of the problem and even justify the present state of things by pompous talk about "cultural democracy"), then it must expect public intervention.

The case for government concern over television is indisputable because government must control the air. The case for government concern over other arts rests on a less clear-cut juridical basis. Yet, as John Quincy Adams said one hundred and thirty-five years ago, "The great object of the institution of civil government is the improvement of the condition of those who are parties to the social compact, and no government, in whatever form constituted, can accomplish the lawful ends of its institution but in proportion as it improves the condition of those over whom it is established." Adams added that this applied no less to "moral, political, intellectual improvement" than to internal improvements and public works.

The American government has acknowledged this responsibility variously and intermittently since its foundation. But the problem of government encouragement of the arts is not a simple one; and it has never been satisfactorily solved. In order to bring some coherence into its solution, Congressman Frank Thompson, Jr., of New Jersey has been agitating for some time for the establishment of a Federal Advisory Council on the Arts, to be set up within the Department of Health, Education, and Welfare and charged with assisting the growth of the fine arts in the United States. "A major duty of the Council," the bill (H.R. 7656) reads, "shall be to recommend ways to maintain and increase the cultural resources of the United States."

There is no automatic virtue in councils. Congressman Thompson and Senator Fulbright, for example, got through Congress a year ago an act establishing a National Cultural Center in Washington. After a protracted delay, President Eisenhower named the thirty-four members of the new Center's board of trustees. Of the whole group, only a handful had shown any evidence of knowing or caring anything about the arts; the typical members include such cultural leaders as the former football coach at West Point, the President's minister (balanced, of course, by Catholic and Jewish clerics), his television adviser, representatives of labor, etc. A Federal Advisory Council on the Arts, appointed on such principles, would be worse than useless. But in due course some President will seek our genuine leaders of the arts and ask them to think through the issues of the government relationship.

Let no one mistake it: there are no easy answers here. But also there has been, in this country at least, very little hard thought. Government is finding itself more and more involved in matters of cultural standards and endeavor. The Commission of Fine Arts, the Committee on Government and Art, the National Cultural Center, the Mellon Gallery, the poet at the Library of Congress, the art exhibits under State Department sponsorship, the cultural exchange programs—these represent only a sampling of federal activity in the arts. If we are going to have so much activity anyway, if we are, in addition, worried about the impact of mass culture, there are strong arguments for an affirmative governmental policy to help raise standards. Nor is there reason to suppose that this would necessarily end up in giving governmental sanction to the personal preferences of congressmen and Presidents—e.g., making Howard Chandler Christy and Norman Rockwell the models for American art. Congressmen have learned to defer to experts in other fields, and will learn to defer to experts in this (one doubts, in any case, whether the artistic taste of politicians is as banal as some assume; certainly the taste of the two most recent governors of New York is better than that of most professors).

Certain steps are obvious. Whereas many civilized countries subsidize the arts, we tend to tax them. Let us begin by removing federal taxes on music and the theater. Then we ought to set up a Federal Advisory Council on the Arts composed, not of presidential chums and other hacks, but of professional and creative artists and of responsible executives (museum directors, presidents of conservatories, opera managers, etc.). This Council ought to study American precedents in the field and, even more important, current experiments in government support of the arts in Europe. A program of subsidies for local museums and galleries, for example, would be an obvious possibility.

There is a considerable challenge to social and administrative invention here. As the problems of our affluent society become more qualitative and less quantitative, we must expect culture to emerge as a matter of national concern and to respond to a national purpose. Yet the role of the state can at best be marginal. In the end the vitality of a culture will depend on the creativity of the individual and the sensibility of the audience, and these conditions depend on factors of which the state itself is only a surface expression.

REFERENCES

1 William Benton, in his testimony before the Senate Interstate Commerce Committee, printed in the 31 May 1951 issue of the *Congressional Record* (A3313-7).

2 John Fischer, "Television and Its Critics," *Harper's Magazine*, July 1959, *219:* 10-14.

3 Frank Stanton, "The Role of Television in Our Society," an address of 26 May 1955.

A General Theory of Mass Culture

Arthur Schlesinger, Jr.: I feel that there is a danger in this discussion of mass culture: the danger of excessive Platonization; that is, taking mass culture as one distinct entity and elite culture as another, each with essences of its own and the product of each having no relation to the product of the other.

Miss Arendt in her brilliant but somewhat artificial analysis suggested that society "produced" culture and mass society "consumed" entertainment. I think that these are useful distinctions if we consider them as representing certain extremes; but if we consider them as corresponding to qualitative distinctions in reality, the consequences are misleading.

I should propose that what is involved is more of a continuum than a deep and essential difference. If this is so, the distinction between mass culture and elite culture is not so absolute as some of the critics and the commentators would suppose. This would imply that the problem of mass culture itself is neither clearcut nor hopeless but rather ambiguous. It is clearly not one of inexorable, unilineal decay, as Mr. Van den Haag seemed to believe. In fact, I felt that Mr. Van den Haag's paper was largely a comparison of the cultural experience of past minorities with the cultural experience of present majorities. In pre-mass societies what cultural experience the few had was purchased at the price of considerable squalor and deprivation for the rest. We are past that stage in history and we have to come to terms with the consequences of social democracy.

Many people in this society cannot bear high level aesthetic experience. But this is not the result of mass culture. It is the consequence of the distribution of vitality and sensitivity in society.

The problem is an indeterminate one. Its very ambiguity means that we can do much more about it than we sometimes suppose. People who criticize the passivity produced by mass culture are often passive in accepting what they regard as a predestined consequence. There are opportunities for leadership and influence in the future of the mass media. There can be administrative intervention to improve standards in the field of public policy through tax power and through F.C.C. licenses. The field of cultural policy has been inadequately considered. As we move into a phase of more affirmative government in the 1960's, I believe this area will require careful thought and will show great possibilities.

One of the indispensable conditions for any advance is criticism, some of which is exaggerated but which still undercuts any tendency toward complacency among those who manage the mass media and those who write for it. They have, many of them, reachable consciences. I think their consciences should be assailed by a constant attack and I condemn the tendency on the part of the mass media executives to react to this criticism with hurt self-defense. The critics of mass media often seem intoxicated by their own rhetoric and sometimes seem misled by a nostalgia for a society which never existed; however, their potential contribution to averting and saving modern society from the fate they seem to fear is great, and I am all for it.

Patrick Hazard: I come not to bury mass culture but to praise it with criticism motivated by love—not rancor or the sullen almost surly stance characteristic of the humanist attitude toward the mass media. Shils has said that mass society is characterized by people making many new kinds of choices; that this has set loose the cognitive, appreciative, and moral potential of the population. He feels that curiosity, sensibility, and privacy are present in mass society and reminds us of the great differences in the cognitive, appreciative, and moral capacities within this society.

The function of the intellectual, I suggest, is not one that he chooses but rather is one that society provides for him: in briefest terms, to clarify the many ambiguities that beset people who have not made these choices before, to help them develop their cognitive, appreciative, and moral potentials.

It seems to me that this whole discussion centers around the term "excellence." When I try to come to any meaningful understanding of this word, I look for instances characteristic of the new kind of society. One of our problems is that we have some free-floating ideal of excellence, the antithesis of which is an equally free-floating conformity. If we are to make any progress at all, we must be more precise in what we mean by these two words.

There is a continuum of excellence available in mass society; one man's excellence is another's mediocrity. The converse is also true. What we want is to get as many people as possible developing their own capacities along that continuum of excellence.

Furthermore excellence exists in a social context. It seems to me that the anti-business bias of most humanists makes it impossible for them to see what excellence exists in a mass society.

We ought to agree that the creation of material abundance is not a minor feat in human history. The problem in America is that there is a serious imbalance between our material productivity and our cultural productivity.

Much of the criticism of mass society reads like a coroner's report. The humanist has been imprudent in the way he has invested his critical energies; humanist criticism is shamefully over-invested in literature. What most humanist critics mean when they contend that mass culture and excellence are incompatible is that the aesthetic forms that flourished in, say, the eighteenth and nineteenth centuries in Europe do not flourish in twentieth century America. It is, of course, perfectly legitimate for serious artists in literature, painting, and music to be concerned with the effects of social change on their genres. But it is an insufficiently acknowledged virtue of our mass society that it is more permissive to a wider range of aesthetic forms than any other culture in history. Never have the elite arts had, in both relative and absolute numbers, larger and more sophisticated audiences; and it is my impression that the opportunities for both creation and appreciation are rapidly increasing.

I suggest that we start reinvesting our critical energies in the new art forms characteristic of mass society. To do this we have to examine the art forms that have come out of mass production and mass communication.

Let me take mass production, to begin with. I have rarely heard critics talking about Charles Eames, George Nelson, or Frieda Diamond. Yet Charles Eames is perhaps the most impressive of our industrial designers. His plastic innovations encompass forms as diverse as colorful building cards for children, chairs and a brilliant color movie popularizing information theory.

George Nelson is another important designer with an articulate rationale. The Information Center at Colonial Williamsburg is an excellent example of how a first-rate designer like Nelson not only humanizes the artifacts and milieu of an industrial society but also makes the past meaningful and accessible.

One reservation about the work of our important industrial designers is that it is so expensive. In recent years, however, this objection has become less significant as designers like Frieda Diamond have aimed for the five-and-dime market and have executed pieces of high quality and low cost for such firms as Libbey Glass. Paul McCobb's furniture has also appeared in reasonably inexpensive lines. Alcoa's Forecast collection—plastic speculations about everyday shapes of the future done by the best designers—promises the convergence of good design with a mass market. The increasing visibility of these patterns of excellence is an earnest of a progressively more attractive physical environment. It is hard to imagine that a generation of school children reared on Eames classroom furniture will be complacent about the over-stuffy designs of the neighborhood furniture store.

Moving from design to mass architecture, Carl Koch in his Techbuilt Homes has successfully used prefabrication and the modular principle to make good architecture available to low income people. He is an unsung hero of mass society. Another is Charles Goodman, who for some years has been designing fine homes for National Homes, Inc., of Lafayette, Indiana, the largest manufacturer of prefabs in this country. Their lowest price house is a striking structure within the reach of the least paid factory worker.

Urban planning is still another area in which mass production has its impact on the new society. I find very few people talking about Victor Gruen's planned shopping centers in Detroit, Saarinen's General Motors Tech Center, and the revival of downtown in cities like New Haven, Philadelphia, and Pittsburgh. At Northland and Eastland in Detroit, for example, thanks to Gruen, shoppers not only have a pleasant time about their business; but the green vistas with contemplative sculpture for adults and play sculpture for children present a strong argument for the indispensability of amenities. The General Motors Tech Center north of Detroit is a vision of what industrial America can be like to live and work in.

It is true that there are very few instances of this excellence, but why should the intellectual feel that its extension ought to be easy? I should think he would address himself to the arduous discipline of extending the beachheads of maturity rather than engage in cerebral whimpering about the lack of excellence.

It is a polite cliché in our circles to talk about advertising as intrinsically debasing to man. Yet recently at the New York Art Directors' Club I saw forty-five minutes of television commercials that were extraordinary in their almost minor lyric art. Anchor Books were only a Jason Epstein away less than a decade ago. When the book clubs started in the 1920's, horrified shouts of conformity echoed through every bookshop in the land, but by now the intellectual has made his peace with this method of distribution in the Mid-Century Book Society. The Teenage Book Club of *Scholastic Magazine* sold over ten million paperback books in one academic year.

The essentially snobbish attitude that humanists have had toward the mass education system in America has contributed materially to its present crisis. Our educational system is part of our multi-purpose mass communication system. It is long overdue for a series of imaginative innovations in instruction, such as the closed circuit TV system financed by the Fund for the Advancement of Education in Hagerstown, Maryland; or the fleet of 16 station wagons taking science teachers to small high schools in the Northwest financed by the National Science Foundation and operated by the University of Oregon. Who would have believed five years ago that Michigan State University, a school built around trips to the Rose Bowl, would found an elite campus at Oakland, Michigan to reassert the primacy of the academic?

Can one find a *via media* between the Pollyannas and Cassandras of mass culture? I should like to see some hard-headed idealism among my humanist colleagues where they use as much imagination trying to develop a new kind of society as they expend extolling what they think is a past one. The trouble with the coroners of mass culture is that they find a morbid fascination writing obituaries on a society just doffing its swaddling clothes. There may not be a satisfying surplus of excellence in contemporary America, but there is just enough around to confute those who don't care enough to look for it, or who wouldn't recognize the excellences of this new kind of society if they saw them. The only significant agenda for the humanities in a mass society is to husband the few archetypes already achieved and settle down to the workaday regimen of seeing that these first faltering steps don't go unnoticed and unimitated. In other words, instead of a doctrinaire Utopianism, I think we ought to have some kind of meliorism about mass society where we try to look for its characteristic excellence and do what we can to encourage its growth.

Sidney Hook: I am concerned with the integrity of culture as a professional educator and as a person interested in values.

I don't like the word "elite," but I think I am committed to what Professor Hazard calls the pursuit of excellence. I don't like the way he generalizes about this excellence, as if one man's excellence is another man's mediocrity. I believe one must take a position which would make it impossible to say that excellence is simply a matter of taste in any field of art or science.

However, I should like to ask: What is the empirical evidence that the diversification of approaches to culture and the existence of plural aspects of culture—and I think that Shils was defending a pluralistic approach to culture—lead to a debasement of what has been called refined or superior culture?

I confess that as a democrat I have no desire to impose my judgments of values and my taste upon other people in the community, and I certainly would resent it if they tried to impose their tastes and value judgments upon me. I am interested in the cultural autonomy which is involved in the pursuit of the best of the past and the present. But no evidence has been presented to show that the best has been degraded because of the existence of mass media in mass society; or that to the extent that we are not satisfied with authentic culture, we cannot improve it even using the instruments of modern technological society.

Dr. van den Haag said that the tales of Grimm are much superior in book form to the versions you hear or see on television. I grant this. But if you are interested in Grimm and can develop a taste for him, how is it affected by what goes on television? Suppose you don't like the television rendition of Shakespeare. If you appreciate and love Shakespeare, how does a poor television presentation affect your appreciation? After all, a good deal of popular science is just superstition. But would anyone say that the dissemination of popular science today has undermined work in pure science? The same thing holds true for the exploitation by writers of popular music of classical melodies. Would this undermine a serious interest in music? The assumption here is that the fact people can consume culture in ways which we disapprove will in the end undermine our own attachment and our own integrity to the higher standards of culture. I challenge those who maintain this to present their evidence. And I would conclude by asking what are the facts to indicate that our position as intellectuals is being threatened or undermined except by the temptation to leave the heights of scholarship or the frontiers of inquiry for the fleshpots? That is a moral question to be addressed to individuals. It hardly seems to me to constitute a general indictment of the nature of culture.

Nathan Glazer: In speaking of the consumption of culture, everyone normally makes a triadic distinction: highbrow, lowbrow, and middlebrow. I think it might be helpful if we were to break up this triad into two variables which involve the quality of the product and the quality of the response to the product.

If you make this distinction, you find you can have high quality with a high or serious response but you can also have low quality with a low or shallow response. And obviously, to complete the possibilities, you can have low art with a high response and high art with a low response.

A person may go to see *The Sound and the Fury*, which was a horrible movie. He may be brought by it to think of serious problems of humanity. This is not an outrageous possibility. People can discuss a mean and cheap art product and come out with a high response. Thus it is useful to keep these two variables in mind when we discuss consumption of culture.

Oscar Handlin: I submit it is important to consider culture apart from the specific mass setting in which we usually think of it or the snob setting in which others have thought of it. I suggest that the use of culture has always been an incidental quality to some other function. That is, when cathedrals were built, people were not building architecture, they were building churches. The architecture was an incidental and almost unpredictable quality that was attached to a function and, to a considerable degree, independent of it.

It is at this point that I found Miss Arendt's statements most suggestive, for she pointed out that in the 18th and 19th centuries in Europe, and I would say in the last quarter of the 19th century in the United States, culture acquired another very important kind of utility: it became a means of identification with society in a special respect.

But even during this period, outside the realm of official culture, there existed another kind of culture in perhaps the more primitive and more original sense. The peasants, the working classes of Europe, had another kind of culture which was not that of the upper bourgeoisie, but which it seems to me showed a greater degree of continuity with the past culture than did the official culture and official society.

The characteristics of this culture were, first, the lack of a set of canons or classics by which it was measured and, second, a close functional relation to the felt needs and the immediate modes of expression of the people who exhibited it.

The question I find interesting is: What is the difference between the mass culture of our society and the type of culture that existed before the appearance of society in its formal sense; or the difference between what we call mass culture today and the popular culture of the 19th and early 20th centuries? I would like to suggest that the difference arises from the dilution of the functional qualities of what we call mass culture; of its ability to serve useful purposes; and of the rapport between the creators of this form of culture and its consumers.

Consider, for example, the extent to which the television playlet or variety performance is different from the performance on the vaudeville stage, which is its lineal antecedent, and yet which is totally removed in quality and relation from the audience from which it descended.

So it seems to me that when we deal with mass culture, the problem is not simply its separateness from other types of culture which may co-exist or not, but whether it is serving a function in the life of those who consume it. Do the people who seek entertainment in the movies or on television actually find it; or are they by the nature of the media so deprived of control over what they find that they must accept it without even being conscious of their dissatisfaction? They may or may not want fins on their cars, but the consumers are themselves often confused and unable to tell what they wish.

From the broadly social point of view, what may be harmful in the present situation is the compulsion under which many people labor of accepting what is not really satisfying and what does not really serve a function in their lives because the range of choices has narrowed and they lack the ability to control the choices available to them.

Bernard Rosenberg: I should like to direct your attention to the political implications of what has been said. The view is—I suppose it starts with de Tocqueville—that somehow mass culture is a consequence of democracy, the price that we must pay for democracy and the price worth paying. This is the major theme suggested by Shils; that we have in modern society some kind of consensual society. I don't know what this can mean; from a political standpoint, it seems to me that primitive society had more consensus, and in that sense perhaps, there was greater democracy among the North American Indian tribes.

It is no longer necessary to develop literacy in order to propagandize and manipulate mass audiences. There have been radios blasting away for a long time in every public square of the Soviet Union, as there are now in the Middle East. We know of Hitler's indebtedness to Madison Avenue for the application of advertising techniques to politics. We are not altogether unfamiliar with this in the United States. But this does not seem to be an enhancement of democracy.

Somehow there seems to be an implication that you are undemocratic if you criticize mass culture; and that you can do so only from the elitist point of view of someone concerned with restoring the aristocratic past. I am concerned that we may establish totalitarianism in the United States without concentration camps through the use of the mass media, which are perfectly neutral in themselves.

When the printing press was first invented it was a liberating force. One can link such historical phenomena as the Reformation and the French and American Revolutions to the uses to which printed matter of all sorts was put. But it should not bewilder us that something used to liberate man has also been used to enslave him. Hasn't this happened before in history? You start with nationalism, which has been a liberating force and then reverses itself. You have the liberating effect of Christianity and then its evolution during the Middle Ages. I have in mind Francis of Assisi, committed to poverty and humility and buried in a marble grave at the expense of a powerful and rich Order bearing his name.

Hook: Are you trying to say anything more than that the mass media may be abused?

Rosenberg: Have been and are being abused.

Hook: Everything can be abused. That is a commonplace. The question is whether you find an inherent tendency here. If you lose political democracy, then literacy becomes a weapon of conformity. The emphasis must therefore lie on democracy. I think the point we are trying to discuss here is whether there are inherent tendencies toward vulgarity in mass culture; and whether literacy must necessarily be used as an agent of conformity.

Hannah Arendt: I stated in my paper that culture is a phenomenon of the world and that entertainment is a phenomenon of life. Culture in its wordly existence is endangered through the human life process and its consumption needs. This danger is not new; it probably exists in all societies. The question is only whether or not it becomes more acute in a mass society.

My point of departure was not man and his "need" for culture, but the cultural objects themselves. Among them, we distinguish use objects and art objects, and the distinction between them is that only the former are meant to meet the immediate needs of human life. Art objects, on the contrary, must be removed from all use if they are to be what they are meant to be. For this reason, we put them into museums or churches or temples; that is, we create a special worldly space where these things are removed and protected from human needs and the functions of human life.

My objection concerns the indiscriminate functionalization of both types of objects. Obviously, use objects were made to be used, to fulfill certain functions, although, by virtue of having forms and shapes, they transcend their use and function. Art objects, however, lose their meaning entirely through this kind of functionalization; they have no function and to think of them in functional terms contradicts their very essence.

I happen to believe that our century is a century of great art. Our political and social troubles are great enough, so great indeed that we do not know whether mankind will survive. No one doubts that this century, however it may end, is outstandingly great in scientific achievement; the same may well be true for achievement in the arts. Yet while scientific progress has long since ceased to be an unmixed blessing, the great art of the twentieth century has been the only oasis in the desert of modern life. Modern sociology and psychology are born from the troubles of life in our century and whenever their conceptual tools are permitted to invade the domain of art, I have the feeling that we carry the sand of the desert into the only oases left to us.

One last word on my use of the word "contemplation." I chose it in order to indicate an attitude of letting things be, of letting them alone, of not using them for one's own purposes, not even for the purpose of self-education or self-perfection.

Ernest van den Haag: I do not think the developments I have described are inevitable. I just haven't found any way to avoid them. I do not think that mass culture involves a decay.

I think mass culture is what it is, as I have tried to describe it, not anything decaying or degenerating.

For a historian it seems to me that Professor Schlesinger was peculiarly unhistorical in refusing to recognize that there is something new in mass culture. Of course there are always continuities, but the important thing is to call attention to what is new.

I have never said that mass culture is necessarily bad. All I am saying is that it is not individual and cannot be. Therefore, the excellence of industrial design, referred to by Professor Hazard, which may indeed be greater than the excellence achieved by an individual artist, is irrelevant.

I think that viewing Grimm's fairy tales on television may not interfere with those who read them separately—though I'm not sure— but it will deter many from reading them. And in these matters half a loaf spoils the appetite.

I do not agree with Mr. Rosenberg. First of all, Hitler did not learn anything from Madison Avenue but rather from Soviet Russia. Secondly, it is very clear that the mass media have fairly little *political* influence, if you recall that Roosevelt and Truman were elected, even though the mass media were strongly opposed to their election. I do not believe that political considerations are important in this context.

The Mass Media

Bernard Berelson: Do we want to understand the phenomenon
of mass culture; do we want to evaluate it; or do we want to
try to change it? The latter objective brings into play a
number of problems involving institutional arrangements that may
not be directly involved if we simply limit ourselves to trying to
understand mass culture.

There ought to be more empirical studies of the effects of the mass
media. There are a large number of facts available and an even
larger number of alleged facts about the "consumption" by a variety
of people of the range of materials in mass media.

It is a fact that people generally like what they get in the mass
media. This is something we cannot ignore if we want to understand and evaluate the mass media, and particularly if we want to
change them.

I should take it as a value that people ought to be free to read
and listen to what they want to read and listen to, provided—and
this is a big proviso—provided that they have relatively equivalent
access to a wide range of communication materials. There are some
very difficult problems involved in that proviso.

Although people generally like what they see, the question remains whether they will not like something else better if they are
exposed to it. But this raises the question—who decides what is
better?

I think if I had to say what the one central value of a communication system is or ought to be, and the one on which we might get
agreement, it is that we ought to maximize the range of material
available to the different social groups and personality types in the
culture. To be sure, the institutional arrangements by which one
maximizes the range of materials is not an easy problem to solve.

Irving Kristol: Mr. Rosten said that the mass media do not sufficiently inform their readers about current events and international affairs. He has a rejoinder which in my opinion is invalid, although I think the accusation itself is misleading.

His rejoinder is: "Look at the articles we have published by Adlai Stevenson and Arthur Schlesinger, Hannah Arendt, Randall Jarrell and so forth." But this is beside the point. The problem of quality in political journalism is not at all a matter of particulars but one of principle. What is wrong with the mass media in political affairs is that their manner of presentation is based on a false premise; namely, that these things are simple. The mass media can't operate without that premise; and yet that premise is false. All political developments are extremely complicated, far more complicated than even the New York *Times* would lead one to believe.

All I think one can ask is that the articles be presented with a restraint, a decorum, a sobriety that would prepare the reader to function as a citizen in a free society.

Remarkably few words have been said about our educational system. We are not educating people to appreciate our high humanist, literary culture in this country. In order to appreciate this culture, you have to have certain years of training. We don't give our children these years of training.

Our educational system is the way it is because a group of people decided that it should be that way. Everyone talks about the intractability of our educational problems, but we forget that we have the blessed right not to avail ourselves of public education. When we talk about the elite culture in England, we should remember that this is not based upon public education but upon private education.

If intellectuals feel strongly enough that they want their children to grow up to read *Partisan Review*, Plato, and Proust, all they have to do is establish the right kind of schools.

The problem of law has thus far not been raised. I am glad Arthur Schlesinger mentioned the F.C.C. because those initials are not to be found in any of the papers. So many of the abominations of mass culture are really trivial matters which could be overcome by the slightest political effort.

For instance, I think that advertising on children's programs is an absolute abomination. I can't understand how it came into existence, and I can't understand why it should be allowed to continue. The F.C.C. has the authority to stop it. All you have to do is get a lot of people to kick up a row and they *will* stop it. This is just a matter of lax administration which is quite within our power to cure.

The last problem I wish to mention is a much more difficult one; it touches upon the question of generations. I think we should make a distinction, when we talk about the mass media, in terms of the generations to which they are directed. On the whole, there is nothing objectionable, in my opinion, in the mass media that are directed to older people. The media are anodyne, trivial, sentimental. They entertain, and that's what the older people want. I think we tend to forget the centuries of endless boredom that stretched behind us. It was not despair, not rebellion, it was just sheer boredom. Millions of people were bored, bored, bored; they took to drink, crime, brigandage; they took to anything they could to dispel boredom. I think TV has made a magnificent achievement here. Where television and the mass media are corrupting is in dealing with youth, the teenagers. The most obnoxious aspects of all of these mass media are those that disorient youth, those that destroy their values and prevent them from achieving anything themselves. This is part of what seems to me at the moment to be a worldwide phenomenon—what Hannah Arendt has called a breakdown of authority—in which youths tend to secede from society and establish a community of their own. How to reach them, I don't know.

Robert Saudek: The intellectual, it seems to me, is in the wholesale trade; the mass media are in the retail trade. If we accept this assignment of roles, the question becomes whether the mass media can intelligently and accurately translate, interpret, or adapt the culture of the intellectuals for the non-intellectuals on a scale that makes this a significant effort.

The mass media go directly to the mass; they speak or should speak its language. They need be no less intelligent in what they choose to say and may even be more intelligible.

The mass media dare not create a cult or a secret society. The vocabulary of the mass media is more difficult to use because it must not depend on the shorthand of the specialist. The mass media must know words so well that cultural expression may be no poorer and may be even richer for the exquisite care taken in translation.

Generally, we who are professionally involved in mass culture are interpreters; and to interpret, one must know two languages, not just one. We must understand ideas first, and we must be able to state them clearly and with an accuracy no less exact than that of their originators; yet in words that will hopefully have a temperature capable of inflaming the minds of otherwise very cool and indifferent people.

I read with some anticipation and anxiety the lists of television programs that Dr. Stanton and Mr. Rosten gave in their papers, and I found none which I felt was a true relative of mine. I therefore feel I have to list a handful of programs which indicate what the mass media can present to very large audiences on a non-profit and profit basis and over a period of a good many years:

Orestes, Ustinov's *The Empty Chair*, Bernstein on Bach; programs on Gershwin and Shostakovitch; *Oedipus Rex*, the *Antigone*, Boswell's *Life of Samuel Johnson*, studies of the Renaissance, of the American Constitution, of Isaac Newton.

And to name some contributors, let me mention: James Agee, Allan Nevins, Arthur Schlesinger, Jr., Richard Hofstadter, W. H. Auden, T. S. Eliot, Shaw, Beethoven, Wagner, and Mozart.

Mr. Rosten has decried the influence television advertisers have in deciding who and what shall appear or not appear in the programs they sponsor. This insidious and pernicious influence exists in television, as I am sure it exists in magazines and newspapers. The scale on which it exists is the important thing today. The degree to which it may be controlled is the important issue for tomorrow.

Mr. Rosten has pointed to the failure of magazines of superior intellectual content. A circulation rise from fifty to one hundred thousand readers would turn them from failures to successes. I should estimate that none of the programs listed above reached less than ten million people. The average number, I should guess, was in the neighborhood of twenty million.

It is not economical to put on television something that will only reach fifty thousand or fewer people, or even a million people. It is as though you hired a passenger car train to carry a family from coast to coast. There are other ways to communicate with this relatively small number of people by television.

Sidney Hook: I confess that I find myself in substantial agreement with Mr. Rosten's point of view, although I find it difficult to square my agreement with my revulsion against so much trash on radio and television.

Why can't there be an American equivalent of the Third Program? The comparison of television and radio to libraries is completely invalid. The air doesn't belong to any particular group; it belongs to me as much as anyone else. There is only a limited number of outlets. Why can't one be made available to people like me?

I am not afraid of government regulation. You cannot rely on private enterprise to provide a Third Program which is not a profitable venture.

> *Alan Willard Brown:* We have forty-three stations operating across the country in META [Metropolitan Educational Television Association]. We don't have any in New York.

> *Hook:* I should like to see that on televison.

> *Brown:* It is on televison, forty-three stations, entirely non-commercial.

> *Hook:* An editor of a widely circulated magazine once said to me in reply to a question about the contents of his publication, "Well, we want to publish something which all our readers can understand."

Is it an assumption made by those working in the mass media that all readers or members of the audience should be able to find the article or program within the limits of their comprehension? Is it impossible for an editor to publish something which only five per cent of his readers could understand? I think that if one did not try to publish things to appeal to everybody in every item, there would be less danger of finding the least common denominator. In other words, why cannot content be diversified?

If it is granted—I am not sure that everyone will grant it—that we are living in a century of great art, great science, great literature, and possibly great philosophy, then popular culture has had little corrupting effect. I should feel very much relieved if this were true. All other questions become academic or merely technical.

> *Gilbert Seldes:* Mr. Rosten said that intellectuals project their own tastes and yearnings on the masses who do not share them.
>
> I should say that the real charge against the mass media is not that they fail to interest the masses in what interests the intellectuals. The real charge is that they satisfy a small percentage, a vital but small percentage, of the interests of their huge audience. It is not that everyone is to be made appreciative of the finer things, but that the media actually stifle sixty per cent of the audience's interests,

or perhaps eighty per cent, by over-feeding the remaining twenty per cent. I should defend the eggheads from the accusation that they are trying to impose their standards on the public. I am only saying the public has many more interests than are served by the mass media.

Ernest Van den Haag: I do not share Hook's private faith in public ownership. In a mass society such as ours I do not think public ownership would improve things very much. It would make them a little duller but it would not make them better. The English do not have the same kind of mass culture society as we do. The contents of their Third Programs are dictated by an educational elite who do not care very much for popularity. A taxpayer in our democracy would say "I want to see what I want to see," how are you going to prevent him? If the Metropolitan Opera House were owned by the government, we would have more musical comedy and less opera. Now that it is being subsidized by small contributions, its standards may be declining already.

Alan Willard Brown: We should remember that the BBC Third Program, which is a radio program, appeals to a very limited percentage of the British population. Interestingly enough, the single Third Program which had the largest tested audience on radio was a full length production of *Hamlet:* this was an audience of around four hundred thousand people out of a population of sixty million. Even in the case of a program service as excellent as that of the Third Program, the material appeals to a limited proportion of the population.

The forty-three educational television stations, although they reach a potential viewing audience of somewhere between fifty to sixty million people, are not a network, and not one of them reaches more than a very small proportion of the viewers in a given area.

There are seventeen million potential viewers in the New York area. Of these, the largest number that has ever viewed an educational program either on META [Metropolitan Educational Television Association] or on Sunrise Semester or Continental Classroom, or any of the other educational programs specifically prepared for educational and cultural viewing, is somewhere around one hundred and forty thousand.

I do not consider this a cultural disaster. If we put on a Russian language course that meets twice a week in the afternoon; and ten

214 : PANEL DISCUSSION

thousand copies of the book used in the course are sold in one New York book store, this in itself justifies the use of television for teaching languages. I think we tend to ignore or fail to realize that there is a difference between the aims of television as a mass medium and as an instrument for the dissemination of culture and education. We in educational television believe we can serve and should serve a wide variety of audiences, and the audience for one program is almost by definition not the same as the audience for another.

Gerald Holton: When the archeologists of the year 5000 A.D. dig down to our stratum, I think they will very quickly dig past our bones and perhaps even past our libraries to that which makes us typical as a mass culture: our cyclotrons, superhighways, hospitals, and supermarkets. So the positive aspect of scientific and technological vitality needs to be put in the foreground of our discussion if we speak of mass culture.

A recent study of the relation of the mass media to science severely criticized the media with respect to the way in which they handle scientific news. Scientific output is fantastic: there are over ten thousand articles a week published the world over; there are also books and government reports. The supply is large and the demand is large, but the available material in the mass media is minuscule. By charitably lumping health, safety, technology, and science together, one finds that the total maximum devoted to science in the mass media is five per cent.

Some of the efforts of the large networks to put science across on a mass media basis are deplorable. It has been asked: What can popular science do to demean science itself? One of the things that popular science does is to change the public image of what science is, and this has an immediate and very striking effect upon what scientists themselves can do.

There is nothing more important about any field, as you well know, than what the public image is, particularly when you have to recruit from the public for support and students. The substitution of packaged ideas of science for valid ideas can have a severe effect. When mass science becomes the image; when the mass medium approach to a very large audience becomes the criterion of success, the effect on the scientific investigator may be destructive.

Melvin Tumin: Much of our discussion concerning different levels of taste and appreciation seems to depend on the assumption you make regarding how many more people could experience high culture than are now experiencing it. If I understood Messrs. Shils and Schlesinger correctly, they asserted that by natural endowment, probably the large majority of people could never experience deep aesthetic sensations.

I should like to ask them whether this is a correct version of their view; and if correct, what is the evidence?

Edward Shils: So far as the evidence is concerned, the general distribution of talents in a normal population follows a normal distribution. There is no point where a line separates, let us say, deep from superficial or great from mediocre. There is a gradual shading off.

The number of people who can appreciate high culture or be artistically creative is probably greater in proportion to the population than it has ever been before. The number is large but it is not infinitely extensible, and it can never become as large as the total population.

Arthur Schlesinger: I don't think we want to inject a Calvinist predestination here. There are only a few who are capable of intense aesthetic experience. But the distribution of talents and the distribution of occupations in society are such that there has never been more than a minority who have had this particular quality.

A society requires a system of priorities, so far as most members of the society are concerned. It is a rare person who has the vitality to meet the administrative imperatives of society and at the same time have deep aesthetic experiences. That is why I add vitality to talents.

Irving Kristol: Someone has said that England could have a Third Program because it is not yet a mass society, and Dr. Brown has pointed out that only a very tiny audience listens to it anyway. But no one has said how utterly dreary the Third Program is. It has excellent music—but you can hear this on most of the FM stations in the country.

I'd like to suggest a problem inherent in the technical consequences of these media. It seems to me possible to read Wittgenstein or to attend a lecture on Wittgenstein; but it is virtually impossible to listen to three people talking about Wittgenstein on the radio.

The intellectuals were all for the Third Program. They made a lot of money from it but most of them did not listen to it. The people who listened were the oddballs of English society—the half educated and the would-be educated.

But the problem I want to raise is whether the mass media can be easily used for high culture, particularly for high culture which has a literary bent in a literary tradition.

Bernard Rosenberg: The mass media are swarming with intellectuals. All you have to do is look around at the entirely new occupations which have been created just to accommodate them—not only writers and musicians, but motivation researchers, people who pre-test, copy test, and do product testing. In view of this, it is a little startling to have many here argue that there is some sort of deep opposition between people we have called intellectuals and the mass media.

William Fitelson: If an intellectual wants to write a book, he writes it on paper. He gets into trouble when he works in the mass media, particularly television, because that is a collaborative medium of art. It does not depend solely on him. It depends on actors, technicians, and a director.

Faulkner finished *The Sound and the Fury* when he wrote the novel. He was not responsible for what Hollywood did with it; in fact, he wasn't very happy with the movie. But the original work remains undestroyed, and there is evidence to show that more people bought more copies of the novel after seeing the bad motion picture.

It seems to me intellectuals are unwilling to participate in the television and movie media. The intellectual is welcome there.

There is another danger which has not yet been mentioned. Our population is increasing rapidly. The number of owners of the most important mass media, and the number of, say, newspapers is decreasing. It is doubtful that there will ever be more than three major networks. There should be more.

Leo Rosten: It is well known that an editor will run a feature that will be read by less than five per cent of the readers. We have singularly exact figures on who reads what, and it has been repeatedly demonstrated that a certain type of article or certain type of editorial will attract only a certain type of reader.

As for the number of intellectuals who contribute to the mass media, if they did not contribute, you would deplore this.

Mr. Hook asked about relying on private enterprise to provide a

Third Program. Suppose you compare a system in which people vote to a system in which they do not vote. Let us say the newsstand is a voting booth; whoever pays a quarter for a magazine, votes for it; whoever buys a different one—or none—has cast a negative vote. I must say that it is my own conviction that it is much safer to rely on the freest possible market and access to the market than on even the most benevolent government control.

> *Sidney Hook:* Can't you combine both; in education we have the government in control without what you fear.

> *Rosten:* But you also have private schools. Mr. Holton's comment on the subject of the media and the scientist depressed me. It is extremely hard to find talented or experienced people today who can serve as communicators between scientists and a less well-oriented people. There is a definite shortage here, and I notice that one of the foundations has just given money to finance the education of competent people in science writing and science interpretation.

I confess I am surprised that after hearing Mr. Saudek's list of programs on *Omnibus*, no one said: "Isn't it extraordinary that twenty million or thirty million people have been given Euripides, not distorted, not interpreted or debased, but straight?" Mr. van den Haag said that mass culture does not produce any new art. I submit that this was said when movies first appeared; I suggest that the introduction of the camera has certainly created new avenues of artistic expression. When Mr. van den Haag said they occasionally, of course, produce a masterpiece, I wondered how one can say with such flippancy, "occasionally a masterpiece." I am grateful if they occasionally produce a masterpiece; there are few fields in which masterpieces are produced more often than occasionally.

It is possible that sometimes something is good and at times it is bad; some aspects of some things are good and some aspects of the same things are bad. This is the way it is, and to deplore this is only to deplore what seems inescapable. I distinguish criticism which is realistic from castigation which is bemused by utopianism.

Mass Culture and the Creative Artist

James Baldwin: In speaking about culture, to me the only thing
that makes sense is that in this country there is a group of
people who are held together by some things they believe in
commonly, some things that threaten them commonly; and that what
they take to be reality is not, for example, what a Frenchman takes to
be reality.

I think there is a confusion about the glories of the past as opposed
to the harshness of the present. I don't think the past was so great.
I don't think there can be any question that no matter how complex
my present situation may be, it is much better than being a slave. I
think too that no matter how complex the American situation is, part
of it is the result of the fact that we have for the first time in the history
of the world a great body of people who are free, who—and this is in
some ways really an affliction—are relatively rich, and who in some
sense hold their fate in their own hands.

In this chaos, I think we find it necessary to create standards which
have never been needed before, which are very painful and very
difficult to work out. Despite the fact that people here are supposed
to be educated, I think we all know that the act of going to school and
reading books, or even the desire to learn, does not make an educated
person. In my view, an educated person has to have a certain independence of mind. He must be able to make choices, even very
dangerous choices, which most other people are not able to make
because they have other things to do: raise their children, earn a
living.

I don't think we can criticize the mass media unless we are willing
to talk about what we believe in, what we want. There is a kind of
confusion between what Americans say they want and say they do:
these are not the things they really want and really do.

It seems to me that the fate of knowledge has not been changed by

218

the twentieth century in America. Ever since there has been art, there has been the same struggle. We have one advantage over the past. We can look back and see what was there. But I don't see any reason to assume that the bulk of the populace was reading Tolstoy and Dostoyevsky.

I am sure most of the populace was doing then what it is doing now: reading bad novels, going to bad plays, listening to bad music; and other people were trying to raise the standards of spiritual life.

I think the pressures of mass culture which seem so threatening are the pressures one has always had. I think the responsibility of the artist is to have a standard, to cling to it, and to maintain it. I don't believe that artists are more threatened now than they were before. If I believed that, I should have to revise my whole belief of what an artist is.

There are people who think they are artists who are not. Also the American artist has a kind of problem which did not obtain before, that is, he can make much more money than others have ever been able to make.

No Frenchman, and I don't think any Englishman until lately, ever assumed that by being an artist he was going to make a lot of money. I think one has to be prepared to give up a great many things for this discipline, if you believe it is worth it.

I think the role the artist plays in relation to his culture is simply to maintain this standard, whether or not it is followed, whether or not it seems to be a dialogue, whether or not he seems to be popular. The whole importance of art is to make real, to bring into the world forever, a standard of possibility of what a man can be and do. This will not necessarily raise the level of the people, but I think without this, the level of the people would be inconceivably lower than it is today.

It is very hard to be an artist. It is not a democratic thing and it cannot be. Nor do I see any reason why it should be. What I mean is that it is there for those who want it, it is there to prove something that nothing else can prove: that a man can be and do what he really wants to be and do.

Leo Lionni: The definition of mass culture at this conference has shifted from one speaker to another, and so I have found myself, as many of you have, in the wonderful position of being able to agree with all sorts of contrasting viewpoints.

But what finally has become clear to me is that what I thought to be my distaste for mass culture, is really a distaste for the mass society. I do not like that marketing society which Mr. Hazard has been telling us about.

As a painter, I find the visual spectacle of the marketing society more damaging than my professional involvement in the mass media. It is becoming increasingly difficult to identify with people in the mass; increasingly difficult to see faces. The evidence of the basic simplicity of man, of his basic condition, is difficult to find and to describe. Man is always on the run, always on a buying spree. He is less discernible as a man, woman, child, mother, worker. He is now as difficult to find as are the classic ingredients for the still life, unless one is willing to paint bottles of California wine and cans of fruit salad.

Nothing is sacred. The manners of marketing have penetrated the universities. The curricula are prepared with the same criteria as the mass media, edited the same way, and for the same motivations. The United States Navy has a public relations office which operates in the same way as the public relations office of Lever Brothers. Even the professors in their public speeches have, for example, become indistinguishable from those who address sales conventions; there is the same pattern of jokes, the same calculated charm. The organization of museums and galleries, Mr. Sweeney has pointed out, follows the pattern that has been established along Broadway.

The marketing aspects of mass culture are the most damaging. They are well echoed in the statement made by an architect who said: "I don't want to be interesting. I want to be good." I think this is a very important statement. What he really meant is: "I don't want to be competitive. I want to be good."

There is a tendency here to lump social scientists and artists together as intellectuals. I must say that as a painter I feel as ill at ease here as with the most illiterate groups in our society. You represent brutal culture to the painter, and he represents refined culture to himself.

In the mass media where the artist should function well, the pressure for novelty and visibility is unbearable to anyone whose standards are absolute values—more unbearable, I think, than the pressures for conformity.

Perhaps it is difficult for the artist to function in a prosperous society. Many creative artists feel that way. Many of us are leaving —ironically enough, with foundation money—for poorer countries.

Gilbert Seldes: Mr. Jarrell's paper is suffused with a kind of melancholy over the fate of the poor artist, this superior, creative man who even if he stands outside the mass media, is doomed because he cannot create as he would have been able to create had the mass media not existed.

Well, this is a tragic figure, and I couldn't care less what happens to him. If my recollection is fairly clear, Mr. Jarrell wrote elsewhere that in a good society Marcel Proust would have made a million dollars, and I have forgotten what riffraff now making a million would be starving in the streets.

Now I really have no sympathy with the whole idea of equating genius, the products of genius with money.

The Dial Magazine paid two cents a word to the best known of our writers and to the beginning writers, not that they were worth only two cents—it was all we could afford. There was no equation between the amount paid and the quality and fame of the author. But if we have to accept this standard, it is a hell of a good society in which Charlie Chaplin made a million dollars and a pretty bad society that turned him into a cantankerous exile. I should rather have Charlie Chaplin than Marcel Proust. I think Charlie Chaplin had much more to give us. I am not making professional jokes. Chaplin has contributed more to the happiness of the world than a neurotic, terribly concerned with himself, reporting on a society which I hope to God will pass.

All of us here are aware that a revolution is taking place. It is the shift in power between the print culture and the electronic culture. But we are all assuming that the change is only quantitative and that this post-atomic, pre-cobalt world of ours is really as safe as, let us say, it was in the age of Shakespeare; that we can tolerate the ignorance, bad taste, and apathy of the masses as well as Shakespeare's age could.

Every time we make a comparison with the past and we find that things weren't any better then, we are relieved. I say that cannot be so. We are in danger of annihilation, and past ages, as far as we can see, were not.

I haven't any statistical or philosophic basis for this, but I suggest at least as a basis for study that the change in quantity, velocity, and force of our mass media is so great as to really make it a qualitative change; that the mass media cannot any longer be compared with anything that went before.

People have talked here as if a rise in the aesthetic qualities of the mass media would make them perfectly acceptable, and we would all love them. I submit that a nation which is passively accepting works even ten times as good as those we have now, passively accepting them, might still be drugged and become entirely apathetic and remain emotionally immature. The need is not so much for improvement in a single product or for so much criticism of the product that comes from the mass media. We need an audience more active than any audience that has ever before been in the world.

It is no use saying to me that three hundred years ago, people were not any more selective or demanding. We cannot run the risk of an undemanding public. We have got to find a way to make the public require things . . . a public which tries to make popular arts responsive to its own needs.

For this I suggest that we take the producers of the mass media at their word. Let us stop being hostile to them. Let us accept the basic statement that they give the public what the public wants and let us try to make the public want a great deal more.

If we can prove to the purveyors of the media that the public really wants something, then they are, by their own principle, committed to fill that want. My objective therefore is the public, the audience, the individual citizen.

Now I can return, happily, to the basic subject—the traditional role of the artist. The artist goes beneath the surface and finds out the real need of a society, a nation, or a community. That is where I think the artist really returns to the mass media, for it is only through the mass media that he is going to be able to fulfill himself at a time when, whether he regrets it or not, these media are dominant and will remain so.

Nathan Glazer: The representatives of the mass media have tended to take an apologetic or defensive position, pointing out that works of high culture are often presented by the media, and there is no argument about this. In fact, more is presented than probably anyone wants. I don't know that there was any great demand for "Orestes" on *Omnibus*.

The problem here is the transformation of the work of art into a fetish: the notion that there are unspoiled works and that these works have to be injected into the media and presented to the people. This conception of the problem is related to the ambiguity of the word "culture." Culture can be found in the high creative achievements of man which do have this unspoiled character and which can be communicated through different media; alternatively there is another meaning of culture which anthropologists use, that is, culture as the expression of life or the accompaniment of life.

I think that the introduction of the high works of art into the mass media has nothing to do with the second meaning of culture. What happened in the shift from popular to mass culture was not only the technical invention of devices which made it possible to reach more people. It was also a change in the character of the people, as they lost those ethnic characteristics which made it meaningful to refer to things in their experience, to use certain kind of jokes or cultural references or language. The cultural forms of these people changed in character. In other words even if the mass media were broken down so that they could reach a thousand people at a time, I don't know that they could get any closer to the people because they have lost so much of these specialized characteristics. The problem, you might say, is the change from popular groups to masses. The question is whether there is a cultural form appropriate for masses, something which does for them what the more specific type of folk and popular cultures of the past did for ordinary people. I feel the problem has to be located in the loss of traditional characteristics and the development of a general type of man rather than in the simple technological problem itself.

Randall Jarrell: I have been trying to think of the fundamental cause for the disagreement among us, and it seems to me that in four out of five cases, the people who have had a direct intensive, extensive experience of works of art are on one side, and the people who haven't are on the other side. The people who are relatively optimistic about accepting mass culture are mostly people who, I believe, have not been primarily interested in works of art. Art does not have final, important, intense value for them.

Often in what sociologists say about art in society there is what seems to the artist a kind of fundamental naïvete or lack of acquaintance. It is something that a person says because he isn't more acquainted with works of art. If he were an artist, you feel that he would necessarily have a discernibly different position.

Several people have said that the artist has always been alienated; there is no difference between past and present. This just isn't true historically. If sociologists will read the history of art or of culture, they will find that the kind of alienation called "romantic" in artists today was extremely rare and quite abnormal before the middle of the eighteenth century.

Nathan Glazer: Mr. Baldwin said that, not the sociologists.

Randall Jarrell: Let me quote to you Arnold Hauser, whose book *The Philosophy of Art* would make good reading for sociologists.

He says: "The consequences of the fact that ever greater masses of people are coming into the market as consumers of art are quite incalculable. The products of mass culture not only ruin people's taste, make them unwilling to think for themselves, educate them in conformity; they also open the eyes of the majority for the first time to fields of life with 'which they never came in contact before. . . .

"Whenever the circle of consumers of art has been widened, the immediate result has been to debase the level of artistic production. . . .

"Today in consequence of the emergence of the lower middle classes and certain sections of the industrial workers as consumers of art, a phenomenon well known in past history is recurring."

Charles Frankel: I am puzzled. This suggests that this phenomenon has occurred many times in the past and that every time there is a widening of the circle standards change, standards fall a little bit, and the creative artist feels a little more alienated during the period of transition. The quotation doesn't prove your point.

Randall Jarrell: Well, a number of people have said there is no debasement or evidence of even a temporary debasement of aesthetic production in this widening of the audience.

Mr. Seldes quoted me earlier on Proust. What I really said was that in an ideal culture, *Remembrance of Things Past* would have made Proust a million dollars and Elvis Presley would be in a gasoline station along with his friends and family.

In an ideally bad society *Remembrance of Things Past* would never be published. In fact it wouldn't even be written. And Proust would write a biography of Presley for the *Saturday Evening Post*.

I was quite shocked by what Mr. Seldes said about Proust and Chaplin. This was a wonderful example of using the good, in so far as you can, to destroy the best. In one sense Chaplin is a kind of Proust of the movies. He is a marvellous artist, but Proust is one of the greatest writers who ever lived, one of the absolute summits of Western culture, and to use Chaplin as a way of sweeping Proust out of existence is, I think, a terrible mistake. It is a kind of negation of values.

Several people have said that the mature artist, the really creative person is all right; we don't need to worry about him. He is always going to produce great works of art, no matter what, if he is that good; and we don't need to worry about his being corrupted or bent or warped or seduced or any of those things. That is a fable.

If you want to know about it, surely the obvious thing to do is, in the first place, to ask the artists whether they are bothered by it; in the second place, to study their lives and the letters they write just before they kill themselves; and finally to study the careers of a number of artists or writers.

For example, the standard thing one says about an American writer—the exception is wonderful—is that he doesn't develop. His best book is almost certainly his first or second or third; and the regular thing for him is to end up hardly writing books at all but writing articles, certainly not developing.

When you have a culture that is profoundly wrong for the artist, he cannot remain unaffected. You will immediately say: "Some artists do." Of course, they are the great exceptions, but generally artists don't keep on unaffected. A number of people have said that creative artists need not be affected by our special kind of world; they can even go into the mass media and manage to create real works of art. A propos, I will say that the best text for a sermon I know is the quotation we heard: "I don't want to be interesting. I want to be good." This is exactly what our commercial culture disbelieves. In fact, it doesn't make the distinction.

I was amused when James Baldwin said that someone once said people in general can't bear very much reality. That someone must have been quoting T. S. Eliot. Baldwin says there is a division of labor in the world, and people have quite enough reality to bear simply getting through their lives.

The implication is: It is hard enough to get through your life without art, simply get through it bare; and with the additional burden of art falling on you, you can't manage it.

But, you see, the reverse is true. Art is primarily to enable us to get through our lives and to help us bear them. In the case of the people Baldwin talks about, who are simply getting through life, does that mean they are getting through without art? None of us do that.

We get through it with good, bad, or indifferent art, but with art of a kind; and it is generally a bad kind which makes our lives as dreary and awful as Mr. Baldwin described.

I should like to talk for an instant about the difficulties of different sorts of artists in this country. Painters have the easiest time, I think. People just swallow them whole. Serious American composers are worse off than American poets. They truly can't even get to hear their own pieces or have them played.

Poets are better off in that they don't have to have an orchestra to play their works. In the past it was taken for granted that intellectuals read poetry. How many of you here do read poetry easily and enjoy doing it? I mean poetry of the past and contemporary poetry. I will wager that a majority of the people here do not. A hundred years ago as many people read Tennyson as read Dickens.

This is extremely hard on poets. It is not so much that they don't have any audience; they have a small audience; and they would be better off without half the audience they have. The kind of thing that happens to an art when it is experienced by only a few people is a terrible thing.

Sidney Hook: When Mr. Jarrell talks about the decline in the appreciation of modern poetry, the assumption is that the development of mass culture is the decisive factor. If this is so, why has there not been a corresponding decline in the appreciation of the modern novel? Perhaps one explanation may be the cerebral character of modern poetry, the fact that to understand it, one can't read it the way one reads nineteenth century poetry. At the same time I can testify to a revolution in the sensibility of the generations of students I have known since the twenties. The appreciation of modern poetry seems to me more widespread than ever. I am wondering whether Mr. Jarrell hasn't over-simplified this, and whether he doesn't owe us an explanation of the casual imputation that the decline in appreciation has been due to mass culture.

Jarrell: If poetry has become more cerebral, harder to read, then easier poetry should be more popular. Poetry since Eliot has become increasingly easier. Richard Wilbur is a far easier poet to read than Tennyson. Similarly, if difficult poetry made people stop reading poetry, this should happen in other countries. But in many European and South American countries, poetry is as difficult as it has been in this country, and yet it is popular.

Hook: What is the explanation for the decline in appreciation of modern poetry?

Jarrell: It is very complicated. I am not sure that we know the answer.

Hook: I guess that is the answer to most of our problems here. We don't know really.

Jarrell: Perhaps as Shils said there has been a real shift in our culture from active to passive consumption, from reading to a passive looking. People are less and less able to respond to a special art form. Poetry is a special art form. You have to have different expectations and training. People don't have the training. Increasingly people who read want everything to be pretty much the same: they don't want to have to change their attitudes.

One of the hardest things artists have to contend with today is the kind of wall between them and the semi-artists. In television, radio, and the movies, on Broadway, and in most magazines there is always someone who knows better than the writer how something ought to be written. There is always someone who can "fix" a piece up the way it ought to be.

Take the *New Yorker*. It's as if the writers always had the *New Yorker* riding on their backs and as a kind of mask over their faces. I know good writers who write for the *New Yorker*, but in the long run they are changed by it. They don't want to be changed; but after a while they begin to develop a *New Yorker* unconscious.

Tennessee Williams is the country's most famous playwright. He says he won't produce another play on Broadway: they so change and falsify his work, the situation is unbearable. If that happens to him, what do you think it is like for playwrights who aren't among the most famous?

It is characteristic of our culture that it is interested in human interest and not in ideas or in works of art. There seems to be nothing more important that one can say in our culture than "I love people." This reminds me that during the war on a number of occasions when our air force bombed a famous cathedral because some Germans were using it for observation purposes, I used to read, "All the cathedrals in Europe are not worth the life of one American boy." Well, if all the cathedrals in Europe are not worth that, they certainly aren't worth much, because just for the slightest gain—crossing a river—the Army was willing to sacrifice from up to five hundred to six hundred boys.

Miss Arendt said that there is nothing you can do with a work of art; in the end all you can do with real values is feel them and be moved by them and see them for what they are. Works of art are in a sense quite beyond any use to society. Constantly talking of function is an awful thing.

When Mr. Hazard talked the other day, I was impressed and frightened, because I thought that more than anyone else here, he was the man of the future. There will be a lot more people like him in ten to fifteen years.

Patrick Hazard: That is very reassuring.

Randall Jarrell: Yes, I know, and they will like it too. But what I mean is there will be people who essentially think of things as functional and will come to terms with a second or third or fourth best. They will be pretty well-adjusted people, but I think that in our culture you ought to be violently ill-adjusted or maladjusted or different from it in many ways.

James Baldwin: Perhaps I said some reckless things earlier. When I said that I didn't think the situation of the artist had changed greatly, I did not mean anything mysterious. I meant that what an artist does is try to interpret experience. What has happened in this culture is that everything is incoherent; people no longer believe what they say they believe; no one believes, for example, in a Presbyterian God.

I myself have never believed for a moment that America was what Americans thought it was. I have believed from my own experience that it was possible for people in a general way to become better. I think it is possible for some people to become better if they want to be. I think that we are really complaining about the fact that no one is related to his own experience.

It is very hard to be an American. The only thing harder is to be a writer, and to be an American writer is almost impossible.

There is a great mass of people who have to get through their lives, and I don't mean that they get through their lives without art. What I mean is that they wouldn't be here at all if there had not been in each generation, in each epoch, in each era, in each country, a few people, maybe ten thousand, a distinct minority who kept showing in cathedrals, books, in their own lives what life was like; who gave back an image of their lives to help people get through life.

Having a baby, paying taxes, living in the country is coherent. People can do that. All the artist can do is describe the world around him and try to interpret that world and make it bearable not only for himself but for everyone in it. This is very hard to do now because we are in a new situation altogether. We are at the end of a whole era . . . the whole European era.

Let me put it this way at the risk of sounding paranoic because it is the only way to make this vivid. As a writer, a Negro writer in this country, by which I mean in the West—what I found out was that I was born into a civilization which is always describing me. I was at the mercy of that description, not only outside but inside. I believed that description.

Now the image that the West has of itself is beginning to break down, and we are beginning to see ourselves as we are. I think just the attempt to describe simply the American chaos is a very valuable thing.

Life in this country is appalling. Human deprivation and misery and want have been abolished, we have no child labor, but we have people going mad. We have people dying for lack of authority. Everything seems to be breaking down. In the time we have left, people, artists—all people—have to live and to work. I think that is all we can do. It is going to be a very bumpy ride but that's it.

Ideals and Dangers of Mass Culture

H. Stuart Hughes: I have been asked by a number of those present how I can be at once on both sides of the cleavage which divides us. I think I can explain.

What we have been discussing for a day and a half is the price we pay for democracy. I shall put it almost as simply as that. I don't think we can begin to understand the subject unless we say this is a price that we should be more than willing to pay. It is a heavy price. This is the paradox of our whole discussion. It is heavier than most of the defenders of the mass media will admit.

I was very much impressed with James Baldwin's moving statement about the past. Those of us who sometimes look back from an elite point of view on the culture of previous minorities should always remember what life was for the majority. Nobody plans to return to the past.

Again and again it has been said here that high or refined culture suffers great difficulties in its production and diffusion. The efforts of the mass media to help are noble but essentially irrelevant to much of our discussion.

It seems to me that what we are talking about is, first, the situation of the artist; second, that of the mass of society.

I am impressed by the fact that none of the practicing artists who have spoken—Messrs. Baldwin, Jarrell, Berger, Lionni—is very happy as far as I can tell; and they do not seem to be extraordinarily difficult human beings. They simply say they do not particularly enjoy the social framework in which they are operating.

I think we are far more in agreement than seems to be the case that high or refined culture will continue to be restricted to very special audiences. The people we like and admire will wall themselves up behind barriers of self-protection with very small audiences. I see

230

no escape from this. What else can you expect of a society that Shils has correctly called a society of consensus, a society in which the artist no longer starves?

It seems to me we cannot understand our mass culture unless we talk about the social substructure. (You will pardon me the Marxist expression, but occasionally Karl Marx needs to be dragged to the forefront.) The one great divisive question left in our society is to be found in the South. Sometimes I think a cynic would say that what is really being fought for is the right of the unhomogenized to join the homogenized.

I agree with Mr. Schlesinger that the problem is to maintain the vitality in our society, but I am extremely sceptical that it can be done. I have much less hope than most of my friends as to what is going to come out of this society in terms of creative values. I agree with James Baldwin that we are at the end of an era. It seems to me that we are going through the transition from the European or nineteenth century to the century of mass society; and that fifty years from now the difference between our society and Communist society will be far less than it is today. I think their society will become more humane. We are going, it seems to me, in a similar direction by a far more humane, slower, and, in our value terms, better process, and I am awfully glad I am going through this transition here rather than in the Soviet Union or China, but I think it is part of a world transition.

The mass media are helping this transition. They are smoothing the way for all of us, for most of the population. They are helping an increasingly gentle and tolerant society bridge its differences. This is a role that has a great social function. It is not a role in which I am interested or in which I think most of you are interested, but if we look at it from a hundred-year or a thousand-year perspective, it may have enormous historical importance.

Alex Inkeles: I am struck by the split to which Stuart Hughes referred. One of the participants, as a matter of fact, said to me: "How come you are playing it so cool?" What was meant was that I was taking a rather dispassionate attitude toward mass culture instead of joining with both feet in stamping on it. This is what I ought to do, a lot of people feel; for mass culture is so evil that to stand back and simply examine it is the wrong attitude.

Others said to me: "I see you have joined the other side." I asked what they meant, and they said: "What is this business of dismissing so many people as incapable of rising in capacity? How can a man with, your background deny the possibility that some day we shall all be people of high culture?"—Something which I personally don't believe.

I am much influenced—although I am not convinced—by some of the things Mr. Jarrell has said and the vigor and persistence with which he has said them. Yet I have doubts as to the capacity of mass culture, however bad it may be, to interfere seriously with the activity of the creative artists.

Much depends on the creative artists you have known and what kind of sensitivities they have. My own reference is to a novelist friend, a teacher, who is unusual in the vigor with which he has resisted the seduction, blandishments, or temptations that people have placed in his way. He puts up a sign on his door: "Students and members of the faculty who wish to speak to me will do so between 9 and 12 a.m. I write between 2 and 5 p.m." He doesn't care what anybody thinks of what he has written. He won't revise his stories. For that reason he won't write for the *New Yorker*.

I think only a rather systematic study will settle the issue as to the extent of harm that has been done and the relation between the pressures of the mass media and creative work. As Mr. Baldwin hints, I personally believe that the travail which a man suffers has an uncertain relation to the quality of the art he may produce; and in fact, it may well be that at least for a certain kind of art and in certain times, the man who suffers most distinctively and uniquely, most deeply, most sensitively, is the one who will produce the work that will be important to us through time.

Under the stimulus of discussion with Mr. Jarrell and others, I have tried to set down some of the elements of the contemporary situation of mass culture. Let me refer to one of these as the problem of diffusion. By this I mean that in the past it was not necessary to build too high a wall for protection. Today one's eyes and ears are constantly assaulted by the products of mass culture. It is almost impossible to escape these assaults unless you go to the high mountains. The air, the streets, the buses, everything is spoiled by the infusion of the products of mass culture. Doubtless the capacity of mass culture to reach the artist, the difficulties he finds in separating himself from it are important.

Another element or problem is that of intrusion: the extent to which mass culture tends to move into areas where previously it could not penetrate. For example, a newspaper like the New York *Times* often carries the same cheap and vulgar ads carried by many other newspapers because of the way advertising contracts are placed. The good magazines tend to escape this kind of intrusion because by and large, they have not been discovered as an advertising source. So far, in the best magazines there are only book advertisements. But as the good magazines win larger audiences, they will be discovered as outlets for the same vulgar ads.

Another element of mass culture may be called invasion: People invade areas which previously were the exclusive reserve of the elite. Homogenization is another problem. Artists find it harder and harder to look for stimulus in popular culture. This special kind of experience is no longer available. Also people lack the awareness of the fact that they do not have the capacity to appreciate works of art. The mass media very often encourage people to believe that they have a level of accomplishment and a right of criticism far beyond what their actual capacity to understand and consume makes possible.

Finally there is the problem of the loss of audience. I don't think audiences are much smaller. But there has been a qualitative change in the audience. It is certainly a real problem to establish contact with people who are part of your audience or who are, like yourself, part of the group of people engaged in the production of works of art. I think many artists have much larger audiences than they realize. The crucial thing is that they don't realize it.

William Phillips: Is cultural coexistence possible? Is it possible for genuine art and mass culture to coexist? A number of people here have either minimized, defended, apologized for, or tended to ignore what might be called the bad effects of mass culture. Let me cite some of their arguments.

First, mass culture or middlebrow culture may be bad, but it does not do any damage.

Second, it is really not so bad.

Third, it is bound to improve.

Fourth, the masses are incapable of anything better; so why try to give them anything better?

Fifth, we try to give them the best we can, and so we feed them special articles by Bertrand Russell and so on.

Sixth, the very idea of an elite is not a democratic concept.

Seventh, a key point which Mr. Hughes developed and which is accepted by a number here, political democracy requires cultural democracy and cultural democracy requires something called mass culture.

Political democracy can be defined as a society which permits a certain minimum or maximum of civil rights, freedom of speech, a certain recognition of differences and the recognition of the basic dignity and worth of individual human beings.

There is no reason whatsoever, as far as I can make out, to assume that this kind of society requires that you have, for example, *Look* Magazine, or *Life,* or our kind of television.

Edward Shils: Has the proposition been asserted during this meeting?

William Phillips: It has been implied. I think Mr. Hughes will agree. He says this is the price one pays for democracy. Is that correct, Mr. Hughes?

Hughes: That is right.

Nathan Glazer: The problem is the word "requires."

Phillips: I will retract the word "requires." You substitute the word.

Glazer: It is likely to happen if you have political democracy.

Phillips: It seems to me that the phenomena we see in mass culture, magazines like *Look* and the big television stations, are the result of two forces: commercial considerations and some sort of egalitarianism which has flourished in this country more than in any other.

To put it crudely, Leo Rosten has somehow left the commercial factor out of his account. One gets the impression that the purpose of *Look* Magazine is to supply culture to the masses, a kind of culture they do not get in the various forms of poetry or the novel which we usually associate with "high" culture. In other words they had to be fed something that was manufactured for them.

It seems to me obvious that the only reason we have *Look* Magazine—and let's be frank about it—is that it makes a profit. I object to the introduction of all kinds of motives or ideologies of uplift, of endless theories of culture which really have only one basic result: to camouflage the reason for the existence of what we roughly call mass culture. Cultural pluralism has been cited by a number of people as another argument in favor of mass culture. The trouble with the word is that it is honorific. When we hear the word "pluralism," we think of democracy, of the fact that people have a right to think as they please; we think of civil liberty, of academic freedom.

It seems to me the notion of pluralism in culture is highly questionable. If all one means by pluralism is that people have a legal right to their opinions, that the editors or owners of *Look* have a legal right to print and publish it, of course everybody will grant that. But what we are concerned with is a question of basic values.

Some years ago, when I was teaching at Sarah Lawrence, the question of totalitarianism arose in a class in literature. To my amazement some of my students said—and they were presenting a kind of pluralistic point of view—"Well, look. Maybe fascism is what the Germans wanted and Communism what the Russians wanted. We should have what we want, and they should have what they want."

One could answer this argument quickly and cleverly by saying that the people of Russia don't vote freely and the people of Poland don't vote freely, etc. But even if people voted, Sidney Hook would be against it. He doesn't take the pluralist point of view.

People say that there are different cultural values; people like different things, but the point is: what do we stand for, what do we value? It seems to me that the whole question of pluralism is basically a cloak to conceal our own values.

We talk about art and culture as though these are subjects or activities which were created so they could be talked about. Somehow we escape the nature of the experience which lies behind art. James Baldwin and Randall Jarrell tried to indicate something of the feeling or tone of that experience.

Nobody objects—it would be insane to object—to getting more readers, more viewers, more hearers for some genuine form of work of art. But this is confusing the issue. Under the guise of saying that one wants to bring things that we all value to larger groups of people, something else is going on. Before you know it, there is a shift of gears, and suddenly we are talking about the fact that there can be an occasional piece by Bertrand Russell in a mass media publication.

I do not object to the products of mass culture; I like to see baseball and football and Westerns. I like to be entertained, and my tastes are sometimes low in that respect. What I object to is the fact that a certain number of people find values that don't exist in these products; that all kinds of theories of art are developed to justify the fact that *Gunsmoke* appears on television, when we all really know why it is presented.

Charles Frankel: The mass media are with us to stay. The question is not whether they are good or bad, but whether we have the wit, intelligence and will—including the artistic intelligence and the political intelligence—to use these things as they ought to be used.

Let me begin by saying what I find wrong with the mass media: First, I find their slickness objectionable. I should immediately add that I admire their professional expertise, and I think that on this level the editors and writers of scholarly journals have nothing to be proud of at all. They do a disservice to their own profession and to the cause of the culture they claim to protect when they write so badly and when they allow so many—at any rate in my field— trivial and unimportant things to be published.

But slickness is not the same thing as professional expertise. Slickness is making things look speciously easy.

Now I don't think obscurity is a virtue; many consumers of elite culture seem to feel that the opposite of slickness is obscurity. But an important argument or idea requires attention. The principle behind mass journalism seems to be that you can absorb serious ideas without paying attention.

Second, I think the mass media in the U.S. have a tendency to confuse facts and ideals. They describe a state of affairs which in fact does not exist, and they do a disservice both to what exists and to the ideals I think decent and sensitive men ought to hold.

Third, the ideals that are held up as ideals America serves frequently seem to me to be meretricious.

I found so much that Mr. Seldes said sympathetic that I hope he won't mind my saying that his remark about Charlie Chaplin stunned me and is an example of what I have in mind.

Charlie Chaplin, he said, has made more people happy than Proust. This may very well be true but that isn't the only way you measure the worth of a work of art. It would seem to me that the values we seek in works of art are the increased intensity of our consciousness, increased self-awareness, increased ability to make discriminations. I don't know whether people will thereby be made happier.

Finally there is the committee system that exists in the production of works for television, the theater, magazine articles and the like.

I suspect that the committee system is unlikely to produce as great works of art as is a system in which the individual can work pretty much on his own.

I think, however, that all these things are due not to the growth of industrial society and not, by the way, Mr. Hughes, to democracy; they are due to factors about which, if you have the guts, you can do something.

A play costs a great deal of money to produce. You have a star system; you have to please the actors; the labor unions are organized in a certain way. It is hardly likely that you can turn out a good play under these conditions. What can you do about it? For one thing, you can have a subsidized theater.

Someone said that the mass media give people what they want. There is no way of knowing that. It is the very rare man, and I should add, the rare intellectual who knows exactly what he wants. Everything would be easier if people knew what they wanted.

One way by which you can find out whether people are getting what they want is to be sure that there is constantly offered to them an interesting range of choices. The introduction of foreign cars into the United States and the interest people show in buying them needs analysis, but perhaps tail fins don't express an innate American prejudice. In any case, the mass media offer a rather thin diet and there is no way of knowing whether people are getting what they want; it seems to me to be fairly plain that there is a relative lack of control by the audience of what is offered to it.

No one here would complain about the mass media if he didn't think that something else was better and possible for a much larger number of people in our society precisely because the mass media exist and industrialization has taken place. The question is: what is possible? And it is in terms of everyone's implicit sense of the possible that these complaints are made. I find it difficult to go along with Mr. Hughes when he says we are paying a heavy price for democracy. I don't think you have to pay as heavy a price as we are paying. This is a problem of power politics, if you want, and involves the structure of power in the U.S. So I should disagree, and most emphatically with van den Haag when he makes an iron law out of his analysis. It seems to me the problem is one in the organization of our political lives.

Daniel Bell: In looking at the proliferation of what might be called contemporary culture, I am reminded of the way I felt when I made my first visit to Calcutta, India. I was prepared for the dirt, the noise, the cows, the people; but one thing I was not prepared for was the sheer quantity of it all.

It seems to me one finds the same problem in the proliferation of contemporary culture. What you have is the breakdown, quite obviously, of the notion of a unified culture, of the concept of a cultivated, educated man capable of the realization of a few central values which are the heritage of his civilization.

I am not saying that this is good or bad, but people find emotional satisfaction in this kind of proliferation.

It seems to me that this is the real issue rather than simply the question of the conventional categories of high, low, or middle.

A second problem I should like to raise is the one of cost, which is involved in the very nature of a mass society. Let me take as an example, *Partisan Review*, which has been over the last three decades the bearer of our culture, and let me also take *Evergreen Review*. You have the problem of the old method of trying to increase circulation by subscription, and this involves high costs. As a result, you may find it easier to put onto the bookstands a magazine like *Evergreen Review* than to raise circulation by subscriptions.

Many problems grow out of the different methods of marketing. With *Partisan Review*, there is a community among readers and writers. They recognize each other. *Evergreen Review* has an audience. It is not a community. But this is the kind of situation which has been created as a result of the cost problem, when you substitute an audience for a community. This problem normally does not receive attention because no one seriously considers the merchandising or the cost problems of the distribution of culture in a modern society.

I should like to make a third point: In the year or so in which I have been engaged in reading material on mass culture, I have been struck by the loose way in which we easily talk about the "public," the "people," "most people," without any sense of whom we are really talking about.

There is a very real problem of evidence and specificity. For example, *Partisan Review* has raised the question as to the effects of the situation wherein the universities have absorbed so much of cultural activity; that poets and writers turn to the university for support; that this is a new institutional form. We do not know the effects. I don't know what kind of study would find out what we need to know, but we are in the realm of opinion rather than knowledge.

There is a whole series of questions whose answers we don't know. Generalizations are made about how art is produced, but really one doesn't know. One would like to know what the results of commissioning music would be. Is this the best way? Mr. Frankel raised the point that there are new problems of creating new institutional forms of support.

I am, finally, troubled by the question that has been raised concerning the coexistence of mass culture and high culture. Regardless of whether or not I have a brief for mass culture, I do not think that many of us here inherited our culture, our education, and our books. By and large we are in a society which gave us some chance to get them. The problem, it seems to me, is how do you create a society which gives those people who want it a chance to become cultured.

This brings us back to Mr. Shils' paper; for the context is a historical one; namely, for the first time masses of people have come into society. The fact that Dostoyevsky was popular in his time is meaningless. Most Russians didn't read in his time. The fact is that you have a mass society which is essentially thirty-five to fifty years old; you have a problem of finding new institutional forms of support; you have the problem of keeping paths open.

Edward Shils: One of the concerns which underlies our discussion and which has not come to the surface sufficiently is the present state of the tradition of high or superior culture, whatever you want to call it. We have made a mistake in not confronting the problem more directly.

The tradition of our high culture is very problematic at present. It isn't that there is not lots of creativity in the United States, England, or France today; there is. These countries have many outstanding people in science, scholarship, literature. Nonetheless, none of us seems to be very happy about it.

We are in a state of distraction about these matters. We have the itch but can't quite locate it. Somehow, we have taken to blaming the poor, miserable middle and working classes for having brought the ants into the house.

But we really ought to inspect ourselves more and see what condition we ourselves have come to. Daniel Bell has emphasized the vast body, the quantities of material available to us. We are caught in a position of mad dilettantism or in a kind of stupefying expertise. We concentrate our efforts on one particular subject which is very narrow, and the literature on the smallest subject is beyond the capacities of any single individual today.

The literary men are free because they don't have to read, except perhaps their own work; nonetheless, they have other difficulties confronting them. In the midst of all this, there is a whole vast body of intellectual development unknown except to a small body of men, the scientists. Most of us' have dabbled in science but we don't know much about it. Our humanist tradition is in danger of being overwhelmed by science. It is in danger because it has not assimilated science sufficiently. It has not appreciated the nonutilitarian elements in scientific knowledge. Of course we don't know much about the utilitarian elements of science but we are blind to its intellectual, moral, and aesthetic elements; we are inclined to think that science has been developed in order to make money or throw bombs on people.

Another of the things wrong with our high culture is that our audience seems to be going to pot, particularly in America. It has not expanded at the same rate as the population. Specialization is one of the reasons for this.

Another is that we don't have enough cultural Philistinism in this country. We have some but not enough. We don't have the serried row on row of the bourgeoisie buying works of Schiller and Lessing, putting more money into the booksellers' pockets, putting more books on their shelves, where they gather dust.

Not that most people who buy books read them. Even when books were copied by hand, most of the people who bought them didn't read them.

We seem to have acquired the technique of acquiring Philistines but not cultured Philistines. How did the Germans and French get so much cultural Philistinism? By the gymnasium and lycée; by a very stiff system of education.

We come back to the point made by Mr. Kristol: that the European educational system is superior. The secondary educational system in the United States seems to be particularly guilty.

One final point: the contention has been made frequently that mass culture is bad because it serves as a narcotic, because it affects our political democracy, because it corrupts our high culture. I don't think there is any empirical evidence for these contentions; and what impressionistic evidence there is does not support them either. I think we are not confronting the real problem: why we don't like mass culture. This seems to me to be the issue. We don't like it. It is repulsive to us. Is it partly because we don't like the working classes and the middle classes?

Some people dislike the working classes more than the middle classes, depending on their political backgrounds. But the real fact is that from an aesthetic and moral standpoint, the objects of mass culture are repulsive to us. This ought to be admitted. To do so will help us select an aesthetic viewpoint, a system of moral judgments which would be applicable to the products of mass culture; but I think it would also relieve our minds from the necessity of making up fictions about the empirical consequences of mass culture.

Stanley Edgar Hyman: I think I agree with everything William Phillips said except on the matter of pluralism, which I think he misunderstands when he calls it a cloak to conceal our own values or implies that behind this pretended pluralism we have no values. To put it clearly, let the rapist be the rapist. That is his way to the good life. I think this is a considerable distortion.

Pluralism assumes that there are many varieties of the good life; that we are not God; that none of us can say: "My form of the good life or my values are for everyone."

The rapist clearly cannot be allowed in our pluralism because he is no pluralist. He is forcing his values on someone else. That is why he is a rapist. I think Mr. Phillips knows about this. I suspect he is for pluralism too, so far as it goes. If we don't have pluralism in culture, we will not have any values probably; I think we have to see it from the other end: that it lets us live.

When I spoke of pluralism, I had in mind that mass culture in producing millions of copies of *Marjorie Morningstar* for whoever wanted them produced thousands of copies of *Finnegans Wake* for those who wanted them. We want to be included in the pluralism.

I want briefly to mention too that our problem is not mass culture but high culture and that is really where we seem to have ended up.

Mass culture will not die if we say "Go die." It will not change itself much if we say, "Go change yourself." It will hear us and be somewhat affected, but fundamentally it goes its own way, and has its past, present, and future.

As a matter of fact, as some people have said eloquently, high culture in some areas is in a desperate state. It is hungry and thirsty, and it is not flourishing. But where we end up is that mass culture ought to do something for high culture not directly, but as patrons, financially.

If William Nichols cannot print any poetry in *This Week* except pious or religious doggerel, perhaps *This Week* can subsidize the publication of volumes of poetry.

I am not going to propose the machinery for this, and it is not my idea. But perhaps the best thing mass culture can do for high culture is to find some way of supplying money without having anything else to do with it.

I propose a kind of wariness, and that is the note I shall end on. We do not have the last word. We do not know the answers. Our creation comes in peculiar fashions, and if we meet and talk about it in humility we may come somewhere to an understanding.

The South East Essex
College of Arts & Technology